KW-223-856

THE NATIONAL INSTITUTE OF
ECONOMIC AND SOCIAL RESEARCH

Occasional Papers
XXVIII

CYCLICAL INDICATORS
FOR THE POSTWAR BRITISH ECONOMY

2 DEAN TRENCH STREET, SMITH SQUARE
LONDON, SWIP 3HE

The National Institute of Economic and Social Research is an independent, non-profitmaking body, founded in 1938. It has as its aim the promotion of realistic research, particularly in the field of economics. It conducts research by its own research staff and in co-operation with the universities and other academic bodies. The results of the work done under the Institute's auspices are published in several series, and a list of its publications up to the present time will be found at the end of this volume.

CYCLICAL INDICATORS
FOR THE POSTWAR BRITISH ECONOMY

D. J. O'DEA

CAMBRIDGE UNIVERSITY PRESS

CAMBRIDGE

LONDON · NEW YORK · MELBOURNE

Published by the Syndics of the Cambridge University Press
The Pitt Building, Trumpington Street, Cambridge CB2 1RP
Bentley House, 200 Euston Road, London NW1 2DB
32 East 57th Street, New York, NY 10022, USA
296 Beaconsfield Parade, Middle Park, Melbourne 3206, Australia

First published 1975

Printed in Great Britain
at the
University Printing House, Cambridge
(Euan Phillips, University Printer)

Library of Congress Cataloguing in Publication Data

O'Dea, Desmond James, 1942–
Cyclical indicators for the postwar British economy

(Occasional papers – National Institute of Economic and Social Research; 28)
Includes index.
1. Economic indicators – Great Britain. 2. Great Britain – Economic conditions – 1945– . I. Title. II. Series: National Institute of Economic and Social Research. Occasional papers; 28.

HC2565.033 1975 330.9'41'085 75–2738
ISBN 0 521 09963 3

CONTENTS

PART II: TURNING-POINTS IN THE TARGET VARIABLES

PART III: THE INDICATORS

TABLES

CHARTS

CONVENTIONS IN TABLES

n.a. means not available.

P and T are used as abbreviations for peak and trough.

Roman numerals are used to indicate quarters of the calendar year.

An asterisk (*) after the number of an indicator series means that the series has been detrended.

PREFACE

This Occasional Paper is an account of research carried out at the National Institute during a period of some two years starting from late 1971. In that time a good many members of the Institute's staff contributed their comments on the results described in the paper. It would not be possible to acknowledge them all by name, but in thanking them all I should like to thank especially the Director, Mr G. D. N. Worswick, for his encouragement at all times and also for his contribution of the Foreword to this paper. My special thanks are also due to Miss Kathleen Fry and Mr Ian Richardson, my assistants during the initial and latter stages of the project. Without their assistance with the handling and analysis of very large quantities of data, the completion of the project would have been impossible. I should like to thank also Mrs K. Jones, the Institute's Secretary, and Miss G. I. Little for arranging the progress of the text through the stages preparatory to publication and Mrs A. Rowlatt for compiling the index.

The cost of the research on this project was met by H.M. Treasury, while much assistance 'in kind', in the shape of computer facilities, was supplied by the Central Statistical Office. I am grateful to both departments. Again it is difficult to single out individuals, but I should particularly like to thank Sir Donald MacDougall, Sir Claus Moser, Messrs Owen Nankivell, John Dryden and Michael Murphy, and all the computer personnel who gave of their time. The statisticians of other government departments were also very helpful in providing both data and advice. Some of the statistical material used is published by non-government sources: the *Financial Times*, Management Selection Limited and the Confederation of Business Industry. The use of their statistics is gratefully acknowledged.

Finally, I must mention a special debt of thanks to Philip Klein and Geoffrey Moore of the National Bureau of Economic Research, New York. Geoffrey Moore played, of course, a major role in the development and publication of cyclical indicators for the United States economy, while Professor Klein has recently been investigating the feasibility of a cyclical indicator system for the major industrial economies. Their visits to London provided stimulating discussions on the methods of cyclical analysis.

The conclusions reached in this paper, and any mistakes which may appear in the text, are of course my responsibility.

October 1974 D.J. O'D.

FOREWORD

BY G. D. N. WORSWICK

The study of leading indicators of economic cycles is most strongly associated with the National Bureau of Economic Research, that most august of economic research institutions, which celebrated its jubilee a few years ago. From Wesley Mitchell through Arthur Burns to Geoffrey Moore, there runs an unbroken succession with which many other distinguished economists have been associated. There is no such tradition in Britain. There have been one or two articles spread over the years, but that is all.[1] The present study by Mr Desmond O'Dea is, so far as I know, the first of book length using recognisably National Bureau methods to study British statistics. It might therefore seem yet another instance of a belated attempt to close a technological gap. But it is possible that the publication may provoke a reaction of an altogether different kind.

When it appeared in 1946, the monumental *Measuring Business Cycles*,[2] embodying the research of twenty and more years, had a rather cool reception from the economics profession. The *Economic Journal* did not review it at all, an omission not wholly repaired by the publication of two separate obituaries for the senior author three years later. However, there appeared in the *Review of Economics and Statistics* an important methodological review article by T. C. Koopmans under the title 'Measurement without theory',[3] which raised the question of the role of the concepts and hypotheses of economic theory in relation to the processes of observation and measurement of actual economies.

The National Bureau method has sometimes been criticised as an arbitrary assembly of economic time-series, in which one plays the game of 'hunt the cycle' without regard to economic motives governing human behaviour. One answer to this criticism has been to point out that the assembly workers themselves were trained economists, who knew instinctively which were the time-series whose movement most economists would wish to take into account. This reply would not have satisfied Koopmans himself, who seemed to be arguing that the economist should not go into empirical action unless he was equipped with a fully articulated economic theory, built upon a foundation of the maximising behaviour of individual units. Koopmans'

[1] The National Institute published the results of a small scale exercise in 1963: C. Drakatos, 'Leading indicators for the British economy', *National Institute Economic Review*, no. 24, May 1963.

[2] Arthur Burns and Wesley C. Mitchell, *Measuring Business Cycles*, New York, NBER, 1946.

[3] *Review of Economics and Statistics*, vol. 29, 1947.

own position in turn is open to a common criticism of contemporary economic theory, namely that so much time and effort is devoted to the refinement of the armour that the brave knight may never get into action at all, and even if he does he may find himself handicapped by the sheer weight of armour he is obliged to carry. The real issue is not one of theory or no theory, but of finding the best mixture of fact and theory. In these terms many economists would regard the Burns and Mitchell mixture as being too thin for their tastes in respect of theory.

A less favourable date for the publication of *Measuring Business Cycles* could hardly have been found. During the 1930s, not only was Keynes' *General Theory*[1] published, but also Colin Clark's pioneer works on the national income.[2] The Keynesian theory of income determination developed side-by-side with the estimation of national income and its principal components in many countries. The process was given an enormous impetus during World War II. It looked in the later 1940s as though economists had got the mixture of theory and fact just right, at any rate for macro-economics. On the more precise quantitative side, econometrics was beginning to flourish in the estimation of consumption functions, investment functions, demand for money functions and the like, and not long afterwards the construction of complete macro-econometric models was begun. All this scientific work appeared to be exactly the kind needed to carry out the policies of full employment charted by the new economic theory. A corollary of the new economics was that the business cycle would cease to exist, being incidentally ironed out in the realisation of full employment policies. The Burns and Mitchell approach seemed to offer little guidance for the new world of managed economies; at best it provided an interesting way of looking at recent economic history.

The economic analysis presented in the National Institute's quarterly *Economic Review* is considered to be characteristic of the Keynesian national income approach and it might therefore seem rather strange that the Institute should return, after more than a quarter of a century, to an approach already considered obsolescent, and an explanation is called for. A cynic might say that we are looking for a new loadstone. Though the Institute may take pride in the scientific purity of its method, its forecasting performance is not so good that it can afford to pass by any alternative approach which promises improvement, even if doubts have been expressed about the approach's methodological credentials. However, we have seen the research reported in this volume not as an alternative to our regular analysis so much as a complement.

To an economic historian studying a period for which virtually all the data

[1] J. M. Keynes, *General Theory of Employment, Interest and Money*, London, Macmillan, 1936.

[2] *The National Income 1924–31*, London, Macmillan, 1932; *National Income and Outlay*, London, Macmillan, 1937.

which can be known are already available, the issue is one of finding the most suitable degree of aggregation of primary statistics. One cannot imagine an historian discarding data on the grounds that they do not fit comfortably into his present picture of an economy. If there are discrepancies or contradictions he will regard it as his primary duty to redraw his picture, to reconstruct his model, so that the apparent contradiction is removed. For the forecaster the issue looks rather different. To the extent that he is working with an explicit model of the economy, he can only include those variables for which the estimates are available fairly quickly. If he is using a quarterly model then essentially he needs quarterly estimates. Statistics available only on an annual basis, or published only after delays of many quarters, are of comparatively little use to him. He may find himself further restricted by the instability of econometric relationships. In the early days of econometric model building for forecasting it was widely expected that models would get larger, the more so that computers were becoming available which allowed the speedy handling of large masses of data. There were and are, of course, strong forces tending towards larger models. It was natural enough to begin with a simple consumption function relating aggregate consumption to aggregate income and then to proceed to break down consumption into various components – durable, non-durable and so on – and to break down income into different classes – wage earners, self-employed and the like. Working against this tendency is the growing experience of the actual behaviour of the estimated equations. Time and again they turn out to be less stable than had been hoped, so that the model-using forecaster may be obliged, at any rate temporarily, to discard good primary statistical series simply because they cannot at the moment be incorporated into behavioural equations which perform satisfactorily.

Under the circumstances, the model-user would find it well worthwhile on occasion to lift his eyes from the particular set of data with which he is able to work and to take a good look round as well at the behaviour of other statistics which are not being incorporated at the moment into any of his equations. A survey of all the indicators may leave an impression of the movement of the economy which can act as a useful check on the more explicitly formulated forecasts generated by the model. The fact is that no regular forecasters ever rely exclusively on a purely mechanical operation of a model; virtually all of them exercise judgement at various points in the preparation of a forecast. Consequently, any significant divergence between the impression left by an inspection of the indicators and the forecast derived from the model could well lead the forecaster to have a second look.

But there is another use for leading indicators, besides acting as a kind of long stop for the econometric model-user. Forecasters are apt to mystify their friends by asserting that their greatest headache is in forecasting the recent past and the present. What they mean is that, for instance, the three different measures of gross domestic product give widely different readings for the change in output in the most recent quarter. In these circumstances some other indicator altogether, such as unemployment, might provide a useful guide. Another instance could be profits, which are reported only annually and some time after they have been earned, and whose final assessment may be delayed several years before the settlement of disputes between the companies and the Inland Revenue. In such circumstances sample surveys can be helpful. Alternatively, research may throw up a good equation showing profits as a function of other indicators more readily available. One possible line for future work might be to concentrate on the potential use of leading indicators in the making of preliminary estimates of key magnitudes.

There are some who may question the wisdom of stressing the importance of timeliness in statistics and the developments of techniques and devices for making speedier preliminary estimates. Will not all this effort encourage Chancellors of the Exchequer to make ever more frenetic efforts to control the course of the economy from month to month and even from week to week? Certainly this result is not logically entailed. Instead of talking of speeding up the forecasting process, we could as well talk of giving quicker information about changes in the immediate past – changes which might make intervention unnecessary. It has often been argued, for example, that deflationary action has been taken at a time when the economy was already slowing down of its own accord. Any improvement in information which enabled one to detect this slowing down earlier would clearly be very valuable. The expressions mean the same thing, but the latter formulation could be said to encourage a calmer and more measured approach to the determination of economic policy.

It was the question of economic forecasting which was the main motivation for the present study and which we hope will ultimately prove to be its principal justification. In this connection the comparison in appendix A of the performance of some of the indicators with random walk series is especially interesting. But there is another use to which this information can be put which is worth mentioning. I have already suggested why the original publication of *Measuring Business Cycles* had a rather cool reception. For the young mainstream macro-economists of that generation, the postwar world was going to be one of managed full employment policies which would simply surpass the old business cycle. If one paints with a very broad brush one can characterise the postwar world in most industrial countries as having come near to full employment in contrast with the fluctuating unemployment of earlier days. But if we look more closely, we see that fairly regular fluctuations of output and other variables have been occurring. We observe that the cyclical character of these movements is more apparent if we express them in relation to a rising trend, which has given rise to the concept of growth cycles. Although they are not the most important of contemporary economic problems, they are worth rather more careful analysis than they have had so far. In the 1930s and the early 1940s it was taken as axiomatic by the majority of macro-economists that a capitalist-type economy left to itself would be subject to fairly substantial fluctuations. It was these fluctuations, combined with a high average level of unemployment, which, after all, gave rise to the Keynesian revolution. Nowadays, however, quite a number of economists appear to impute the greater part of such fluctuations in output and employment as we do observe to mistaken timing of government policies. Implicitly they appear to be assuming that the capitalist-type economy left to itself will be rather stable. Meanwhile the majority of econometricians go on correlating time-series without worrying themselves about the ultimate causes of the fluctuations in the variables they observe. But it is, on the face of it, improbable that the same type of analysis would be appropriate irrespective of whether the fluctuations originate within the system or are imposed on it by government actions. Whether or not conventional macro-economic theory has been fully adapted to the new circumstances of the managed economy, progress will ultimately depend on returning to the economic statistics themselves. We are in Mr O'Dea's debt for his careful charting of some of the main economic indicators, his study of the duration of their fluctuations, and the relations between the peaks and troughs of different series; it is to be hoped that they will provide useful signals to the practical forecaster and will prove valuable source-material for the economic theorist.

CHAPTER I

INTRODUCTION

OBJECTIVES

As originally conceived, the objective of this project was to apply the techniques of indicator analysis and to examine the results from the point of view of improving current forecasting, either by giving earlier or better warning of turns in certain key economic variables, or by improving current estimates fed as basic data into economic models. During the course of the research the objectives have, as usually happens, become rather more precise and also somewhat modified. The aims of the project would, with hindsight, be spelt out as follows:

(i) To establish a business cycle chronology for Britain in the postwar period.[1] A fine chronology is required, to the nearest month where possible.[2] This is essential if we are to have some framework in which to describe the timing relationships to each other of a large number of economic time-series. But other useful purposes are also served by a business cycle chronology provided it becomes widely accepted by economic analysts. For example, exact comparisons of cyclical characteristics and locations can be made with other countries which possess similar chronologies.[3] Also the move from annual data to a monthly (or quarterly) chronology permits the economic historian much more precision in his description and analysis of the cycle.

(ii) To establish timing relationships for all the more important cyclically sensitive indicator series, using the fixed chronologies as the benchmarks from which leads and lags are measured. There are a large number of series available, certainly several hundred, which are influenced in one way or

[1] The term 'business cycle' is used to describe a fluctuation in aggregate economic activity, or in the major sub-aggregates or other important economic variables, varying in duration from just over a year up to several years (a more precise definition is given later in the text). The term should not be taken as implying anything about the cause of the cycle. Cycles resulting from the actions of Government fall within the scope of the definition equally with those cycles resulting from other exogeneous causes and 'shocks', or from endogeneous causes. 'Trade cycle' is sometimes used as an alternative.

[2] Some postwar chronologies are already available: Drakatos in 'Leading indicators for the British economy' developed a monthly chronology for the period up to 1960; another chronology based on annual data was given in R. C. O. Matthews, 'Postwar business cycles in the United Kingdom' in M. Bronfenbrenner (ed.), *Is the Business Cycle Obsolete?*, New York, John Wiley and Sons, 1969.

[3] Particularly the United States, but also Japan, Canada, Italy and Australia. Other countries for which cyclical chronologies have been compiled are New Zealand, South Africa and West Germany.

another by the economic cycle. Over a hundred of these series are reported on in this paper, while many others were given an initial scanning.

(iii) To find whether any of the timing relationships so established can be used to improve current forecasting procedures and to give better forecasts.

This last objective, it will be noted, is open-ended in the sense that the exact method of improvement is quite unimportant; that is, it does not matter whether better forecasts are obtained directly from the use of leading indicators, or indirectly by feeding the indicator information as supplementary data into, say, a large-scale economic model, or simply from obtaining better estimates of the current values of certain economic aggregates.

An important feature of this project, and one in which it differs from the work undertaken at the National Bureau of Economic Research in connection with the United States economy, is that there is not simply one chronology or 'general reference cycle' to which all the indicators are related. Instead three chronologies are developed for different 'target variables' – certain key economic variables whose cyclical movement is of vital importance to policy-makers. In order of treatment they are production, investment and unemployment, and a 'reference cycle' chronology has been established for each of them. (An attempt to define cyclical chronologies for other target variables proved unsuccessful.) Using more than one chronology does complicate the analysis. However, it also allows for the fact that some indicators will be more closely tied, say, to investment than to production; thus it is likely to deal more adequately with variations in the relationships between the target variables and to reduce the variation about the average lead or lag of the indicator. Naturally the construction of separate chronologies does not rule out the construction of a general reference cycle based on the individual chronologies. The construction of a general cycle is discussed in chapter 7 of this paper and a general chronology is tentatively defined.

In talking of a reference cycle chronology we are really talking solely about a chronology of the peaks and troughs in the target variable. This limits the scope of all the succeeding analyses. The measurement of leads and lags between series and of the past consistency of these relationships is made only for peak and trough points, not for other points of the cycle except in so far as transformations, such as detrending or growth-rate computation, throw up new peak and trough locations; that is, although it is reasonable to think that a large part of the cyclical behaviour of a series can be summed up in its behaviour at peaks and troughs, a considerable amount of information on the characteristics of the series over the whole cycle is lost. This can be justified on grounds of simplicity and because there are other methods of time-series analysis more appropriate to analysis over the whole cycle.

Further, one is not committed to any particular view as to the behaviour of series between peaks and troughs, and turning-points in the target variables are of sufficient importance to policy-makers, whether as indications of the need for policy-change or as showing the result of recent actions, to justify a degree of concentration on economic relationships at or near the turning-points. It would in fact be possible to extend the methods outlined in this paper, even though they are of a non-mathematical, descriptive type, to an examination of other points of the cycle. For example, the path-breaking work of Wesley C. Mitchell and that of his successors at the National Bureau included statistical analyses of the movement of each series over the various phases of the cycle (generally splitting each cycle into nine segments), and of measures of amplitude and its rate of change.[1] Matthews also used fairly simple techniques to measure relative amplitudes.[2]

OUTLINE OF PROCEDURE

In broad outline, the procedure was first to establish cyclical chronologies for the target variables. An initial problem was to decide which statistical series most appropriately represents each such variable; in other words the target variable must be precisely defined. For instance, 'investment' becomes 'private sector non-residential gross fixed capital formation at constant prices'. In a few cases alternative series, and hence alternative chronologies, are listed out.

Sometimes data transformation was necessary before work could proceed. For prices and wages, for example, it is almost self-evident that the analysis must deal with rates of change. The major economic aggregates of production and investment also require transformation; the cycle in these aggregates is not clearly apparent until the growth component is removed by detrending the series. Analysis is then in terms of the 'growth cycle', the cycle relative to the long-term trend.[3] However, although these target variables and a few of the indicators are analysed in detrended form, this is not true of the generality of indicator series. There is some inconsistency in this.

Next, some hundreds of series which met the basic requirements (see chapter 2) and which seemed likely *a priori* to be related in some way to the business cycle were given an initial vetting. This consisted in graphical inspection to see whether there was cyclical movement in the indicator series and whether this corresponded, even if very roughly, with the general

[1] In particular, see Burns and Mitchell, *Measuring Business Cycles*; Geoffrey H. Moore (ed.), *Business Cycle Indicators: contributions to the analysis of current business conditions*, Princeton University Press, 1961; Geoffrey H. Moore and Julius Shiskin, *Indicators of Business Expansions and Contractions*, New York, Columbia University Press, 1967.

[2] 'Postwar business cycles in the United Kingdom.'

[3] For further discussion see chapter 3 below.

economic movements known to have occurred during the period of analysis. Sometimes the series would be highly erratic and it became necessary to smooth them to bring out the cycles – although this procedure has its dangers.[1] The net result was to eliminate a large number of series, either because the cyclical movement was ill-defined, or else, even if cycles could be defined, because the series was of relatively minor economic significance.

The selected indicators were then put through much more detailed tests. The first was to identify the cyclical turning-points for each indicator, which were then matched against the appropriate reference cycle turns, and leads or lags computed for all those turns which could be compared. It was then possible to compute the average lead or lag at peaks or troughs. Other information, such as dispersion about the average, general conformity of the indicator to the cycle, extra turns in the series and its smoothness, was also obtained (see chapter 2 and appendix A for details on how this was done).

All this information led to an assessment of the quality of the series for analytical or forecasting purposes. The way chosen here of summarising this information was to give an indicator a score under each of a number of headings and to weight these together to give an overall score (separate scores were computed for peaks and for troughs). The indicators could then be ranked in order of their overall score, a preliminary step being to classify them in terms of a given reference chronology as being leading, lagging, or roughly coincident (turning on average within three months either way of the reference turning-points). Some series were so inconsistent that they could not be classified under any of the three headings. The principal results of this analysis are detailed in Part III of this paper.

A second use for the scores given to the series was to summarise the information yielded by a selected short list of indicators. Alternative techniques are to weight together either the directions of movement in the selected indicators or the sizes of changes in the indicators. Suitable weights for combining the series in the latter case are the overall scores computed for the individual series. Tests on these indices ('diffusion' indices and 'amplitude-adjusted composite' indices) were carried out and are reported on in chapter 12, where a look is taken also at experience across the Atlantic in forecasting from indicators.

An obvious use of the leading indicator series is for forecasting. Given an average lead of some months over a particular target variable, these indicators should be valuable for predicting future peaks or troughs in the

[1] These result from the 'Slutsky–Yule' effect, i.e. the fact that moving averages applied to a purely random time-series can produce an apparently cyclical trend. The seriousness of the effect depends on the size of the irregular component relative to the other components of the indicator series and also on the variance-reducing properties of the particular moving average chosen, which will depend again on the coefficients of the moving average.

target variable. In practice, various complications (such as high variability in the leading series or 'false alarms') rather reduce the value of these forecasting techniques, but the results of this project suggest that they can still be fairly useful.

CONCLUSION

An element of personal judgement inevitably enters into the type of analysis discussed in this paper, and there can be honest disagreement as to where, for instance, a particular peak should be located. The basic data from which such decisions were made have either been tabulated in this paper (within, of course, the limitations imposed by the economics of publication) or else are available from the main statistical publications.

This information should enable other workers to alter turning-point locations should they think this appropriate. At least, the chronologies set down in this paper should be a useful starting-point for the description and analysis of postwar cycles, whilst the results for individual indicators will suggest various potential forecasting uses. They will also suggest, or help to check and verify, various economic hypotheses, whether set in the framework of indicator analysis or of some other technique.

Part I

METHOD

CHAPTER 2

THE INDICATOR APPROACH TO BUSINESS CYCLE ANALYSIS AND FORECASTING

THE BUSINESS CYCLE

Some fifty years ago Wesley C. Mitchell gave the following definition:

> Business cycles are a type of fluctuation found in the aggregate economic activity of nations that organize their work mainly in business enterprises: a cycle consists of expansions occurring at about the same time in many economic activities, followed by similarly general recessions, contractions, and revivals which merge into the expansion phase of the next cycle; this sequence of changes is recurrent but not periodic; in duration business cycles vary from more than one year to ten or twelve years; they are not divisible into shorter cycles of similar character with amplitudes approximating their own.[1]

Mitchell's definition is sufficiently general and flexible to be retained, with one major modification, for this paper. The modification is required by the tendency in recent years for the business cycle to be much more clearly apparent as fluctuations about an upward trend than it is in the 'classical' form of fluctuations in the original absolute values. This is discussed in more detail in the next chapter, but the effect on Mitchell's definition is that some phrase about long-run trends needs to be inserted.[2] Since appropriate methods of trend elimination will convert the new 'growth-cycle' form of the business cycle to the old 'absolute' or 'classical' cycle, the discussion in the rest of this chapter is restricted for simplicity to the classical form of the business cycle.

[1] Wesley C. Mitchell, *Business Cycles: the problem and its setting*, New York, NBER, 1927, p. 468. The definition given here differs slightly from Mitchell's original version, see Burns and Mitchell, *Measuring Business Cycles*, p. 3.

[2] For further discussion see Ilse Mintz, 'Dating American growth cycles' in V. Zarnowitz (ed.), *The Business Cycle Today*, New York, NBER, 1972, p. 41.

INDICATOR ANALYSIS

In essence, indicator analysis involves the examination of large numbers of economic time-series and the identification of cycles in those series. The cycles, or rather their peaks and troughs, are then compared with a 'reference cycle'. The reference cycle consists of a chronology of the peaks and troughs in the general business cycle, or in some major economic aggregate. Thus timing relationships between the individual indicator series and the reference cycle averaged over several complete cycles are obtained. These, assuming reasonable stability, can be used as the basis for further analyses of the cycle and, in appropriate cases, for forecasting. It follows that *leading indicators* – those which on average reach their turning-points ahead of the general cycle, as against those coinciding or lagging on average – will be of particular interest and value.

We now consider the indicator method of cyclical analysis in detail. The first requirement was a reference chronology or chronologies of business cycle peaks and troughs against which the individual indicator series could be compared. A separate chronology was derived for each of three cyclically significant major economic variables. The details of the derivation of the chronologies are given in Part II of this paper.

Identification of cycles in individual indicators

The next step was to examine the individual indicator series in order to identify cyclical movements in them and to determine the dates of their turning-points. This was based, after preliminary vetting, simply on inspection of a graph of the individual series,[1] proceeding further only if there was a reasonably obvious cyclical pattern (perhaps after a degree of smoothing for a series with a strong irregular component). More objective operational rules were needed, however, for those series surviving the initial sifting. For a sequence of generally upwards movements in a series followed by a sequence of generally downwards movements to be classed as a 'cycle' the following criteria of duration and amplitude had to be satisfied:

(i) The total length of the cycle from peak to peak or from trough to trough should not be less than fifteen months.

(ii) Each phase from peak to trough or trough to peak should not be less than five months.

(iii) The cyclical movement should be of sufficient amplitude to be reasonably easily discerned; also it should not be possible to split the cycle into other cycles of approximately the same amplitude.

These rules served to distinguish genuine cyclical movements from short-term irregular fluctuations. An occasional exception may have been

[1] A few such graphs for particularly important series are given in appendix E.

made to the rules, particularly where some event such as a strike introduced extraneous movement into a series, but in general they provided an objective framework for the identification of cyclical behaviour in an individual economic time-series.

In eliminating irregular movements, these rules also, in a number of cases, eliminated some 'expansions' and 'contractions' which were too long to be irregular and appeared in several economic sectors at about the same time, but yet were too short and, particularly, of insufficient amplitude to be classed as major cyclical phases. Perhaps some form of aborted cycle, they are given the label 'sub-cycles' and in general excluded from further analysis except, of course, that their effect on forecasting needs some discussion.

Matching indicator cycles with reference chronologies

Cycles identified in individual indicators were now matched against a reference cycle, or possibly against two or more different reference chronologies. Frequently there is not an exact one-to-one correspondence between the turning-points in indicators and in the reference cycle. Sometimes the indicator series may skip one or more cyclical phases; alternatively, it may have extra cyclical turns. Occasionally this creates difficulty in matching the series to the reference chronology, but generally it is possible to match most of the turns. The number of months by which the indicator series either leads or lags each reference cycle turn is then immediately available.

A small variation in treatment is required for those series which move contra-cyclically, that is expanding during the course of a general contraction and contracting during the expansion; the series measuring unemployment are an example. The simplest approach is to proceed as though the series had been inverted; a peak in, say, unemployment then becomes a trough in the inverted series, which is matched against the corresponding trough in the reference cycle. Series which are treated thus in this paper are labelled 'inverted', although the graphs show these series in their original form.

Timing classification and qualities of a 'good' indicator

The next step was to check for the existence of a stable timing relationship between turns in the indicator and in the variable represented by the reference chronology.

First, the average over all the leads or lags at the reference cycle peaks which had been matched gave an initial indication as to whether the indicator tends to lead or lag at peaks. Similarly the average lead or lag over all the matchable troughs could be calculated. The average taken was the median value, as a precaution against being over-influenced by extreme observations when only a small number of turns was being matched.

The average lead or lag gives only the roughest of pointers to the nature of the timing relationship between the indicator and the reference cycle, and to the general usefulness of the indicator for analysis and forecasting. A good deal more information is needed, particularly on the consistency and stability of the timing relationship. A short list of the desirable characteristics of an indicator series is as follows:

(i) Economic significance: other things being equal, a series with broad economic coverage is preferable to a series of narrow coverage whose cyclical path might be distorted by events peculiar perhaps to only one industrial group. Likewise, a series representing a theoretically significant economic process would normally be preferred to one of no particular theoretical importance.

(ii) Conformity: there should ideally be a one-to-one correspondence, over the period covered by the indicator, between turning-points in the indicator series and in the reference cycle. Put differently, the indicator series should, after allowance for the average timing difference, be expanding during the expanding phase of the reference cycle and contracting during the contracting phase of the reference cycle (vice versa for an inverted series).

(iii) Timing stability: from the point of view of forecasting in particular, the two aspects of the turning-point leads and lags which are of most interest are the variability of the leads and lags about their average, and the consistency with which the indicator series either leads or lags.

Considering first the consistency of the timing relationship: if a specific series leads on average at peaks (troughs) and also leads at almost every individual reference peak (trough), then it can be labelled a *leading indicator*. Likewise, if an indicator lags on average and also lags at most individual peaks (troughs), it can be called a *lagging indicator*. Finally, those series which have a small or zero average lead or lag and most turns occurring within three months of reference cycle turns can be denoted as *roughly coincident indicators* (at peaks or troughs as the case may be). Naturally a series may have a different timing classification at reference cycle peaks from that at reference cycle troughs. Quite frequently too the individual leads and lags are insufficiently consistent for the series to be assigned a timing classification.

Even if the series can be allocated to one or other timing classification, it still may not be particularly useful for analysis unless the timing relationship is reasonably stable as measured by the variability of individual leads and lags about the average. It is useful to know that a particular series will always, say, lead general cycle downturns, but rather less so if the indicator leads on one occasion by fifteen months and on the next by two.

(iv) Smoothness:[1] in a smooth series a turn can be recognised almost immediately. If, on the other hand, there is a good deal of 'noise' or irregularity in the series, then there can be a lengthy recognition lag before a turning-point is seen to have occurred.

(v) Currency: the recognition lag may be additional to an already lengthy reporting lag. Some statistical series, for example unemployment and vacancies, are reported almost immediately, others only after considerable delay.

Smoothness and currency are highly desirable attributes when using leading indicators for forecasting. The other three – cyclical conformity, timing stability and economic significance – are important for both historical analysis and forecasting.

The types of statistical measure used to assign arithmetic values for these various attributes are set out and discussed in detail in appendix A.

Scoring of indicators

Given that statistical measures of an indicator's performance are available under the several headings just outlined, it is necessary to combine the information conveyed by the separate measures into one single figure or index, so that the analytical or forecasting value of one indicator can be compared with that of another and, in general, so that the various indicator series can be ranked. As always, a certain amount of detailed information is lost when compressing information into a single figure, but this is made up for by greater ease of comparison.

The scores under each of the five criteria were combined using the following weights to give an overall score, and also scores for peaks and troughs separately: economic significance 15 per cent, cyclical conformity 25 per cent, timing stability 30 per cent, smoothness 15 per cent and currency 15 per cent. These weights were determined subjectively (as also to a certain extent were the scores under each heading) and so the resulting scores should be regarded as giving an approximate rather than a mathematically exact assessment of the quality of the indicators.

Some tests made on the scoring system seem to show reasonable results. These tests (described in detail in appendix A) consisted in finding how well 'random walk' series would score on average, as against the scores obtained in general by the cyclically sensitive time-series discussed in this

[1] This was measured by the MCD statistic (months for cyclical dominance), details of the computation of which are given in appendix C. In non-mathematical terms, the change in the series from period to period is taken to be made up of two components: one is the long-term cyclical change (including any trend component), the other the result of period to period changes in the irregular component of the series. In the short term the irregular movements may 'swamp' the underlying cyclical movement, but over a long enough period the irregular movements can be expected to cancel and the change in the series is predominantly cyclical. The MCD statistic is an estimate of the number of months required before, on average, the cyclical movement dominates the irregular movement.

paper. To illustrate the results of the test (shown in detail in table A.3), 10 per cent of the random walk series had basic scores better than 38, and 25 per cent scored better than 32. Of more than a hundred indicators matched against the production cycle, 41 per cent scored 38 or better and 65 per cent 32 or better; that is the scoring system shows a significant difference in performance between cyclical indicators and random series.

The score calculated for an indicator series serves principally to compare it with other series and to rank the series in order of merit. But another use is when we wish to combine the information from a number of indicators into one statistical time-series. Two different methods of doing this – diffusion and composite indices – are discussed in chapter 12, but the important point is that the score given to an indicator serves very nicely as the appropriate weight to use when weighting the various series together.

CONCLUSIONS

Commencing with an empirically based definition of the business cycle, this chapter has outlined the methods of indicator analysis as applied to the timing relationships at peaks and troughs between individual indicator series and the reference cycle. The characteristics required for an indicator to be of value and, in general terms, the measurement of these characteristics were also discussed.

For simplicity the discussion has been limited to the case of the classical cycle, that is cyclical motion in trend-free time-series. However, in reality many of the most significant cyclically influenced time-series have an important trend component. In the next chapter the changes required to the classical methods of indicator analysis, or rather the transformations required to bring trend-dominated series within the scope of the classical methods, are discussed.

CHAPTER 3

TREND REMOVAL AND GROWTH CYCLES

In chapter 2 we discussed the classical business cycle and its analysis. By 'classical' we mean cycles whose contractions are marked by absolute declines in all or most of the major aggregates of employment, production, consumption, investment and, in general, prices and wages. During the interwar period it was customary to think of the trade cycle in terms of absolute fluctuations rather than fluctuations about a trend, and one result of the Great Depression of the 1930s must have been powerfully to reinforce this habit of thought. Over the longer term, prewar as well as postwar, there has unquestionably been an upward trend. Probably the best way of stating the position is to say that between the wars the mix of cycle and trend was mostly cycle with little trend; it followed that cyclical analysis in terms of absolute fluctuations did not depart too far from reality.

As has been frequently noted, the postwar business cycle has taken on a much milder character. Indeed the change was so marked that by the early and mid-1960s some observers were prepared to announce the demise of the traditional business cycle, and in 1967 a conference was held on the subject of its obsolescence.[1] The effect of this change was to make cyclical movements in the main national income aggregates much less clear-cut. The existence of such movements in the economy is still strongly indicated by fluctuations in unemployment and, to a lesser extent, employment, but the principal production, consumption and investment aggregates are more likely to show a decline in the rate of growth rather than an absolute decline, except in the case of a severe or prolonged contraction. That is, the presence of a cyclical pattern is clearly established from consideration of the growth-rates of these aggregates, but the basic cycle is not easily identified because of the upward trend in the statistical series. (The same holds true for statistics on prices and wages, but for these series the growth-rate, rather than the absolute level, is the natural focus of attention.)

It is natural then, when examining cyclical movements of the national income aggregates, to attempt to remove the trend-component from the statistical material. The possible methods of doing this are discussed below. Presuming the trend removal is correctly carried out, the cycles exposed in

[1] See Bronfenbrenner (ed.), *Is the Business Cycle Obsolete?* To quote the dust-jacket 'The answer to the question "Is the business cycle obsolete?" is, in general, affirmative regarding major depressions, but the case is "not proven" for smaller ones. Several writers suggest that contemporary cycles are "growth cycles", in which economic growth rates oscillate, but seldom fall below zero.'

the detrended series can then be subjected to the methods of analysis described in the previous chapter.

As a convenient term for the cycles in the detrended series, or, regarded slightly differently, the cycles relative to the long-term trend, we use the phrase 'growth cycles'. An important point is that growth cycles are not the same as cycles in the growth-rates, and indeed the former could be expected to be something like a quarter of a cycle out of phase with the latter.

However, the analysis of cycles in growth-rates can sometimes be of considerable interest in itself. It is appropriate for those series, such as many for prices, which are very smooth and are dominated by a long-term trend component. It is a much less appropriate technique for more irregular series, particularly where they exhibit the classical cyclical pattern with a decline in the absolute level, or show a vestigial pattern of that sort. In all such cases cyclical analysis should be either of classical cycles in absolute levels, or of growth cycles (cycles in the detrended series). Analysis of growth-rates is difficult or inappropriate because:

(i) they are extremely irregular unless the original series is very smooth (although this can be helped somewhat by smoothing with moving averages);

(ii) even where an aggregate series shows little evidence of cyclicity in its original form, other series which are economically related to the aggregate (for example, employment and unemployment series which are related to total production) can be found to display cyclical movement closely related to cycles in the detrended aggregate. On the other hand, any timing relationship to cyclical movement in the growth-rate tends to be highly erratic.

METHODS OF TREND REMOVAL

Given the necessity of trend removal so that analysis can proceed on the detrended series, the question is which is the best method of doing this. The possible approaches are as follows:

(i) to fit a mathematical trend-line, either linear or polynomial (normally to the logarithmic rather than the original values);

(ii) to estimate the trend by fitting a moving average of very long duration, sufficient in length to separate the trend-component from any cyclical element, except that cycles of length longer than the moving average will still be included, at least in part, with the trend (this could well be what is desired if we are interested only in those cycles whose length varies from about two years up to, say, six or seven years);[1]

[1] This approach is one of those used by Ilse Mintz in *Dating Postwar Business Cycles: methods and their application to Western Germany, 1950–67*, New York, NBER, 1969 and more recently in 'Dating American growth cycles'. She uses the term 'deviation cycles' to describe that subspecies of growth cycle obtained by removing a moving average estimated trend.

(iii) to revert to the growth-rate approach, but using the points of inflexion of the cycle (that is, the transition points from above-average rates to below-average rates) as the reference points rather than the peaks and troughs (this brings the growth-rate approach back into phase with the original cycles).[1]

Of these three approaches, the third (step cycle) technique, has been rejected here on the grounds of being rather artificial and difficult to present clearly in graphical form. The second approach is more attractive; in particular it has the advantage of dealing much more readily than the first method (though still with a lag of two to three years) with major breaks in the long-term trend. Also past trend-values and deviations from them do not require re-computing every time there is a revision in the more recent data. The disadvantages, however, are sufficient to outweigh these advantages; they are two. The first is that it is, as a technique, rather more difficult to explain clearly to a public audience than the first approach. The more fundamental objection is that the latest available trend-value, assuming say a 75-month moving average, is some three years in the past. This seriously reduces the value of the trend-adjusted series for forecasting, and is the reason for preferring, in this work, to estimate the trend as a mathematical curve which can be extrapolated to any desired time-period succeeding the estimation period.

Having settled on the general method of trend extraction, there is still room for choice in the selection of the function to be fitted as the trend. The simplest possible function, an exponential growth-rate (linear in the logarithms of the original values), has been used for all the detrending work in this paper, basically because of its simplicity. However, one researcher, Waterman, preferred log-quadratic trends to log-linear trends, since the former showed a noticeable tendency to reduce the dispersion of reference points in the indicator cycle. He found also that peaks and troughs in the detrended series were less dispersed than peaks and troughs in the original series. This supported the assumption of the independence of the trend and cyclical components of economic time-series and led to the conclusion that trend elimination was, in the Australian context, a useful operation.[2]

To sum up, our selected method of trend elimination is the estimation of a simple exponential growth curve (log-linear); the cyclical analysis then

[1] Ilse Mintz uses this as her second method of identification of growth-cycle reference points, labelling the cycles so obtained 'step cycles' and using them to check against the 'deviation cycles' of (ii) above. The method is an iterative one and is outlined in the references quoted. Generally the dates obtained compare well with those from the deviation cycle approach.

[2] A. M. B. Waterman, 'The timing of economic fluctuations in Australia: January 1948 to December 1964', *Australian Economic Papers*, vol. 6, June 1967, pp. 77–102. The paper carefully distinguishes the reference points in the original cyclically affected curve, the detrended curve, and the growth-rate curve, reaching a total of eight reference points for each cycle.

concentrates on the deviations from this trend. This does not, of course, mean that it would not be of interest to see the results of other methods and how they compare with this approach.

EFFECTS OF ESTIMATION PERIODS ON TURNING-POINT LOCATION

If least-squares methods are used, then one factor affecting the estimated value of the trend, and hence possibly the location of turning-points in the detrended series, is the time-period over which the trend is estimated. The effects of changes in the estimation period can be tested quite easily and some results are given here. Later it will be seen that to obtain reference chronologies for two of the target variables, production and investment, it is necessary to detrend the series. Obviously any errors in the reference chronologies determined from these detrended variables would have serious repercussions on subsequent work, so the tests were carried out on these series.[1]

The principles used to determine the various time-periods over which the trends were estimated were as follows:

(i) The end-points of the estimation period should be at corresponding phases of the cycle, for example, both near a trough value or both in the middle of an expansionary phase, or a bias in the estimated trend is almost unavoidable. (Of course there is some leeway in fixing the exact dates of the end-points. A few months makes little difference in practice, so that the use of turning-points based on the unemployment cycle is justified.)

(ii) Only in exceptional circumstances (say following a major change in secular trend, or a period of prolonged economic disturbance such as a major war) should the trend be estimated over a period shorter than two complete cycles. This normally implies an estimation period of at least eight years or 30 quarterly observations.

(iii) The trend should not be fitted through any major change affecting the long-term trend. This assumes of course that such a change can be identified, if not at the time, at least reasonably soon thereafter.

Production series

A monthly and a quarterly index of production were tested, both for total industrial production. Table 3.1 shows the different estimation periods. The trend-values are impressively stable, ranging from a minimum of 2·8 per cent a year to a maximum of 3·2 per cent, despite the quite marked

[1] The tests were carried out on the old 1963-based production series. Spot-checks on the recently available 1970-based series confirm the conclusion from the 1963-based series, that is that turning-point locations are quite stable for different trend estimation periods. Having said this, it also needs to be said that there are two changes in turning-point dates when the 1970-based series are used, but these are a result of changes in the composition of the series and in no way connected with the estimation period.

Table 3.1. *Tests of trend stability: production indices (1963-based)*

Monthly index of production[a]			Quarterly output index[b]		
Estimation period	No. of cycles covered	Estimated growth-rate	Estimation period	No. of cycles covered	Estimated growth-rate
		(% p.a.)			(% p.a.)
50/6–58/9	2	2·9	52/III–63/I	2	2·9
50/6–63/3	3	2·8	52/III–67/III	3	3·1
50/6–72/3	5	3·0	52/III–72/I	4	3·0
51/2–60/3	2	2·9	55/IV–65/I	2	3·1
51/2–65/1	3	3·1	55/IV–68/IV	3	3·1
51/2–68/12	4	3·1			
52/7–63/3	2	2·8			
52/7–67/8	3	3·2			
52/7–72/1	4	3·0			

[a] For all industries.
[b] For all industrial production.

differences in the spans of the different time-periods. It follows that turning-point locations are unlikely to be seriously affected by the estimation period selected, and this turns out to be the case. Not one turning-point (the detailed results are not given here) would be shifted by a change from one to another of the estimation periods listed.

Investment series

Private non-dwelling fixed capital formation at constant prices is the reference series, although for some purposes it is useful to concentrate on

Table 3.2. *Tests of trend stability: gross domestic fixed capital formation*[a]

Estimation period	No. of cycles covered	Estimated growth-rates	
		Private non-dwelling GDFCF	Manufacturing GDFCF
		(% p.a.)	(% p.a.)
57/I–65/I	2	5·7	2·6
57/I–69/III	3	5·2	3·2
59/I–67/IV	2	4·6	3·3
59/I–72/IV	3	4·7	3·0
61/III–69/III	2	4·9	3·1
63/III–72/III	2	n.a.	3·2

[a] At 1970 prices.

capital formation in the manufacturing sector only. Growth-rates over different periods are given in table 3.2 for both series. The range of growth-rates is rather larger than for production, at least for private sector investment. Again, however, turning-point locations turn out to be quite stable. Peaks and troughs in private sector investment are not shifted by a change from one to another of the estimation periods listed. For manufacturing investment one turn is affected – that in mid-1970; if the estimated growth-rate is 3·0 per cent or lower, the date of the peak becomes the fourth rather than the second quarter. In other words, manufacturing investment in the latter part of 1970 was growing at close to the long-term trend rate, making the turning-point date rather susceptible to changes in the estimated trend.

Overall, however, turning-points in the two detrended capital formation series are almost as stable with respect to the trend estimation period as are the production series.[1]

CONCLUSIONS

Turning-point locations in the detrended reference series for production and investment (both private non-residential and manufacturing sector) are not much affected by changes in the period over which the trend is estimated. Indeed they are rather more stable than expected in advance. The results, at least for these two target variables, appear sufficiently robust to justify the use of reference chronologies based on the detrended series for further analysis. More generally, they give partial justification for the use of detrended series (the trend being a simple exponential) as indicators, although other tests on total consumers' expenditure showed that this is not without hazard.

It should not be forgotten that the estimation period is only one of the possible factors affecting the location of turning-points. For example, the method of trend estimation, either, say, by moving averages or by least-squares, is highly relevant. Also, changes in the statistical content, or the procedures adopted by the official statisticians can be significant. An example of this last point is the effect of the recent rebasing of many statistical series from 1963 to 1970.

[1] This conclusion does not, however, apply to other capital formation series. Total capital formation, for instance, including both dwellings investment and public sector capital formation, seems to be a lot more susceptible to the estimation period.

Part II

TURNING-POINTS IN THE TARGET VARIABLES

CHAPTER 4

TARGET VARIABLES AND REFERENCE CYCLES

GENERAL COMMENTS

In this part we consider the 'target variables', that is, those broad economic processes which economic policy is generally intended to affect.[1] The cyclical turning-points are identified for each variable (it may sometimes be represented by more than one series) and so a reference chronology is obtained. The individual indicator series can then be tested against the appropriate reference chronology.

The three target variables for which reference chronologies were established are production, investment (gross domestic fixed capital formation at constant prices) and unemployment. Tentative chronologies were also established for consumption (in constant prices, detrended), for the foreign trade balance, and for the rate of inflation of prices and wages. However, various defects were apparent; for example, cyclical turns in consumption were particularly susceptible to the method of trend estimation used. More generally, these variables are, to a much greater degree than the three target variables listed above, susceptible to intervention of one type or another, whether by the Government in the form of exchange rate changes, changes in hire purchase regulations, or prices and incomes policies, or by others, as for instance dock strikes or disruptions caused by war. The effect is to make inter-period changes more erratic and 'true' cyclical movements more difficult to discern. Amongst other considerations are that consumption and, to a lesser extent, the foreign balance, are leaders in terms of the general cycle and more conveniently treated as individual indicators to be matched against the other target variables.

Analysis was therefore concentrated on the target variables production, investment and unemployment. Production (in trend-free form) is the best

[1] Following the convention from J. Tinbergen, *Economic Policy: principles and design*, Amsterdam, North-Holland, 1956, where economic variables, such as taxation and public expenditure, the exchange rate, and Bank Rate (formerly), which policy-makers use to influence the economy, are labelled 'instruments', and variables which the policies are intended to affect 'target variables'.

summary indicator for the economy as a whole; that is, it most closely approximates to the 'general cycle' determined for some other countries (chapter 7 takes up this theme). Investment (detrended) and unemployment are both of considerable importance (politically as well, of course, as economically), and can be described as 'lagging' target variables. Thus there is a good likelihood of finding a number of leading indicators for them, with obvious implications for forecasting.

For both production and investment trend removal is necessary before they display clear cyclical movements; that is, these reference chronologies are growth-cycle chronologies or chronologies of cycles relative to the long-term trend. The reference chronology for the third variable – unemployment – is however determined from the original undetrended series. This may seem inconsistent, particularly as chart 6.1 shows there has been an upward trend in postwar unemployment – at least since the mid-1950s. Trend estimation over the period covered by the graph gives a significant value for the growth-rate in excess of 3 or 4 per cent per annum. Nevertheless the cyclical turning-points are quite distinct. Also it seems rash to assume either that the number wholly unemployed will remain more or less permanently in excess of half a million, or, if one does expect this, that this higher level is due to a steady upward trend rather than to a sharp change in previous relationships between unemployment and production occurring about 1965–6. Many observers believe that there was such a break. In the circumstances, it seems wisest not to try and eliminate the trend from unemployment, although this is at the cost of a loss of consistency in treatment with production and investment.

The fixing of a reference chronology for the three main variables is given in detail in the next two chapters. The questions discussed there include such matters as the selection of an appropriate reference series, of the time-period over which the trend is to be estimated, and of the turning-points. It will be clear that there is an element of personal judgement, sometimes a considerable element, involved in answering these questions. The turning-points finally given are those which seem reasonable, but are not necessarily those which would be selected by another person. The selections and the reasons for selection are set out in some detail so that users of the chronology can question the dates and, should they disagree, have sufficient information to substitute their own.

THE GENERAL CYCLE

Carrying out the analysis in terms of individual target variables, rather than in relation to the general cycle in the whole economy, gives possible gains in precise estimation of lead or lag relationships, but also a loss in simplicity.

For some purposes, for instance international comparisons, it is particularly useful to have a general cycle chronology.

The details of how such a chronology might be constructed and the difficulties involved are described in chapter 7. Briefly, it is not possible to construct a general cycle by detailed consideration of a selection of major economic variables, as in the National Bureau's approach for instance, because of data difficulties and also some puzzling incongruities between the cyclical chronologies established for the individual target variables. However, if one assumes that the reference series used to determine the production cycle (the output index for all industries) is a suitable proxy for gross domestic product and hence probably the best single variable to represent the general cycle, it is possible to claim that the production cycle chronology is an adequate approximation to a general cycle chronology. Going a stage further, the evidence of some other series (and also the diffusion and composite indices presented in chapter 12) can be used to make adjustments to the chronology at those turns where the production index seems a little out of line with other evidence. On this basis a tentative general cycle chronology is set out in chapter 7, but it will be apparent that, even following the adjustments, the chronology is still closely linked to the production cycle and so can be criticised as not being truly representative of all economic activities. The analysis of individual indicators in Part III is related to the target variable chronologies and not to a general cycle.

CHAPTER 5

PRODUCTION AND INVESTMENT

There are some difficult problems in determining postwar cyclical chronologies for the two target variables production and fixed investment. The initial problems are caused by the quality of the data available and the need to select a 'reference series' from which to determine the turning-point dates. Data on fixed investment, for example, are only available more frequently than annually from 1955 onwards and then only quarterly. The same applies to the estimates of gross domestic product, with quarterly values of the output estimate available only from 1958. This is one reason for rejecting this as the reference series for the production cycle in favour of the monthly indices of industrial production, which, although having much less extensive coverage of the economy, have a far longer time-span. But the monthly indices have statistical deficiencies too, being based on estimates subject to sampling and response errors, and to errors in price deflation. The recent rebasing of the indices from 1963 to 1970 led to quite significant movements in the series and affected estimates of turning-point location. The rebasing also had effects on turning-point dates in the series selected as the reference series for fixed investment – that is private sector non-residential gross domestic fixed capital formation at constant prices.

Troublesome too is the extent to which cyclical movements in these variables are masked by an upward trend. This is frequently strong enough to leave only traces of cyclical movement, except to the extent that the cycle is shown by levelling off or acceleration in the growth-rate rather than by absolute decreases or increases in the original series. To reveal these cyclical movements it is necessary to remove, as completely as possible, the trend-component. The alternative methods of tackling this have already been discussed (see chapter 3) and the procedure followed here was to extract a simple exponential time-trend from the data.

PRODUCTION

Statistically we are fairly well off for material on production cycles. Our main reference series are the two monthly indices of production – one for all production industries (including mining and quarrying, construction and gas, electricity and water, but not the agricultural and service industries) – and the other restricted to manufacturing industry. They are shown, both in

Table 5.1. *The chronology of the production cycle (detrended)*[a]

Months

Peaks	Troughs	Phases		Cycles	
		Peak to trough	Trough to peak	Peak to peak	Trough to trough
51/2	52/7	17	41	58	74
55/12	58/9	33	18	51	52
60/3	63/1	34	24	58	55
65/1	67/8	31	22	53	54
69/6	72/2	32			
Mean duration		29	26	55	59

[a] Based on the monthly index of production (all industries).

the original and in their detrended forms, in chart 5.1.[1] Table 5.1 gives the production cycle turning-points determined from the detrended index for all industries. A check using the quarterly series of gross domestic product at constant prices, following trend extraction, generally confirms the turns in table 5.1, at least at cyclical troughs. At cyclical peaks there is a tendency for gross domestic product to turn down earlier, most noticeably in 1968–9 where there is a rough 'plateau' in all the series concerned and so turning-point dates tend to be more variable relative to each other.

Generally, there is little difficulty in determining peak and trough dates. The reference series is unsmoothed, as is the case throughout this paper. One noticeable feature is the existence of two extreme troughs in January 1963 and February 1972. The first was caused by unusually severe climatic conditions, and the second is a result of the coalminers' strike of early 1972. In both cases the trough appears to have been exaggerated rather than shifted (the decline in late 1962 commenced well before the severe weather, thus justifying the choice of 1963 over early 1962 as the trough date). However, the double trough of 1966–7 poses a problem. Detrended the index is lower in late 1966 than in the autumn of 1967, but only marginally so. The difference is sufficiently small to apply the rule that the later of two equal

[1] All the series in chart 5.1 are on a base of 1970 = 100. As the official monthly series have at this date been rebased back only to 1963, the earlier 1963-based data have been linked to the official series on a 1970 base, using the revised quarterly (back to 1952) and annual series as a guide. This is a little arbitrary, particularly using annual data, so the turning-points for the earlier period are those determined on the basis of the 1963-based series. For the most recent period, however, the 1970-based series is used. The rebasing was not without effect on the estimated location of turning-point dates, the peak now located in mid-1969 being previously fixed at the end of 1968, while the trough in 1967 is now less clear-cut than before.

Chart 5.1. *Indices of production, original and detrended*

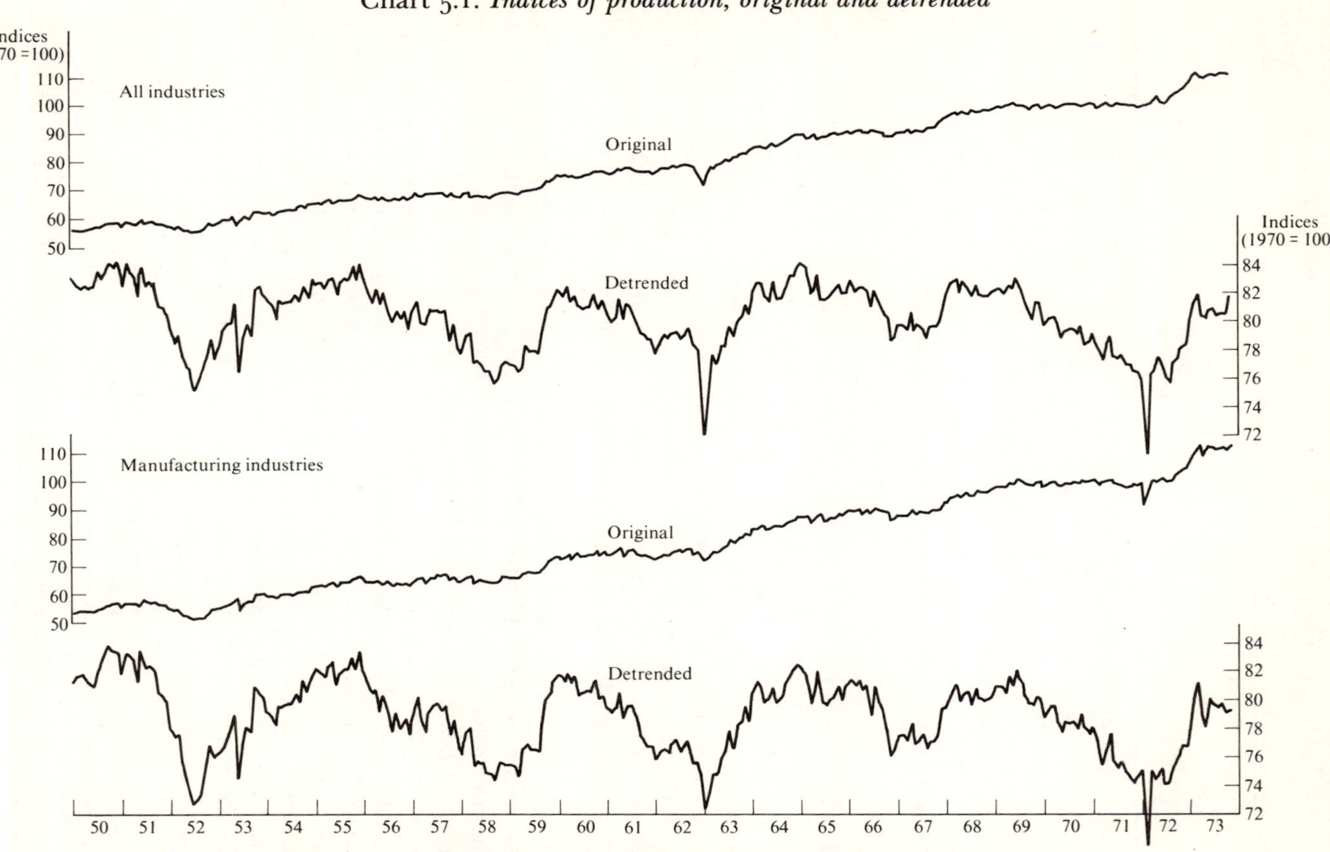

Notes: (i) Both indices detrended between July 1952 and January 1972, with T = 1 at January 1963.
(ii) Index for all industries has a trend annual growth-rate of 3·1 %, for manufacturing industries one of 3·2 %.

or very nearly equal values should be taken as the turning-point date. On this basis, the recession commencing in 1965 is taken to end in August 1967 rather than in November 1966.

Examining table 5.1, we see that postwar cycles have averaged four and a half to five years in duration. The contraction phase of the cycle has been slightly longer on average than the expansion phase – indeed only the 1952–5 expansion is of greater length than its neighbouring recessionary phases.

From chart 5.1 it can be seen that sub-cycles are present in the reference series, that is upward or downward movements which are of insufficient total amplitude and duration to rank as fully fledged cycles, but clearly somewhat more than temporary and irregular fluctuations in the data. The first is the expansion lasting from the end of 1956 to mid-1957 (more noticeable for manufacturing than for all industries). The most clearly marked, however, is the expansion lasting from January to September 1962, while other, though less clear-cut and obvious expansionary phases extending over periods of several months can be identified during 1965, late 1966 to mid-1967, and early 1970.

The analysis in this report is, for simplicity, based solely on the main cyclical turning-points, ignoring the sub-cycles. The sub-cyclical turns cannot, however, be completely ignored, for quite a few of the indicator series also show sub-cyclical movements, sometimes in fact dominating the main cycles, and an idea of how the underlying reference sub-cycle relates to the reference cycle can assist in deciding which is the true cyclical turn in the indicator series.

INVESTMENT

The second target variable we examine is fixed investment or, more precisely, gross fixed domestic capital formation at constant (currently 1970) prices. This still leaves some question, however, as to which investment aggregate is most appropriate for determining the investment reference cycle. Total investment is inappropriate, as the public sector investment which is included is unlikely to conform very well to any cyclical pattern and, in any case, is presumably controllable (with some time-lag) by policy-makers. Also it is undesirable to include investment in dwellings, since residential investment is influenced by factors different from those affecting other types of fixed investment.

These considerations led to private sector investment excluding dwellings at 1970 prices being selected as the reference series for the investment cycle. An alternative series, but much narrower in coverage, would be manufacturing investment at 1970 prices and a cyclical chronology is established for this variable too. Quarterly data for the two investment series

Table 5.2. *The chronology of the fixed investment cycle (detrended)*[a]

Months

Peaks[b]	Troughs[b]	Phases		Cycles	
		Peak to trough	Trough to peak	Peak to peak	Trough to trough
		Based on private non-dwelling GDFCF			
57/2	58/11	21	33	54	57
61/8	63/8	24	18	42	51
65/2	67/11	33	21	54	57
69/8	72/8	36			
Mean duration		28	24	50	55
		Based on manufacturing GDFCF			
57/2	59/8	30	24	54	48
61/8	63/8	24	30	54	51
66/2	67/11	21	30	51	60
70/5	72/11	30			
Mean duration		26	28	53	53

[a] At 1970 prices.

[b] Turning-points taken as mid-months of the relevant quarters.

extend back to 1955 if earlier series are linked with the latest at 1970 prices, but unfortunately no earlier. Monthly data are available for the housing sector only.

The two series are shown in chart 5.2, first in original form and then detrended. The detrending operation brings out the cyclical movement much more clearly, although the turning-points are sufficiently well marked in the original manufacturing series to be little affected by the removal of the trend.

Even after trend removal it is still not easy to determine with certainty the dates where turning-points in private sector investment occurred, at least in recent years. The last peak is taken as having occurred in the third quarter of 1969, but the recovery in 1970 brought investment back to levels not far short of the 1969 peak.[1] The latest trough, in late 1972, now looks to be more firmly established following the upward revision of the initial estimates for

[1] Prior to the rebasing on 1970 prices, the selected peak date was in fact in 1970. One possible factor causing this switch was a change in the treatment of investment by the shipping industry in ships purchased from overseas (see *National Income Blue Book, 1973*, p. 112), their procedure being to record cumulated expenditure at the time of delivery, rather than in instalments as before. However other factors such as revisions to price indices could also have had a considerable effect.

Two other factors affecting movements in the data also require mention, although not specifically connected with the 1970 rebasing. They are the nationalisation of the steel industry in 1967, which shifted some investment out of the private sector, and the alterations made by the official statisticians to counter the bringing forward of investment from early 1969 to late 1968 because of changes in investment grants.

Chart 5.2 *Gross domestic fixed capital formation at 1970 prices, original and detrended*

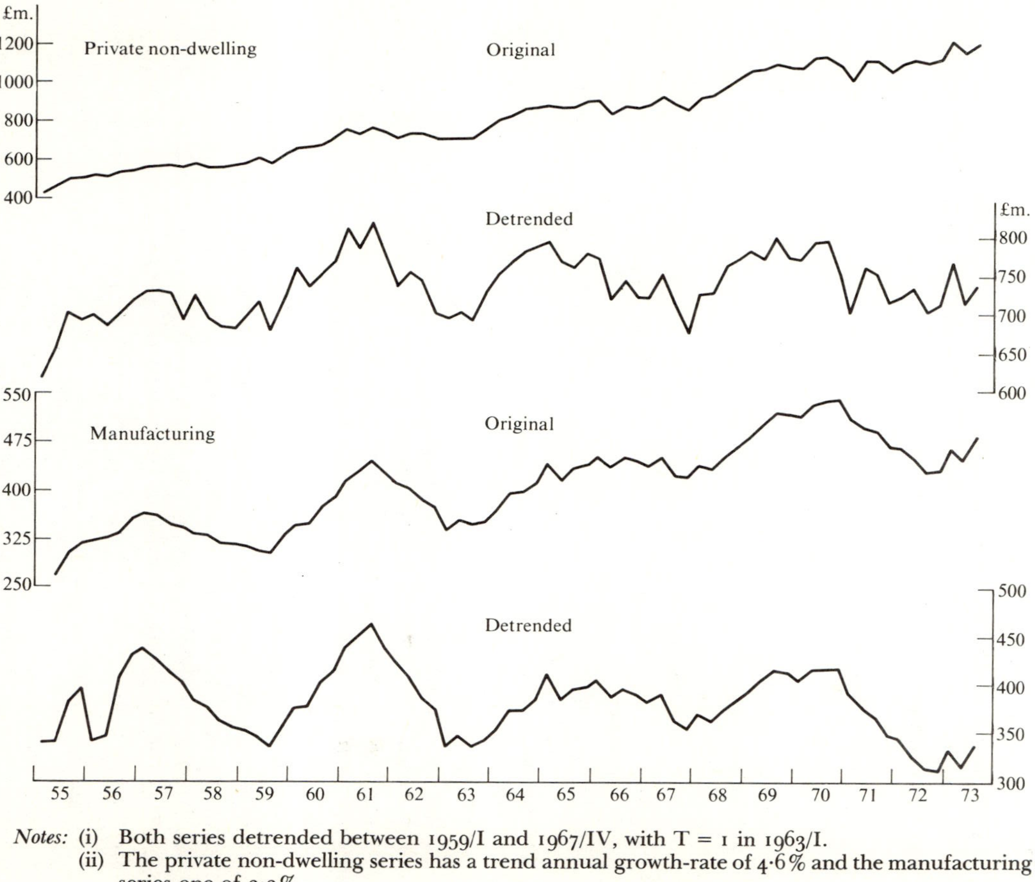

Notes: (i) Both series detrended between 1959/I and 1967/IV, with T = 1 in 1963/I.
(ii) The private non-dwelling series has a trend annual growth-rate of 4·6% and the manufacturing series one of 3·3%.

mid-1973, although it is still necessary to assume that the dip in the first quarter of 1971 is an extreme value; an assumption which graphically looks reasonable.

Table 5.2 sets out the reference chronology finally decided for the investment cycle; the chronology for manufacturing investment (de-trended) is also listed. Whether on a peak-to-peak or trough-to-trough basis, cycle durations for both the private non-residential sector and manufacturing average out at about four and a half years, that is approximately the same as for production.

CHAPTER 6

THE LABOUR MARKET: UNEMPLOYMENT AND VACANCIES

While for production and fixed investment it was necessary to remove the trend-component prior to cyclical analysis, this is not the case for unemployment and unfilled vacancies, as shown by chart 6.1. Admittedly there is an apparent trend upwards in the level of unemployment since 1948 and, more doubtfully, a corresponding downward movement in the level of unfilled vacancies. These long-term changes, however, are comparatively small relative to the cyclical amplitude of both series. Consequently, cyclical turning-points are easily identifiable and there is no need to identify and extract a trend-component.

Unemployment is selected as a target variable in this paper for both its economic significance and its political sensitivity. But cyclical movements could also be represented by unfilled vacancies, or again by the ratio of unfilled vacancies to wholly unemployed, as shown in chart 6.1. The object of this chapter is to derive a cyclical chronology for unemployment, but, having done that, it is a comparatively easy matter to go on and derive subsidiary chronologies for unfilled vacancies and for the ratio of vacancies to unemployment.

In the course of the discussion it is also necessary to touch on some important changes which have occurred in the labour market during the postwar period. One such change is the marked reduction in normal hours (that is, in the standard working week) which occurred in the 1960s, affecting the relationship between the production cycle and the unemployment cycle, and also the timing patterns of individual labour-market indicators relative to these two target variables. The second change is the apparent shift, about 1966–7, in the relationships between unemployment, on the one hand, and variables such as vacancies and production on the other.

UNEMPLOYMENT

Chart 6.1 shows total unemployed in Great Britain (excluding school-leavers and adult students) seasonally adjusted from July 1948 onwards.[1] In

[1] The exclusion of unemployed adult students from the wholly unemployed total is of quite recent origin. Up to 1971, the main unemployment series excluded unemployed school-leavers (because of their irregular seasonal component) but not adult students. The new official series now excludes adult students back to 1963, the numbers registered as unemployed prior to that date being negligible.

An earlier paper on labour-market indicators (D. J. O'Dea, 'Leading indicators of cycles in

Chart 6.1. *Total wholly unemployed, adult unfilled vacancies and the vacancy–unemployment ratio*

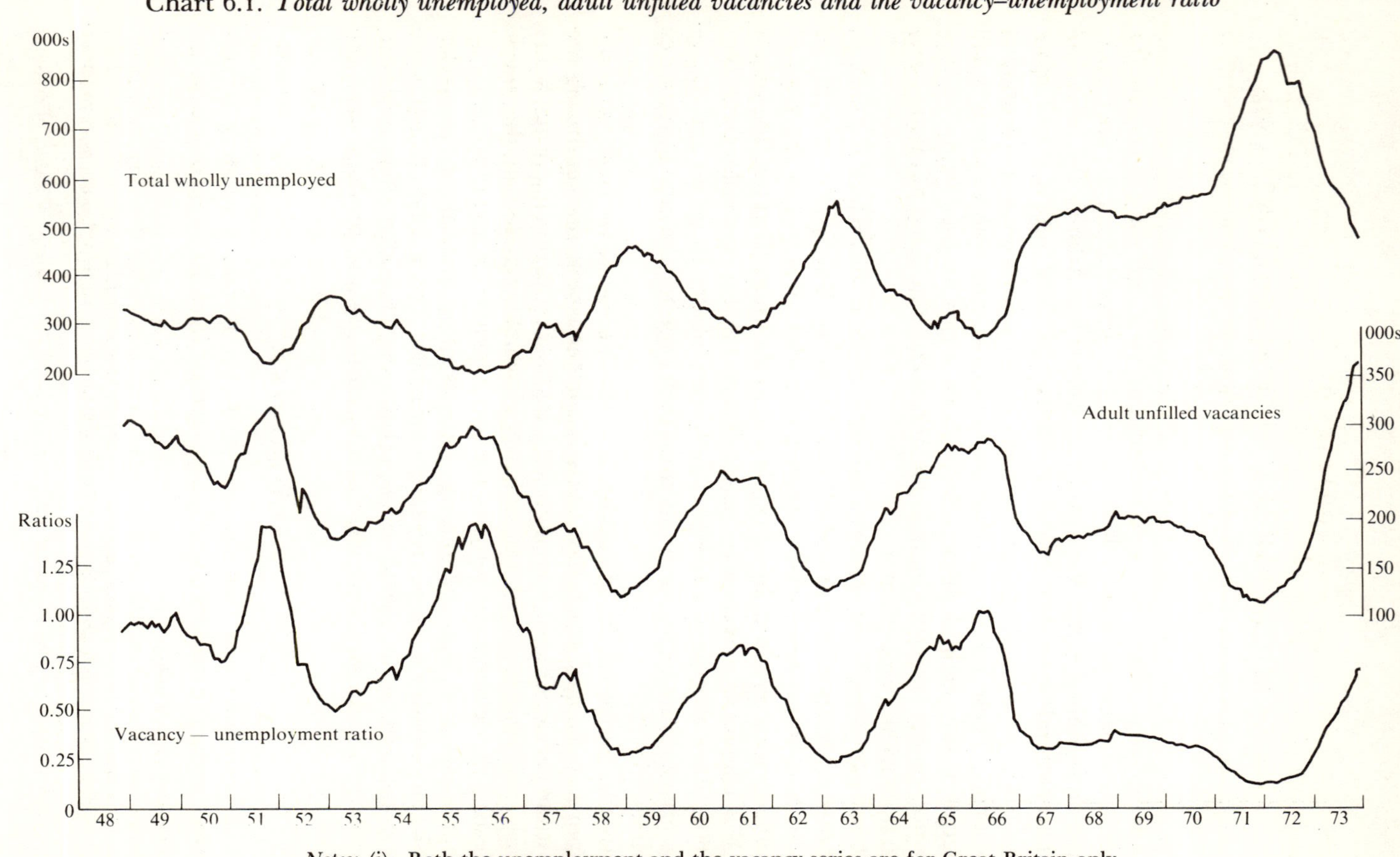

Notes: (i) Both the unemployment and the vacancy series are for Great Britain only.
(ii) The unemployment series excludes school-leavers and adult students.
(iii) All series are seasonally adjusted.

most cases the dates of peaks and troughs in this series can be determined quite easily. For instance the peaks in 1950, 1952, 1958 and 1963 are all reasonably clear-cut, as are the troughs in 1951, 1955, 1961 and 1966. The peak in early 1963 coincided with severe weather conditions, but this appears to have exaggerated rather than shifted the turning-point.

The difficult problem lies in deciding whether there exists a genuine cycle over the period 1966 to 1969. More precisely, is there a genuine contraction in unemployment from mid-1968 to mid-1969, or should the whole period be regarded simply as a not too long-lived plateau in the generally upwards trend in unemployment since 1966?

The decision taken here is that there was indeed a genuine cyclical expansion (reduction in unemployment) in 1968–9. The expansion is certainly weak in terms of its effect on unemployment, but is of reasonably long duration. A similar pattern is shown by almost all other labour-market time-series and, in the last chapter, by the reference series for production and investment.

As an extra check, the series was tested on the Bry and Boschan program for turning-point identification.[1] The program, in addition to confirming all the turns listed earlier, also identified a peak and a trough in mid-1968 and mid-1969 respectively. Overall the evidence points fairly conclusively to a cyclical expansion between 1968 and 1969.

Two other fluctuations can be discerned from the chart: a mild expansion (a contraction in terms of unemployment) extending over most of 1957, and a short-lived contraction (increase in unemployment) in mid-1965. Clearly both are of minor amplitude and duration compared with the major postwar cycles in unemployment. Perhaps they can be appropriately regarded as sub-cycles; in any case they have been excluded from the analysis, which concentrated on statistical relationships at the major turning-points.

Table 6.1 shows the turning-point dates finally selected. Durations of cycles in Great Britain average, for the period covered, about 4½ years, although individual cycles range from approximately 2½ years up to 6 years.

The reduction in normal hours worked in industry (that is, the 'standard' number of hours worked at ordinary time rates) from approximately 44 hours a week in the 1950s to 40 hours in the late 1960s was concentrated in two periods, with about half the decrease occurring in each: the first was the calendar year 1960, and the second the period between the end of 1964 and early 1966. As it happens, both these periods are in the neighbourhood of cyclical peaks, and it does appear that the change in

unemployment: an interim report' in G. A. Renton (ed.), *Modelling the Economy*, London, Heinemann, 1975) used the old, wholly unemployed series, which peaked one month later in 1966, but otherwise shows little difference.

[1] The program is one of those described in Gerhard Bry and Charlotte Boschan, *Cyclical Analysis of Time Series: selected procedures and computer programs*, New York, NBER, 1971.

Table 6.1. *The chronology of the unemployment cycle*[a]

Months

Peaks	Troughs	Phases		Cycles	
		Peak to trough	Trough to peak	Peak to peak	Trough to trough
	50/7		13		28
51/8	52/11	15	37	52	72
55/12	58/11	35	28	63	52
61/3	63/3	24	35	59	63
66/2	68/6	28	11	39	45
69/5	72/3	34			
Mean duration		27	25	53	52

[a] Inverted, so that a trough represents a 'high' in unemployment and a peak a 'low'.

normal hours at least partially affected some of the timing relationships between unemployment and the labour-market indicators – in particular, the series for average hours and total hours as discussed below. This means that the timing relationships at peaks established for these particular series are unlikely to provide a good guide to future events in the British labour market without some adjustment. For this reason the experiment was tried of adjusting them by means of the normal hours index (a series published by the Department of Employment). The results, as discussed later, look on the whole more reasonable when matched against the unemployment cycle.

A second consequence of the change in normal hours is less easily overcome; this was the effect on the estimated average time-span between peaks in production and peaks in the unemployment cycle (actually troughs in the original unemployment series, but for all subsequent analysis we regard the turning-points as occurring in the inverted unemployment series). If the effect in both 1960–1 and 1965–6 is to retard the peak in the unemployment cycle in relation to that in the production cycle, then the average lag will be over-estimated. Whether there has in fact been such a retardation is not easily established; there are too many factors whose influence cannot be easily ascertained – for instance the extent to which an increase in the demand for employees as a result of reductions in normal hours affected the level of unemployment and unfilled vacancies (possibly having a greater impact on turnover than on absolute levels). From graphical inspection and checks on the numbers involved, it does seem likely that the 1965–6 peak in the unemployment cycle was delayed, explaining incidentally the 1965 sub-cycle; alternatively the continuance of the boom in late 1965 is sometimes thought to be a consequence of businessmen believ-ing that national economic planning would thenceforth eliminate the 'stop' part of the 'stop–go' cycle. It is less likely that the unemployment turning-point was delayed in 1960, when there is some evidence that the peak in production is dated a little early relative to other variables.

This possible divergence assumes importance if, in addition to reference chronologies for the individual variables, a general reference cycle is also being established based on a consideration of all major economic activities. There are sound reasons for linking such a chronology to the production cycle (discussed at more length in chapter 7), but it is also highly desirable to possess confirmatory evidence from variables such as unemployment and employment. The effect of the postwar reductions in the average working week is to make labour-market indicators less reliable at identifying general cycle turning-points than they otherwise would be.

VACANCIES

An alternative measure of cyclical movements in the labour market is the monthly series recording the number of vacancies notified by employers and as yet unfilled. It will be shown later that cyclical turning-points in unfilled vacancies in general lead those in unemployment, more particularly at peaks. Thus the series, in addition to being a measure of current trends in the labour market, can also give a forewarning of changes in unemployment.

No discussion of the cyclical fluctuations in unfilled vacancies would be complete without some reference to the extensive literature on the interpretation of data on vacancies and the problems caused by its deficiencies.[1] The latter can be quite serious, and there can be a substantial degree of under- or even over-statement of vacancies reported by employers, though probably most observers would believe that unfilled vacancies, and also other measures such as the 'gap' between unemployment and vacancies, can be used to give a fairly reliable ordinal measure of demand pressure.

This conclusion has looked rather more doubtful in recent years. There has been quite widespread criticism of the vacancy statistics, generally in the context of discussion of potential 'bottlenecks' and 'overheating' during the course of the 1972–3 expansion in the United Kingdom economy. Much of the discussion has centred round changes in administrative practice and whether these may be inflating the number of vacancies, but in a recent article Colin Leicester has suggested a number of other factors, notably the

[1] J. C. R. Dow and L. A. Dicks-Mireaux, 'The excess demand for labour: a study of conditions in Great Britain, 1946–56', *Oxford Economic Papers*, vol. 10 (new series), February 1958, pp. 1–33; NBER, *The Measurement and Interpretation of Job Vacancies*, New York, Columbia University Press, 1966; Charlotte Boschan, 'Fluctuations in job vacancies – an analysis of available measures', (unpublished) 1967; John G. Myers, *Job Vacancies in the Firm and the Labor Market*, New York, National Industrial Conference Board, 1969.

Table 6.2. *The chronology of unfilled vacancies and its ratio to unemployment*

Months

Peaks	Troughs	Phases: Peak to trough	Phases: Trough to peak	Cycles: Peak to peak	Cycles: Trough to trough
		Unfilled vacancies			
	50/8		9		27
51/5	52/11	18	33	51	70
55/8	58/9	37	25	62	52
60/10	63/1	27	39	66	54
66/4	67/7	15	17	32	53
68/12	71/12	36			
Mean duration		27	25	53	51
		Ratio vacancies–unemployment			
	50/7		10		28
51/5	52/11	18	34	52	72
55/9	58/11	38	27	65	52
61/2	63/3	25	37	62	52
66/4	67/7	15	17	32	53
68/12	71/12	36			
Mean duration		26	25	53	51

duration of vacancies, which will change over the cycle and tend to invalidate inter-period comparisons even on an ordinal basis.[1]

While it would be unwise to ignore the possibility of changes, both secular and cyclical, in the vacancies series, it does seem that indicator analysis is less likely to be affected by them than other means of analysis, and that the turning-point locations in the series are unlikely to be seriously affected. Table 6.2 sets out the peak and trough dates, and phase and cycle durations. The average durations are very close to those obtained for unemployment; the turning-point dates are also normally close to those established for the unemployment cycle, with the exception of the 1967–8 trough where the upturn in vacancies occurs almost a year before the corresponding turn in unemployment.

This last divergence is seen also in the other variable in table 6.2, the ratio of unfilled vacancies to numbers wholly unemployed. Overall, the cyclical timing of the ratio lies between vacancies and unemployment. The ratio, like the vacancies series, is frequently used as a measure of the pressure of demand for labour. Its particular virtue is that it can be expected to have

[1] Colin Leicester, 'Vacancies and the demand for labour', *I.M.S. Monitor*, vol. 2, October 1973. One apparent change at employment exchanges has been to set targets for the number of vacancies to be registered, this change taking effect from about the end of 1972 (see *Financial Times*, 4 April 1973).

relatively sharp and well-defined turns at both peaks and troughs, whereas this is not necessarily true of its two components. The reasoning is that in a comparatively tight labour market unemployment declines to near 'frictional' levels and thereafter changes only sluggishly, whereas vacancies can continue to increase without any obvious ceiling. Conversely, in a slack labour market, vacancies can decline little further, whereas numbers unemployed can still increase.[1] Thus the vacancy–unemployment ratio should be sharply defined at all turns. In practice, however, as shown in chart 6.1 it is difficult, at least from visual inspection, to see any marked improvement.

Any defects in the vacancies data, of the type discussed above, will equally affect the ratio. Also it has clearly been affected by the marked change in the relationship previously existing between unemployment and vacancies which appears to have taken place in the period 1966–8 – explaining incidentally the different dates tabulated for the 1967–8 trough. There has been a good deal of controversy about the causes of this change, centring largely on the factors determining the numbers registered as unemployed.[2] Whatever its cause, the effects can be seen in chart 6.1.

A final point about the series for both vacancies and the vacancy–unemployment ratio is that two sub-cycles corresponding to those in unemployment are again apparent – a short-lived recovery in 1957 and a brief contraction in mid-1965.

[1] The reasoning here follows that in Charlotte Boschan's unpublished paper.

[2] See for example the exchange between J. Taylor and D. Gujarati, 'The behaviour of unemployment and unfilled vacancies. An interchange', *Economic Journal*, vol. 82, December 1972, pp. 1352–68. The question posed was on the relative merits of a supply-based or demand-based explanation for the 1968 increase in unemployment (i.e. the introduction of redundancy payments and income-related benefits versus a labour shakeout). The most recent experience supports the latter hypothesis (*National Institute Economic Review*, no. 66, November 1973, pp. 25–8). See also David T. Llewellyn and Paul Newbold, 'The behaviour of unemployment and unfilled vacancies', *Journal of Industrial Relations*, vol. 4, Spring 1973, pp. 30–42.

CHAPTER 7

A GENERAL CYCLE?

This paper concentrates on chronologies for distinct target variables rather than a single chronology for cycles in the whole economy. A reason for this is implicit in the very name 'target variable' – certain components of the overall economic structure are particular targets of economic policy, or at least objects of particular interest and comment. This approach is made, however, at the cost of a considerable loss of simplicity, initially in the computations, but also in the description of cycles in the United Kingdom economy. As matters stand we cannot refer to the '1960 downturn in the British economy' without making it clear that we are speaking of production, say, rather than employment. Likewise any comparison with the cyclical chronologies of other countries becomes a good deal more difficult.[1]

It seems then, that it would be worthwhile for some purposes to develop a general cycle chronology, even though our detailed analysis of individual indicators will continue to be related to specific target variables. We examine first alternative methods of determining such a general reference cycle.

General chronologies have been determined for a number of countries,[2] whether in terms of the 'classical' cycle in the original series, or growth cycles in the detrended series. Although all have been conceptually influenced by the work of the National Bureau, the actual methods used have in practice varied widely.

Frequently it is suggested that the obvious variable is gross domestic product or gross national product, and occasionally this has been used.

[1] An important point in view of the proposals for a system of international indicators contained in a paper by G. C. Moore and W. C. Shelton, 'International economic indicators: a proposal', *Business Economics*, vol. 7, May 1972. At the time this project was under way, the Moore–Shelton proposals were being put into effect as the International Economic Indicator Project at the National Bureau under the direction of Professor P. A. Klein. A joint attempt was made by Professor Klein, research staff at the Central Statistical Office and the author of this paper to establish an agreed general reference chronology for the United Kingdom. Although the attempt was not successful, much of the material in this chapter has been influenced by our discussions.

[2] For a list see Mintz, *Dating Postwar Business Cycles*, p. 7. Four recent publications and articles can be added: M.G. Bush and A. M. Cohen, *The Indicator Approach to the Identification of Business Cycles*, Sydney, Reserve Bank of Australia, 1968; E. Haywood, *The Dating of Post-war Business Cycles in New Zealand 1946–1970*, Wellington, Reserve Bank of New Zealand, 1972; Gunther Tichy, *Indikatoren der Österreichischen Konjunktur 1950 bis 1970*, Vienna, Österreichisches Institut für Wirtschaftsforschung, 1972; D. J. Smit and B. E. van der Walt, 'Business cycles in South Africa during the postwar period, 1946 to 1968', *South Africa Reserve Bank Quarterly Bulletin*, September 1970, pp. 21–46 (also June 1973 issue, pp. 33–9).

Matthews used annual detrended data on gross domestic product to represent the general cycle;[1] and most recently Gunther Tichy used detrended gross national product.[2] But the objections to gross domestic product are decisive: the uncertainties in its measurement and the frequency with which it is revised; to this it should be added that even quarterly data are available only from 1955 (1958 for some measures).

Drakatos for the British economy and Bush and Cohen for Australia used the medians of clusters of turning-points, computed for a considerable number of indicators.[3] A look at their graphs shows that one difficulty is that sometimes the clusters are rather widely spread. A more general objection is that the results depend too much on the indicators selected, and the selection could easily be biased towards a certain type of series and could also have a biased representation of the different timing classes.

Finally the National Bureau examines in detail those major economic aggregates (gross national product at constant and current prices, employment and others) which are known to have cyclical movements approximately coincidental with each other and therefore with the general cycle. The process is not mechanical but involves a high degree of expert judgement.

Ideally it is the last of these methods we would wish to use, but unfortunately our results for the target variables, and also for other series such as employment, show that the turning-points in the different series are sometimes quite scattered (for example in 1960–1 or 1964–6) and that any chronology based on all of them would have a large element of subjectivity. This is clearly shown by chart 7.1, which sets out in simple schematic form the cycles in the target variables. The unfilled vacancies series is also included and shows quite clearly that the 1968 trough in unemployment is an aberration, with the other target variables pointing to a much earlier general trough. The investment series, with its lengthy and variable lags, is not particularly useful for determining the general cycle, so essentially we must rely on those series measuring cyclical changes in the labour market and in production.

This, however, raises the difficulty touched on in an earlier chapter, namely the divergence between the production and unemployment cycles at the cyclical peaks in 1960–1 and 1964–5, which appears to have been at least partly a result of reductions in normal working hours taking effect about those times. The net result of all these considerations is to force us to use a single target variable, namely production, to define the general cycle

[1] 'Postwar business cycles in the United Kingdom'.

[2] *Indikatoren der Österreichischen Konjunktur 1950 bis 1970.*

[3] Drakatos, 'Leading indicators for the British economy'; Bush and Cohen, *The Indicator Approach to the Identification of Business Cycles.* Drakatos states that, as a check on the cluster centre-point method 'six series which are thought to provide a good guide to the movement of the general level of activity were examined'.

Chart 7.1. *Schematic diagram of cycles in the target variables*

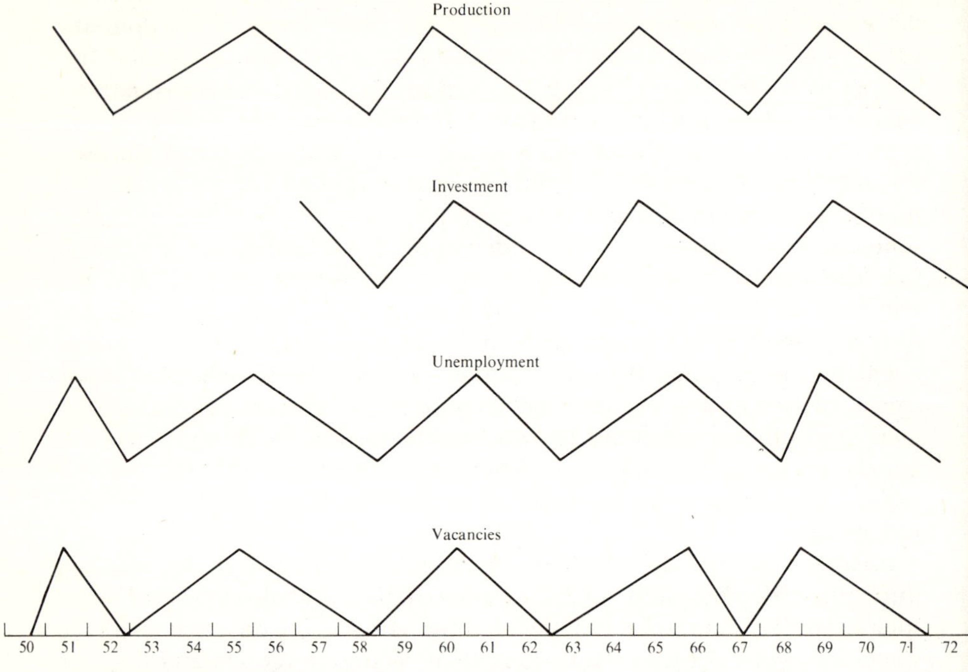

SOURCES: tables 5.1, 5.2, 6.1 and 6.2.

chronology. Production is the logical variable to use, being closest to the ideal of an accurate monthly measure of gross domestic product. However, the indices of production are themselves subject to various types of measurement error. Hence, in trying to define a general chronology, a sensible procedure is to modify those turns in the production cycle where there is strong evidence from other series against the location of the original turning-point.

Table 7.1 displays the leads and lags of the other target variables (and also the subsidiary target variables discussed in chapters 5 and 6) at individual turning-points in the production cycle. Also included in the table are corresponding figures for two composite series whose derivation is described in chapter 12. They summarise the evidence of a number of individual indicators, the first being based on twenty series which customarily lead the production cycle and the second on fourteen series which generally lag it. (A similar index is also available for those series which approximately coincide with production. However its principal components are so closely related to the production indices that it can hardly be regarded as providing independent evidence.)

Table 7.1. *Leads and lags of other target variables over turning-points in the production cycle*

Months

	Unemployment	Investment (detrended)		Vacancies	Vacancy/unemployment ratio	Composite indices	
		Private non-dwelling	Manufacturing			20 leading series	14 lagging series
Turning-points:							
51/2	+6	n.a.	n.a.	+3	+3	−5	+6
52/7	+4	n.a.	n.a.	+4	+4	−3	+6
55/12	0	+14	+14	−4	−3	−6	+4
58/9	+2	+2	+11	0	+2	−7	+4
60/3	+12	+17	+17	+7	+11	0	+17
63/1	+2	+7	+7	0	+2	0	+7
65/1	+13	+1	+13	+15	+15	−12	+13
67/8	+10	+3	+3	−1	−1	−9	+3
69/6	−1	+2	+11	−6	−6	−9	+17
72/2	+1	+6	+9	−2	−2	−11	+3
Median lead or lag:							
Peaks	+6	+8	+13·5	+3	+3	−6	+13
Troughs	+2	+4·5	+8	0	+2	−7	+4
All turns	+3	+4·5	+11	0	+2	−6·5	+6

Note: Leads are shown as negative and lags as positive.

Table 7.2. *A chronology suggested for the general reference cycle*

Months

Peaks	Troughs	Phases		Cycles	
		Peak to trough	Trough to peak	Peak to peak	Trough to trough
51/2	52/7	17	41	58	74
55/12	58/9	33	22	55	52
60/7	63/1	30	24	54	55
65/1	67/8	31	19	50	54
69/3	72/2	35			
Mean duration		29	26	54	59

In examining these series, any marked deviation of an individual lead or lag from the median for that series will suggest a possibility that either the turning-point in that series or the corresponding turn in the production cycle is displaced by some irregularity from its 'true' position. If a number of the series show a deviation in the same direction, the likelihood is that it is the production cycle which requires modification.

On this basis it can be seen that the doubtful turns are the three cyclical peaks occurring in 1960, 1965 and 1969. In 1965 a combination of reductions in normal hours plus confidence engendered in businessmen by the National Plan is sufficient to explain the lengthy lag behind production shown by some series. A general cycle peak in early 1965 looks reasonable. On the other two occasions, however, there is a strong case for supposing that the general cycle peak does not coincide exactly with the peak in the detrended index of production. The 1960 peak appears too early by a few months; the 1969 peak, although not so clearly, seems to be fixed too late.

Following this reasoning the general cycle is taken as having turning-point dates identical to those in production, with two exceptions: the 1960 peak should be placed in July rather than March, and the 1969 peak should be placed in March rather than June. With these adjustments the chronology in table 7.2 is obtained with the usual measures of phase and cycle duration. As is to be expected, the mean durations are nearly identical to those for the production cycle.

Whatever can be claimed for the general cycle chronology determined in this chapter, it can hardly be said to be the last word on the subject. The subjectively determined modifications to the production cycle require further testing, and the basic reliance on the production cycle is also debatable. In spite of these limitations, the chronology is put forward here as a provisional dating of the general cycle, which possibly will both inspire further development and serve as a basis for it.

Part III

THE INDICATORS

CHAPTER 8

CLASSIFICATION OF INDICATORS AND PRESENTATION OF RESULTS

The performance of the individual indicators, analysed by the methods explained in chapter 2 and appendix A, is tabulated and discussed in this section. First, the determination of the timing class given to a series is explained, and then the classification of the indicators according to economic category is outlined. Overseas experience is relevant here and those indicators found to be particularly useful in the United States are tabulated.

The three chapters following describe in detail the results obtained from matching the indicators with the three target variables – production, investment and unemployment. The tabular material presented in these three chapters is substantial, and so a guide to its organisation is given later in this chapter.

The final chapter in Part III deals with the techniques used to combine information from a number of indicators into one summary index, that is with the construction of diffusion and composite indices. These indices, especially those constructed from leading indicators, have obvious potential for forecasting, and so lead naturally to the subsequent section dealing with forecasting.

CLASSIFICATION BY TIMING CLASS

The indicators are classified as being leading, lagging or roughly coincident relative to a specified target variable or, if not falling within one of these classes consistently, simply remain unclassified. The classification applies to peaks and troughs separately, but can also be applied over all turning-points.

The timing class for a given indicator is determined first by the average lead or lag of the series against the peaks or troughs of the reference chronology, and secondly by whether the turns in the series fall with reasonable consistency within the same timing class as the average. The test of 'reasonable consistency' makes use of the timing probability defined in appendix A. Thus we have the following rules for classification:

(i) A leading series has an average (median) lead of three months and upwards (though sometimes of only one or two months if nevertheless the series is a more consistent leader than a coincider) at reference cycle peaks (or troughs) and will lead at most individual peaks (or troughs).

(ii) A lagging series has an average (median) lag of three months or more (or sometimes less if nevertheless the series is a more consistent lagger than a coincider) at reference cycle peaks (or troughs) and will lag at most individual peaks (or troughs).

(iii) A roughly coincident series will have an average (median) lead or lag in the range plus or minus two months, and most individual leads or lags within the range plus or minus three months of the reference cycle peaks (or troughs).

It should be noted that the timing classification appropriate at peaks might not be that appropriate for the troughs of the same series; in fact, they quite often differ. Another point is that the timing classification will depend on the target variable against which the indicator series is being compared. The consistency with which individual turns fall in a particular timing class and the variability of the leads or lags about the average lead or lag gives some guidance on the target variable with which an individual indicator is most appropriately matched.

CLASSIFICATION BY ECONOMIC CATEGORY

Table 8.1 lists the principal economic categories – seven in all – into which the indicators are classified. The system is based closely on that used by Moore and Shiskin in their last general review of indicators for the United States, although the category measuring government activity, for instance tax receipts and expenditure, which appears in the Moore and Shiskin work, is omitted.[1] Some series were examined, but the effect of frequent policy changes in tax rates, etc., was to conceal any relationship between the series and the general economic cycle. In all some 150 monthly or quarterly time-series appear in the tables in this section, with most of them being tested against the production cycle. These indicators are those which survived an initial vetting given to a substantially larger number, but, even so, many of them do not score particularly well against any of the listed target variables, or, for other reasons discussed later in this paper, do not contribute much of value to cyclical analysis. Thus, taking the selection process a stage further, we selected a short list of indicators tabulated in the summary sections of the next three chapters. Table 12.1, with a similar layout to table 8.1, gives the classification of shortlisted indicators.

From table 8.1 we see that the most indicators fall into the employment and unemployment category, although a sizeable proportion of those are

[1] Moore and Shiskin, *Indicators of Business Expansions and Contractions.*

Table 8.1. *Economic categories of indicators analysed*

Numbers of series

	Target variable			Totals		
	Production	Investment	Unemployment	Monthly series	Quarterly series	Overall
Labour-market	28	7	61	43	19	62
Output, consumption and income	22	12	7	14	9	23
Fixed investment[a]	16	17	5	4	16	20
Stocks (levels and changes)	11	11	0	0	11	11
Prices, costs and profits	15	5	3	8	7	15
Money and credit	12	8	2	10	2	12
Foreign trade	13	0	0	9	4	13
All categories	117	60	78	88	68	156

[a] Includes series for orders and anticipations.

matched only against unemployment. With that exception the indicators examined are spread roughly evenly across all categories.

SHORTLISTED INDICATORS IN THE UNITED STATES

We digress briefly at this point to consider those indicators which have been found most useful in the United States. Because of the use in this paper of separate target variables and because also the production chronology is based on growth cycles, it is not particularly meaningful to try and compare results from this study directly with those for the United States.[1] However the listed series do suggest where good indicators for cycles in the British economy can be expected. As will be seen later, the British series analogous to those listed in table 8.2 are generally high-scoring and also generally fall within the same timing class (when matched against the production cycle) as that found for the United States indicators. There are some exceptions: thus the new companies series is not a useful leading indicator for the British

[1] For a study which compares average leads and lags between countries, see Kathleen H. Moore, 'The comparative performance of economic indicators in the United States, Canada and Japan', *Western Economic Journal*, vol. 9, December 1971, pp. 419–28. She found that there is 'a broad similarity among the three countries in the length of leads at peaks and at troughs, respectively'. The paper reports only a comparison of composite indices for the three countries, but the conclusions were based also on unpublished material comparing individual indicators. A comparison between labour-market indicators of unemployment for Britain and the United States, made by the author of this paper, reached similar conclusions (D. J. O'Dea, 'The cyclical timing of labor market indicators in Britain and the United States' to be published in a forthcoming issue of the NBER journal, *Explorations in Economic Research*).

Table 8.2. *Indicators suggested by United States experience to be of particular value*

Category	Leading	Roughly coincident	Lagging
Employment and unemployment	Average work week in manufacturing Placements Initial unemployment claims	Non-agricultural employees Unemployment rate	Unemployment rate, 15+ weeks
Production, income and consumption		GNP at constant prices Industrial production Personal income Manufacturing and trade sales Retail sales	
Fixed investment	Net business formation New orders, durable goods Contracts and orders, plant and equipment Housing permits		Business expenditure on new plant and equipment
Stocks	Change in manufacturing and trade inventories		Manufacturing and trade inventories
Prices, costs and profits	Industrial materials prices Stock prices Corporate profits after tax Ratio prices to unit labour costs		Labour costs per unit of output in manufacturing
Money and credit	Change in consumer instalment debt		Commercial and industrial loans outstanding Bank rates on business loans

Source: Moore and Shiskin, *Indicators of Business Expansions and Contractions*

cycle, and neither are the income series (even in growth-rate form) of much use as coincident indicators. Also, closely matching British series are not available for a number of the series listed. Nevertheless, there is a substantial overlap between the series in table 8.2 and the British series found later in this paper to be among the better cyclical indicators.

One series not included in the United States short list, doubtless because of the comparative unimportance of foreign trade in the United States economy, is the external balance, which is however a leading series for both the Canadian and Japanese economies, and is, of course, one of the series to be tested as an indicator for the British cycle.

LAYOUT AND PRESENTATION OF RESULTS

In view of the large amount of material analysed in the next three chapters, it will be helpful at this point to outline briefly how the material is organised.

Each chapter deals with one of the three target variables. For each target variable the individual series are classified into the seven broad economic categories listed in table 8.1 for presentation of results and comments. (The series being matched against unemployment are treated slightly differently, with a finer breakdown of the employment and unemployment category, and some amalgamation of the other groups.) Thus the detailed material is presented in seven tables,[1] which are followed by two summary tables, listing the 'best' indicators and drawing together the results from the earlier tables together with some additional material.[2] The discussion of the tabulated material does not go very far beyond setting out the empirical findings; some indication is occasionally given of the theoretical reasons for expecting particular cyclical sequences, but the reasoning is verbal and not particularly detailed. The mass of statistical data presented within the comparatively short compass of this paper has prevented the exploration in a good deal more detail of the tabulated results. However, for those requiring a more analytical treatment, there are a number of references on cyclical indicator analysis of particular aspects of the United States economy.[3]

[1] Unfortunately it was not possible to include tables of turning-points in the individual indicators, but duplicated tables of such dates for indicators appearing in the summary tables are available on application to the author.

[2] Further details for the indicators shortlisted in the summary tables are given in appendix B.

[3] For the United States, because little material using this method of analysis is available for other economies, including the United Kingdom, although there are of course many relevant analyses based on other approaches. One work which is particularly worth citing is Moore (ed.), *Business Cycle Indicators*, which contains in vol. 1 a number of papers specifically analysing the cyclical behaviour of certain types of leading indicators, such as business formation, business failures, profits, manufacturers' orders, the average work-week and other labour-market indicators. Among other recent works of importance are Geoffrey H. Moore, 'The cyclical behavior of prices' in Zarnowitz (ed.), *The Business Cycle Today*; P. A. Klein, *The Cyclical Timing of Consumer Credit, 1920–67*, New York, NBER, 1971; V. Zarnowitz, *Orders, Production and Investment: a cyclical and structural analysis*, New York, NBER, 1973; Thor Hultgren, *Costs, Prices and Profits: their cyclical relations*, New York, Columbia University Press, 1965.

CHAPTER 9

INDICATORS OF CYCLICAL TURNS IN PRODUCTION

In this chapter we turn to a detailed examination of the individual indicators, and how they relate to cyclical turning-points in production. The two other target variables, investment and unemployment, are examined similarly in the two succeeding chapters. The target variable production is taken to be satisfactorily represented by the monthly index of production for all industries, following the removal of the trend component from the series (see the earlier discussion in chapter 5).

LABOUR-MARKET SERIES

Details on statistical sources and peculiarities of the various labour-market indicators can be found in chapter 11, where the series are matched against unemployment. A selection from the series considered there is given in table 9.1. A particularly interesting question is whether the series can be readily classified into two separate groups – those linked closely to cyclical movements in unemployment and those more closely linked to the production cycle, to the extent that cyclical movements in the two variables diverge.

Before proceeding, however, to the discussion of such points, a brief digression on the layout of table 9.1 and succeeding tables is in order. The indicators are all identified by a code number used in the original computations; a detailed description of the series and their sources is given in appendix D. The code numbers have no significance in themselves, although the letters M or Q indicate whether the series is monthly or quarterly. A few of the series carry an asterisk; this shows that they have had the trend component removed. Taking Q7, which is the series for net engagements in manufacturing, as an example, the table shows that it leads on average at both peaks and troughs, the median leads being recorded in the first three columns of the table.

This information, however, is not too meaningful without further information about the stability and consistency of the leads or lags. While an examination of leads and lags at individual peaks and troughs in the reference cycle would give some idea, the summary figures in table 9.1 are a great deal more convenient to use. The standard deviations in the next two columns measure stability about the average lead or lag. At troughs the standard deviation for Q7 is satisfactorily low, but at peaks the standard deviation of eight months is higher than is desirable. The next three

Table 9.1. *Labour-market series as indicators for production*

Series no.	Median lead (−) or lag (+) P	T	P & T	Standard deviation P	T	Timing class[a] P	T	P & T	Basic score[b] P	T	P & T	Total score[c] P	T	P & T
	(months)			(months)										
Labour turnover in manufacturing														
Q1	−7·0	0·0	−1·0	8·1	3·6	U	U	U	31	37	34	37	43	40
Q4	−1·0	+4·0	+2·5	8·6	3·2	U	+	+	31	44	37	37	50	43
Q7	−12·0	−3·0	−6·5	8·0	3·3	−	−	−	38	44	41	44	50	47
Temporarily stopped and short-time (inverted)														
M1	0·0	−1·0	−0·5	1·5	3·5	C	C	C	49	38	44	70	59	65
M10	−6·5	−1·5	−4·0	3·4	4·2	−	C	−	45	30	38	54	39	47
Overtime in manufacturing														
M5	+2·0	−1·0	−1·0	6·8	3·0	U	C	U	32	36	34	44	48	46
M7	+2·0	−1·0	−1·0	6·1	3·0	U	C	U	33	36	35	42	45	44
M8	+0·5	−1·5	−1·0	5·4	1·6	U	C	C	38	58	48	41	61	51
M9	+0·5	−1·0	−1·0	5·9	3·0	U	C	C	33	36	35	42	45	44
Hours in manufacturing														
M15	−6·0	−1·0	−3·0	3·7	4·3	−	C	−	44	33	38	53	42	47
M60	−1·0	+1·5	+1·0	2·5	4·0	C	+	C	36	34	35	48	46	47
Vacancies														
M25	+3·0	0·0	0·0	7·6	2·0	+	C	U	31	44	38	58	71	65
M37	+3·0	+2·0	+2·0	8·0	2·2	+	C	+	30	44	37	57	71	64
Q11	−3·0	−6·0	−5·0	1·0	0·0	−	−	−	24	25	24	45	46	45
Employment														
Q16	+13·5	+1·0	+7·0	6·8	2·6	+	C	+	36	34	35	48	46	47
Q25	+13·0	+2·0	+7·0	9·6	4·2	+	+	+	33	32	32	45	44	44
M48	+6·0	+4·0	+5·0	9·1	3·8	+	+	+	37	53	45	52	68	60
M49	+6·0	+7·0	+6·5	4·5	3·5	+	+	+	52	53	52	67	68	67
Wholly unemployed by industry (inverted)[d]														
M70	+6·0	+2·0	+3·0	5·8	3·2	+	+	+	32	51	42	59	78	69
M90	+4·0	+2·0	+2·0	6·6	3·4	+	+	+	31	51	41	52	72	62
M91	+4·0	+1·0	+1·5	6·8	0·5	+	C	+	32	56	44	53	77	65
M92	+6·0	+5·0	+5·5	7·3	4·1	+	+	+	21	41	31	39	59	49
Wholly unemployed by duration (inverted)[e]														
M78	+4·0	−1·0	0·0	7·4	3·3	+	−	U	27	32	30	42	47	45
M99	+4·0	0·0	0·0	7·0	4·8	+	U	U	28	30	29	43	45	44
M100	+4·0	0·0	0·0	7·0	5·2	+	U	U	28	30	29	43	45	44
Q58	+4·0	+3·0	+3·5	5·5	3·9	+	+	+	47	39	43	62	54	58
Q59	+7·0	+5·0	+5·0	4·6	1·5	+	+	+	48	51	50	66	69	68
Q60	+14·0	+10·0	+12·0	6·5	2·7	+	+	+	43	48	45	61	66	63

[a] U = unclassified; C = coincident; − = leading; + = lagging.
[b] Total for items (i) to (iii) on p. 10.
[c] Total for items (i) to (v) on pp. 10–11.
[d] Excluding school-leavers and adult students.
[e] Including school-leavers and adult students.

columns record the timing class in which the indicator falls, for peaks and troughs separately, and also combined. The fact that an indicator can be placed in one or other timing class shows that its timing differences are fairly consistently in one direction. Conversely, a series which is unclassified under the heading 'timing class' does not possess a high degree of consistency.

Scores for each variable are given under two headings. The first, the 'basic' score, is the weighted sum of part-scores given to the series for economic significance, cyclical conformity, and timing consistency and stability. This score is in effect the basic measure of the performance of the series as a cyclical indicator. The total score, on the other hand, takes in also the criteria of smoothness and currency ('up-to-dateness'), and is the more appropriate score when ranking the series for use in forecasting. The smoother the series and the more promptly it is published, the greater the difference between the two scores. A small difference, if combined with a good basic score, may indicate a situation where an investment in improving the smoothness of the series, and in speeding its availability for publication, could yield a useful return in improving economic interpretation.

When the indicators are ranked by their scores, the three timing classes should be kept separate. Lagging series are often quite smooth with few or no extra turns and, if the mean lag is lengthy, are bound to be reasonably consistent in their timing classification. Leading series on the other hand are quite noticeably more variable and prone to extra turns. Yet the resulting lower scores in comparison to lagging series do not, of course, reflect their relative utility for analysis.

Examining now the indicators in table 9.1 in detail, an immediate observation is that the series for quarterly engagements and discharges (Q1 and Q4) are not very useful as leading indicators for production. The same goes for most of the other 'marginal adjustment' indicators, such as the series measuring overtime (M5, M7, M8 and M9) and average hours in manufacturing industry (M15). A comparison of their variability and overall scores with those given in chapter 11 shows them to be better indicators for unemployment.

A few series, however, do agree closely with the turning-points in production. For forecasting this can be valuable as, even though a series might be only approximately coincident at peaks and troughs, it may be easier to recognise an upturn or downturn in the series than in the target variable; that is, the indicator may have a 'recognition lead'. Examples of such approximately coincident series are vacancies (M25) at upturns, total hours (M60) at production peaks, and the series on temporarily stopped (M1) at both peaks and troughs.

The temporarily stopped series is a particularly interesting example of one which is clearly more closely related to changes in production than to movements in the level of unemployment. Normally, during the course of expansionary or steady-growth periods, the series oscillates in the range 10,000 to 20,000 temporarily stopped each month. Only as the downswing gathers momentum does the series climb well above this range; so it is not particularly useful for marking production downturns, that is not as useful as the results in the table might suggest. At production upturns, however, the reversal in numbers temporarily stopped is dramatic; also the turns occurred, with one exception, within one month of the production upturn. The short-time series (M10) not unexpectedly follows a very similar pattern, although with rather different timing at downturns.

Looking now at those indicators measuring changes in employment, the first two, Q16 and Q25, are quarterly series measuring economy-wide employment. They extend back to 1952 and differ only in that Q25 includes employers and self-employed as well as employees in employment. Both lag by over a year at peaks, but have a much shorter lag at troughs. This is the sort of timing pattern we would expect of a lagging series with a strong upward trend imposed; the lag at cyclical peaks would be increased and that at troughs reduced. And checking graphs of the series we do find strong upward trends until 1966, when there is a switch to an equally strong downward trend.

These trends are also present in the two monthly series on employment in the production industries and (more restricted in coverage) in manufacturing – M48 and M49 respectively. These are both summary series, based on a monthly figure of numbers employed linked to quarterly data for the early 1950s, and in recent years corresponding to the seasonally adjusted monthly indices published by the Department of Employment. They lag production cycle turning-points (determined in fact from the detrended series for the same group of industries) by a few months at both peaks and troughs.

For all these series any attempt to interpret the mean leads or lags must take into account the existence of the trend component and its effect on the timing relationships. Bearing this in mind, the series do confirm that cyclical movements in employment for the economy as a whole lag behind cyclical movements in production about its long-term growth-rate.

Finally we compare unemployment series with the reference cycle – first total unemployed (M70), then unemployment for the principal industrial groupings (M90, M91 and M92) and then with unemployment classified by duration.

Series M70, total wholly unemployed (excluding school-leavers), is the series used to define the unemployment reference cycle. The series lags production by a few months, noticeably at downturns. This might be an over-estimate of the normal lag, a result of the unusually long lags in 1960 and 1965. Apart from this the series has quite consistent timing relationships with production at both peaks and troughs, although of course less stable at peaks than at troughs.

The series giving numbers wholly unemployed in the production industries (M90) and in manufacturing (M91) match closely the reference series for total wholly unemployed. The same holds true of unemployment in the construction industry (M92), except for a tendency to longer lags at troughs than for other industrial groupings.

From their variances, the series for short-duration unemployment (M78, M99 and M100) are better indicators for the target variable unemployment than they are for production. In particular they lag the production peaks in 1960 and 1965 by substantial margins; hence on average they lag production at peaks. The long-duration series (Q58, Q59 and Q60), which would be expected to lag anyhow, are affected in the same way, giving high standard deviations and increasing the average lags.

OUTPUT, CONSUMPTION AND INCOME SERIES

The initial block of indicators in table 9.2 are detrended series for gross domestic product. Q231* is an average of the expenditure estimate (Q193*) the output estimate (Q230*) and also the income estimate (not given here). The results are not as consistent as could be wished. At troughs the three series do not depart too far from coincidence with the target variable; at peaks the results are more variable. On the evidence of the output estimate it is perhaps a fair claim that the detrended index of production is a reasonable proxy for the 'ideal' series for gross domestic product, and has the advantages over actual gross domestic product of being available over a longer period, published more frequently and more speedily, and subject to fewer major revisions. The detrended index of production for manufacturing (M120*) is of course almost exactly coincident with the target variable.

The two detrended labour productivity series (M114* and M115*) are also closely linked to the reference cycle. The leads shown by the two series are too short to be of use for forecasting.

Turning next to the series on production of individual commodities – steel, bricks and cars; we find generally that the series do not score well. However, the most useful of all the indicators given in this table is the series on new car registrations (M206). This is a leading series (although classed as coincident at peaks, it is in fact on the borderline of being leading and does lead on average by a couple of months). As seems generally true of consumption series, the lead at upturns is much longer than at downturns. Its high overall scores are attributable in part to the promptness of its publication.

Examining the principal consumption aggregates (all in detrended form) we see that the three consumers' expenditure series – durables (Q166*), non-durables (Q158*) and total (Q163*) – all lead by fairly lengthy margins. Surprisingly the total series out-performs its two components. The drawback to all three series is, as pointed out earlier, the rather high susceptibility of turning-point locations to the period used for trend estimation.

The series for retail sales represent two different approaches to re-

Table 9.2. *Output, consumption and income series as indicators for production*

Series no.	Median lead (−) or lag (+)			Standard deviation		Timing class[a]			Basic score[b]			Total score[c]		
	P	T	P & T	P	T	P	T	P & T	P	T	P & T	P	T	P & T
	(months)			(months)										
GDP at constant prices														
Q193*	−7·0	+2·5	+2·0	8·7	1·9	U	+	+	37	59	48	43	65	54
Q230*	−2·0	+0·5	−1·0	6·8	3·9	–	U	C	43	36	40	52	45	49
Q231*	−7·0	+1·5	0·0	3·1	1·1	–	C	C	48	54	51	57	63	60
Output and productivity														
M120*	0·0	0·0	0·0	1·0	1·4	C	C	C	50	49	50	65	64	65
Q92	+5·0	+1·0	+2·0	6·1	3·8	+	C	+	42	35	39	54	47	51
M114*	−1·0	−2·0	−1·0	2·2	4·5	–	–	–	51	41	45	60	50	54
M115*	−1·0	−1·0	−1·0	2·6	5·0	–	–	–	46	29	38	55	38	47
Production of steel, bricks and cars														
M147	0·0	−1·0	−1·0	9·8	2·9	U	C	–	18	33	26	36	51	44
M160	+2·0	−6·0	−2·0	10·7	7·1	U	–	U	14	18	16	32	36	34
M153	−2·0	−10·0	−5·5	4·2	9·2	–	–	–	26	27	26	44	45	44
M154	−3·0	−9·0	−4·5	3·2	9·4	–	–	–	29	15	22	47	33	40
Consumption of steel and new car registrations														
Q156	+1·5	−1·0	+1·0	3·4	4·3	+	C	C	26	25	25	41	40	40
Q157	+2·0	0·0	+1·0	1·4	2·4	C	C	C	45	35	40	57	47	52
M206	−2·0	−15·0	−9·0	6·3	7·0	C	–	–	30	39	35	48	57	53
Consumers' expenditure at constant prices														
Q163*	−2·0	−8·0	−6·0	6·7	4·5	–	–	–	38	41	39	47	50	48
Q166*	−1·0	−11·0	−10·0	7·2	11·1	–	–	–	30	34	32	39	43	41
Q158*	−2·0	−8·0	−6·0	9·7	4·5	–	–	–	25	39	32	34	48	41
Retail sales														
M185*	+12·0	−6·5	−4·0	13·8	4·9	U	–	U	18	24	21	27	33	30
M189*	−9·0	−10·5	−9·0	11·6	6·3	U	–	–	22	41	31	37	56	46
M198	−13·0	−6·0	−7·0	6·6	2·1	–	–	–	29	45	37	38	54	46
M199	0·0	−10·0	−6·5	9·2	10·1	U	–	–	13	22	18	19	28	24
Wage rates and earnings														
M181	+10·0	+9·0	+9·5	5·3	8·2	+	+	+	49	29	39	73	53	63

Notes: see notes *a* to *c* of table 9.1.

moving the trend component. From M185* and M189* the trend has been removed in the same manner as for the analogous quarterly consumption series (Q163* and others) – by simple estimation of an exponential trend. The total series (M185*), dating from 1957, proves of limited value, but M189* for durables looks more useful as a leading indicator at troughs, although again turning-point locations are very sensitive to the choice of period over which the trend is estimated. The alternative approach is to take annual rates of increase; the value series on this basis (M199) scores poorly, but the corresponding volume series (M198) could be a useful leading indicator, again more particularly at troughs.

INVESTMENT AND INVESTMENT ORDERS SERIES

The series in table 9.3 fall into two main groups. The first measures actual fixed capital formation in manufacturing, housing, etc.; the second comprises series measuring investment orders, for example, contractors' new orders (Q173), engineering orders (M270); also housing starts (M267), or expectations, as measured for example by the Confederation of British Industries' (CBI) surveys of investment intentions.

Table 9.3. *Investment, orders and anticipation series as indicators for production*

Series no.	Median lead (−) or lag (+)			Standard deviation		Timing class[a]			Basic score[b]			Total score[c]		
	P	T	P & T	P	T	P	T	P & T	P	T	P & T	P	T	P & T
	(months)			(months)										
Orders														
Q173	−2·0	−21·0	−17·5	15·2	7·8	U	−	−	14	27	21	26	39	33
M270	+14·0	+5·0	+11·0	0·0	7·8	+	+	+	50	31	41	65	46	56
Private housing														
M267	−2·0	−21·0	−12·0	11·7	7·0	−	−	−	17	30	23	38	51	44
M287	−2·0	−5·0	−4·0	11·7	9·4	U	−	−	22	30	26	43	51	47
CBI survey														
Q305	−6·0	−7·0	−6·5	5·0	2·6	−	−	−	40	44	42	58	62	60
Q306	+6·0	+1·0	+2·5	4·5	4·2	+	U	+	26	26	26	44	44	44
Q309	−3·0	−5·0	−4·5	2·9	1·7	−	−	−	35	47	41	56	68	62
New companies registered														
M253	−1·0	−8·0	−4·0	3·0	5·0	U	−	U	22	20	21	28	26	27
GDFCF at 1970 prices														
Q212*	+8·0	+4·5	+4·5	7·1	2·1	+	+	+	43	49	46	52	58	55
Q209	+6·0	−9·5	−4·0	12·3	8·9	+	−	U	18	19	19	27	28	28
Q214	+15·5	+6·5	+12·0	1·8	2·9	+	+	+	47	46	47	56	55	56
Q214*	+15·5	+8·0	+10·0	6·6	3·0	+	+	+	51	55	53	60	64	62
Capital expenditure by manufacturing sector at 1970 prices														
Q223	+8·0	+7·5	+7·5	8·0	4·3	+	+	+	35	39	37	44	48	46
Q224	0·0	−10·0	−3·5	3·7	5·0	C	−	−	36	48	42	45	57	51
Q225	+17·0	+6·5	+12·0	1·7	2·9	+	+	+	43	42	43	52	51	52
Q225*	+15·5	+8·0	+12·0	1·8	3·0	+	+	+	52	51	52	61	60	61

Notes: see notes *a* to *c* of table 9.1.

The indicators measuring investment intentions and expectations are most logically matched against the reference chronology for fixed investment (private sector, non-residential). But they can also provide a guide to the expected path of the production cycle. Naturally, any leads over peaks and troughs in production can be expected to be much shorter on average than leads over investment upturns and downturns. This is apparent with contractors' new orders (at constant prices) (see also table 10.3 below), which score badly for the production cycle.

Both housing starts (M267) and housing completions (M287) look useful indicators with long leads at troughs, but also with fairly high variability about the average. Housing completions lag the series for starts by some months, but are frequently easier to interpret. For short cyclical phases, the lead shown by housing starts is sometimes sufficiently long to produce apparently contra-cyclical movements, as in the early 1950s – a dubious result.

On the basis of United States experience, new company registrations (M253) should be a useful leading indicator. Unfortunately, actual experience is that the series performs very inconsistently, generally leading when it does conform to the cycle, but commonly skipping the turn altogether. The steady growth in the formation of new companies (apart from breaks caused by changes in the Companies Act) is mainly responsible. A restriction to industrial companies might give an improved indicator, but unfortunately monthly data classified by type of company are not available.[1]

The origin and derivation of the CBI survey series need some explanation before their cyclical behaviour is analysed. An industrial trends survey among CBI members is carried out each quarter (until recently every four months). The survey, whose coverage is extensive, particularly of the larger manufacturing concerns, seeks information on expected trends in output and employment, current capacity restraints on output, and other information. The two questions made use of in this investigation are, first, whether the individual being questioned is more or less optimistic about the general business situation in his industry than he was at the date of the previous survey, and, secondly, whether he expects to authorise more or less capital expenditure in the succeeding twelve months than in the previous twelve months (on buildings and on plant and machinery separately).

From the first question, a series has been constructed in the National Institute, known as the 'optimism balance' (Q305), which is quite simply the proportion reporting themselves as more optimistic less that proportion who are less optimistic. (Those in the unchanged category are excluded.) Cyclical peaks and troughs can be clearly identified in the 'optimism balance', but the points where it switches from optimism to pessimism or vice versa are also of interest. To present these more clearly, and also to give a smoother series, a second series, called the 'cumulative optimism balance' (Q306), was constructed by cumulating the values of the optimism balance. The final series in the group (Q309) – the balance of manufacturing investment – is derived as an average weighted by actual investment in the previous quarter of the intended investment 'balances' in buildings and in plant and machinery. An appropriate interpolation then transforms the

[1] Modifying the series by deducting the number of business failures did not give an improved indicator.

combined series into a quarterly series for those periods in the past when the survey was carried out only thrice-yearly. This last series is more likely to be a useful leading indicator for investment than for production, but *a priori* there seems little reason for the two optimism series to be more closely related to one target variable than to the other. In fact a comparison of their standard deviations suggests they are about equally closely related to both.

The properties of these indicators can be described quite briefly: the cumulative optimism balance (Q306) is a lagging indicator; the optimism balance itself (Q305) and the balance of manufacturing investment (Q309) are both leading indicators. The latter both score highly, suggesting that they could be useful for forecasting production turning-points, more particularly the upturns.

The first of the aggregate capital formation series listed (Q212*) is private sector non-residential fixed capital formation (detrended and gross at constant prices). This is of course the reference series selected to give the cyclical chronology for the target variable investment. As is characteristic of most capital formation series, peaks and troughs in the reference cycle chronology lag by some months (almost a year at peaks on average) behind the corresponding turns in the production cycle.

Capital formation in the private dwelling sector (Q209) takes on different cyclical characteristics however. The series leads on average by almost a year at cyclical troughs; a consequence, one assumes, of the downturn in interest rates at some period after the preceding downturn in the general cycle, although the existence of a lag on average at peaks is rather puzzling. At both peaks and troughs, individual leads and lags show a high variability. In its original form the series shows a strongly pronounced upward trend, although cyclical characteristics are still readily observable. It was tested also in detrended form, but this gave a worse rather than better indicator.

The remaining capital formation series (Q214 and Q214*, as well as the final group) are all to do with capital formation in manufacturing. Frequently the trend component is sufficiently weak in relation to the cyclical movements to make it questionable whether the series require detrending or not. Two of the component series, manufacturing fixed capital expenditure on new building work and on vehicles (Q223 and Q224), are given solely in their original form. The other two series, total fixed capital formation in manufacturing (Q214), and its main component, fixed capital expenditure on plant and machinery (Q225), are analysed also as detrended series. For these two series, detrending does seem to result in a definite improvement, although median lags are little affected.

Apart from capital expenditure on vehicles (Q224), whose cyclical behaviour appears akin to that of the private dwellings series, perhaps from similar causes, all the manufacturing series display characteristically lengthy lags behind the production cycle. Indeed the manufacturing sector has much longer lags than the private sector as a whole. As lagging indicators the series score quite well, although normally interest lies more in production as a leading indicator of investment, a consideration which will be taken up later.

STOCK SERIES

The series shown in table 9.4 are all quarterly, measured in constant prices, and indicate either the *level* of stocks (sometimes including work in progress) at the end of each quarter, or else the *change* in stocks from quarter to quarter. The few monthly stock series available, notably retail stocks, proved too irregular for analysis.

Table 9.4. *Stock series as indicators for production*

Series no.	Median lead (−) or lag (+)			Standard deviation		Timing class[a]			Basic score[b]			Total score[c]		
	P	T	P & T	P	T	P	T	P & T	P	T	P & T	P	T	P & T
	(months)			(months)										
Stock-levels at constant prices														
Q247	+19·0	+5·5	+14·0	1·3	2·3	+	+	+	53	52	52	65	64	64
Q264	+16·5	+5·0	+10·0	7·9	8·2	+	+	+	40	32	36	55	47	51
Q267	+15·0	+11·0	+13·0	8·9	6·2	+	+	+	37	31	34	52	46	49
Stock-ratios at constant prices														
Q254	+22·0	+15·0	+21·0	5·0	0·8	+	+	+	47	49	48	59	61	60
Q258	+28·0	+14·0	+21·0	6·4	3·6	+	+	+	51	50	50	63	62	62
Q259	+22·0	+15·0	+21·0	5·0	3·6	+	+	+	55	53	54	67	65	66
Changes in stocks at constant prices														
Q269	−2·0	+2·0	0·0	2·4	3·0	C	+	C	54	39	47	57	42	50
Q270	−3·0	+6·0	+5·0	5·4	1·9	U	+	+	27	46	37	33	52	43
Q275	+6·0	−2·0	−1·0	9·3	4·3	U	−	U	23	29	26	29	35	32
Q276	+6·0	+6·0	+6·0	6·6	1·9	+	+	+	37	46	41	43	52	47
Q286	0·0	−8·0	−3·0	6·1	7·8	U	−	−	24	29	26	33	38	35

Notes: see notes *a* to *c* of table 9.1.

To give an impression of overall magnitudes: stocks and work in progress at 1970 prices amounted, economy-wide, to £16,300 million at the end of 1972, of which manufacturing stocks and work in progress amounted to £9,300 million or 57 per cent of the total. Of total manufacturing stocks, materials and fuel accounted for just over a third, work in progress for about 40 per cent, and finished goods for a quarter. (These ratios can of course be expected to vary somewhat over the cycle.)

The first series, Q247, material and fuel stocks for manufacturing, displays a very clear cyclical movement. Even though this is combined with a fairly strong upward trend, there is no difficulty in fixing turning-point locations. As expected beforehand, the series is a lagging indicator, and one with high consistency of timing and low variability about the average lag.

The remaining components of manufacturing stocks, as also total manufacturing stocks and total economy stocks, cannot be analysed quite so easily. The upward trend is of sufficient strength to prevent easy identification of the cyclical component. One approach would, of course, be to detrend the series. However, a rather more intellectually satisfying procedure is to take the ratio of aggregate stocks to the relevant output variable. Thus Q259 is the ratio of total stocks and work in progress to gross domestic product (output estimate), all at constant prices, and the other two series (Q254 and Q258) represent the ratios of manufacturing stocks (total and finished goods) to manufacturing output. The resulting series are again lagging indicators of high quality with very lengthy lags.

The only stock series considered at a more restricted level are the quarterly series for merchants' and consumers' stocks of finished steel (Q264). Total stock-levels, whether measured as such or in terms of the number of weeks supply at current consumption levels (Q267), display exceptionally clear and trend-free cyclical movements. Stocks of steel, like stocks of manufacturing raw materials in general, continue to increase for a considerable period after a production downturn, and to decline for some time following a general upturn.

Whereas stock-levels lag the cycle, changes in stocks might be expected to lead or at least coincide with cyclical turning-points. The material presented in table 9.4 shows this not to be the case. While changes in total stocks (Q269) are approximately coincident or lag by a small margin, changes in manufacturing stocks (Q270) and the corresponding series for finished goods (Q276) lag the production cycle by a substantial margin. Changes in manufacturing stocks of materials do however lead the reference cycle at upturns, although only by a very short period.

A point worth noticing about the stock-change series is the smallness of the difference between the basic and total scores, a reflection of the highly irregular character of all these series. Estimates of stockbuilding are probably more subject to errors in measurement than any other major economic aggregate.

PRICES, COSTS AND PROFITS SERIES

The series in table 9.5 can be further classified into four groups:

(i) indices of stock exchange share prices and yields;

(ii) annual rates of change of wholesale and consumer prices;

(iii) profit-margins (or, to be more exact, a crude approximation provided by the ratios of output prices to unit costs);

(iv) aggregate profits.

Table 9.5. *Prices, costs and profits series as indicators for production*

Series no.	Median lead (−) or lag (+) P	T	P & T	Standard deviation P	T	Timing class[a] P	T	P & T	Basic score[b] P	T	P & T	Total score[c] P	T	P & T
	(months)			(months)										
Share prices and yields														
M313	−4·0	−7·0	−5·0	7·4	3·3	U	–	–	25	46	36	52	73	63
M384	−5·0	−7·0	−6·5	4·9	3·9	–	–	–	36	46	41	63	73	68
M385	−9·0	−15·0	−15·0	4·9	6·4	–	–	–	30	33	32	57	60	59
Wholesale prices, annual rate of increase														
M363	−3·0	−2·0	−2·5	6·2	12·4	–	–	–	19	15	17	43	39	41
M557	−2·0	−5·0	−3·5	2·3	4·1	C	–	–	38	45	42	62	69	66
M560	+12·0	+5·0	+6·5	8·4	4·2	+	+	+	43	39	41	70	66	68
Retail and consumer prices, annual rate of increase														
M378	+11·0	+5·0	+8·0	9·9	7·9	+	+	+	37	40	38	58	61	59
Q332	+23·0	+5·0	+7·0	8·3	5·7	+	+	+	38	45	41	50	57	53
Q333	+17·0	+2·0	+7·0	6·6	3·1	+	+	+	27	20	24	39	32	36
Price–cost ratios														
Q328	−10·0	+0·5	−1·0	5·4	7·0	–	C	–	37	25	31	46	34	40
Q336	−10·0	+0·5	−1·0	5·4	4·4	–	C	–	37	28	32	43	34	38
M382	−13·0	−14·5	−13·0	1·0	5·5	–	–	–	28	22	25	40	34	37
Company profits														
Q345	−1·0	−11·0	−9·5	4·8	12·3	C	–	–	27	21	24	36	30	33
Q345*	−10·0	−10·0	−10·0	5·4	5·0	–	–	–	46	50	48	55	59	57
Q366	−10·0	−3·5	−6·0	5·4	4·4	–	–	–	46	37	41	55	46	50

Notes: see notes *a* to *c* of table 9.1.

The share price index (M313) is the well known Financial Times (FT) price index for thirty leading industrial ordinary shares, based on 1 July 1935 = 100. In 1962 the Financial Times, together with the Institute of Actuaries, introduced a considerable number of new prices and yields indices (known as FT–Actuaries indices) with more comprehensive coverage than the old indices. For this study, however, the greater time-span covered by the old indices outweighs the more comprehensive coverage of the new. In general, peaks and troughs in the two sets of indices agree closely, apart from the flattish trough in late 1970 to early 1971. The FT industrial ordinary index leads overall and at troughs by a few months, but at peaks the average lead is unstable. That is, in terms of our chronology, stock exchange investors appear to anticipate the upturn well, but the downturn with a good deal less certainty. The series scores very well as a leading indicator at troughs.

Closely related to the share price index are the two FT indices measuring movements in dividends and earnings yields (M384 and M385). Again these are the older 1935-based series, not the more recent FT–Actuaries indices based on 10 April 1962 = 100. The yields are obtained by expressing the latest data on dividends and earnings as a percentage of total market valuation. Thus, to a first order of approximation, these series would be expected to move inversely to the share price index. In fact a more exact examination, as given in the table, shows that they lead the share price index, especially at peaks. The chain of causation is readily apparent – from earnings to dividends to share prices – and implies that earnings, or profits, play a key role in business cycle gestation. The more immediate implication is that the two series should be very useful forecasting tools – their record marred only by a tendency to false alarms. (The corresponding FT-Actuaries dividends and earnings yields series again match the FT indices fairly closely in the post-1962 period, although leading by some months at the 1970 trough.)

Of the wide variety of price indices available for economic analysis, the share price index is the only one analysed here in its original form. The other price series examined were in general relatively smooth and dominated by an upward trend component, and so were transformed to annual rates of increase. The more sensitive wholesale price indices of raw materials do exhibit some cyclical behaviour, but even for these series the pattern becomes much clearer on differencing.

The wholesale input indices – those measuring price changes of the basic materials required by manufacturing industry – exist in a number of variants. Some indices cover fuel as well as basic materials, other indices exclude commodities going to food-processing industries. Thus, in table 9.5, series M363 measures price changes of basic materials and fuel going to all manufacturing industry, whereas M557 refers to prices of basic materials only for non-food industries. (The latter series incidentally covers a considerably longer time-span, back to 1949–50.) In practice, the inclusion – or exclusion – of fuel seems to make little difference to the location of cyclical turns in price changes; the exclusion of materials for the food industries makes, however, a significant difference. Graphical examination makes it clear that such commodities (largely of course agricultural commodities on the world market) have price cycles bearing little relationship to the British domestic cycle. This is shown in the low scores and high variability of M363 as compared with M557.

The latter series scores quite well as a leading indicator. This was an unexpected result, but perhaps reflects the impact of forward orders in anticipation of production changes. In the United States, an index of industrial material prices (not even in rate of change form) is one of the shortlisted leading indicators. The British series can be seen from a detailed check on individual turns to have been a near-perfect indicator until 1967. From that date the distortions and uncertainties induced in the cyclical pattern by the 1967 devaluation, plus an extra-cyclical decline in the rate of increase in 1971–2, make the matching of the series to the production cycle much less certain.

Wholesale output or sales indices are likewise available in a number of different forms. Food products can be included or excluded, and the index can include either total sales or just sales to the home market.[1] Again the inclusion of food products makes the analysis more difficult, so the series in the table, M560, represents prices of non-food products going to home sales. Again, this particular index can be extended back to 1950. This series is seen to lag the production cycle consistently at turning-points. At troughs the lag is fairly stable, though with one lapse in 1967, when the relaxation of the prices and incomes policy in mid-year may have been responsible. At peaks individual lags are not so stable, though the variability is not extreme if one considers only the period up to 1968. From then onwards the old relationship seems to have broken down, at least temporarily (as seems true of most of the price series), as a result of both the 'impact' inflation caused by the 1967 devaluation and the inflationary surge through 1970 to mid-1971. Nevertheless, if this turns out to be only a temporary aberration, the median lags may still be suitable, after appropriate adjustments for shifts in the foreign exchange rate, for forecasting the approximate timing of shifts in the rate of inflation.

Prices paid by consumers are measured either by the quarterly consumers' price index (Q332) – the implicit deflator of consumers' expenditure at current prices – or by the monthly retail price index (M378) – covering, despite the name, such items of expenditure as housing and electricity. A series of retail price indices on different bases can be linked to cover the whole postwar period and longer; the quarterly consumption deflator dates only from the late 1950s. Despite differences in construction and coverage, turning-point dates in the quarterly and monthly series match each other quite closely. This is not apparent from an examination of the median lags in table 9.5 for series Q332 and M378, because extremely long lags in both at the 1960 and 1968 peaks in production have a greater impact on the quarterly series than on the monthly series with extra readings from the 1950s. The high standard deviations which result reduce the analytical usefulness of the results for both series.[2]

The quarterly series for increases in prices of consumer durables (Q333) is a low-scoring series.

Three series (two quarterly, one monthly) represent in different forms the ratio of prices (either at output or final expenditure stage) to unit labour costs or to unit wage and salary costs. (Broader measures including other costs were not obtainable, at least in simple form.) The monthly series M382 refers to the manufacturing sector only; the other two, Q328 and Q336,

[1] Publication of total sales figures ceased at the latest rebasing to 1970.

[2] A point worth noting is that the turning-points in the retail price index since 1963 have been obtained from an index excluding those items showing seasonal movements. The effect is sometimes to shift the turning-point by a month or two.

cover the whole economy. These series act as rough measures of movements in profit-margins. Obviously they have defects, particularly in measuring only one component of costs, and also in making no allowance for the effects of tax changes, capital grants and the like. Nevertheless they may identify reasonably reliably cyclical turning-points in underlying profit-margins.

The series for the whole economy take the implicit deflator of total final expenditure as the measure of overall price movements; the unit wages and salaries and labour costs are the series computed and published by the Department of Employment dating back to 1955. Both indicators lead at peaks, but display a less consistent pattern at troughs. A strongly downward trend in Q336 reflects the greater rate of increase of 'fringe' labour costs.

The corresponding monthly series for the manufacturing sector (M382) dates only from 1963. The relatively short time-span covered imposes a harsh penalty on its score. Despite not having been tested over many cycles, the consistency and stability of the series suggests, however, that it is definitely the 'best buy' from this group of indicators and is possibly a leading indicator of very high potential value.

From indicators measuring (or purporting to measure) profit-margins, the next step is to consider those measuring actual profits. The basic series measuring company gross trading profits (Q345) is a leading indicator. However, the series exhibits very high variability about its average lead at troughs, while it is clear that the upward trend in the series has reduced the average lead at production downturns. As an experiment, the series was detrended and the analysis repeated. This resulted in a considerable improvement.

Alternatively, gross company profits can be analysed as a percentage of total gross domestic product (series Q366).[1] This method of detrending has the advantage of being much less arbitrary. The series is clearly an important leading indicator, a result of considerable analytical importance. For forecasting too, the indicator should be of considerable value, although the total lead will be reduced by both publication delay and variability in the series.

MONEY AND CREDIT SERIES

A good number of the statistical series measuring monetary variables date only from 1960–3 and so can be tested against only a small number of cyclical turning-points. Other series of considerable theoretical interest are either of too recent origin, for example bank advances classified by econ-

[1] There are a few traps in interpreting trends in the profits–GDP ratio, see *National Institute Economic Review*, no. 66, November 1973, pp. 20–4. In particular, allowance must be made for capital grants on the one hand, and increased depreciation and stock appreciation on the other.

Table 9.6. *Money, credit and interest-rate series as indicators for production*

Series no.	Median lead (−) or lag (+)			Standard deviation		Timing class[a]			Basic score[b]			Total score[c]		
	P	T	P & T	P	T	P	T	P & T	P	T	P & T	P	T	P & T
	(months)			(months)										
Changes in money supply														
Q375	−7·5	−21·0	−11·0	5·5	12·0	−	−	−	19	14	17	25	20	23
Q376	−4·5	−21·0	−11·0	8·5	12·0	U	−	−	13	14	13	13	14	13
M400	+2·0	0·0	+1·5	9·8	5·7	+	U	+	38	36	37	53	51	52
Hire purchase and other instalment credit														
M403	−4·0	−10·0	−10·0	7·3	12·5	−	−	−	19	5	12	31	17	24
M407	−3·0	−9·5	−9·0	7·1	12·1	−	−	−	20	30	25	32	42	37
M409	−6·0	−9·5	−9·0	4·8	9·9	−	−	−	33	31	32	45	43	44
M428	+13·0	−13·5	−6·0	10·0	10·0	+	−	−	15	29	22	36	50	43
Total business failures (inverted)														
M474	−10·5	−4·0	−10·0	0·5	9·0	−	−	−	38	36	37	47	45	46
Interest rates														
M449	+2·0	+2·0	+2·0	8·7	9·5	+	+	+	24	30	26	51	57	53
M453	+10·5	+3·5	+4·0	8·6	2·7	+	+	+	30	23	26	54	47	50
M465	+17·0	+5·0	+17·0	2·3	11·2	+	+	+	48	22	35	75	49	62
M468	+18·0	+8·0	+16·0	3·0	11·7	+	+	+	50	25	37	77	52	64

Notes: see notes *a* to *c* of table 9.1.

omic sector, or else have been affected by major changes in the banking system in recent years, for example the former statistical material on advances and deposits of the London clearing banks. All this reduces both the number and the quality of those series measuring monetary aggregates, particularly for an investigation such as this, where a long run of consistent data is needed to provide a few observations (cyclical peaks and troughs) for analysis. Statistical material on interest rates and yields is, however, much more easily available on a long-term consistent basis, and such series figure prominently in table 9.6.

There are two principal quarterly series measuring money stock. The narrower definition 'M1' represents most closely the function of money as a medium of exchange, and includes, as well as currency in circulation, current accounts in sterling of private sector residents. The broader definition 'M3' takes in all resident deposits with the banking sector, whether in sterling or foreign currency, and includes deposit as well as current accounts. Quarterly changes in these two money stock series are the two best-known measures of changes in money supply. A third measure is domestic credit expansion (Q375 in the table), which allows additionally for changes in banking sector transactions with non-residents, and external financing of the public sector.[1]

[1] For complete definitions of the different money stock measures, the annual 'Notes and definitions' supplement to *Financial Statistics* (Central Statistical Office, monthly) should be consulted.

The usual measures of performance are given in table 9.6 for domestic credit expansion and the quarterly change in 'M3' (series Q376).[1] Both series lead in general, but both score very poorly, partly reflecting the relative shortness of the period covered, but also the variability of the lead at cyclical turns. Thus, an upturn in the growth of money stock dated approximately mid-1969 was not succeeded by a corresponding upturn in real terms until early 1972. It is this lengthy individual lead which produces the long median lead at troughs. On the evidence here, the rate of growth of money stock is not a useful leading indicator. However the shortness of the series examined makes this a rather qualified conclusion, and a longer run of data might suggest more stability in the timing relationship.

Taking a narrower definition of money, as being simply currency in circulation, analysis is possible over a much longer period. The monthly series M400 measures annual changes in currency in circulation. The series seems on average to coincide approximately with the production cycle, although it shows, like other monetary or prices series, a pronounced divergence from the 'real' cycle over the period 1968–71.

Data on monthly hire purchase (and other instalment) credit extended to consumers by both retailers and finance houses are available from the late 1950s. The first three series listed in the table, measuring either new credit (M407), or the increase in net credit after repayments (M403 and M409), are all leading indicators with average leads of significant length. The most comprehensive series, M409 for the total increase in hire purchase debt, has the best rating, scoring significantly better than the other two series. Again the usefulness of the series for forecasting is impaired by the signal of the 1972 upturn being so far in advance (some 30 months) of the actual upturn. If this observation were to be excluded, all the series listed in the table would show much smaller standard deviations at troughs. The series are all in current prices; however, a conversion to constant prices using an appropriate deflator did not decrease the variability of individual leads.

A further point to watch in graphical observation of the hire purchase series is a tendency to 'overshooting'; that is, following government relaxation of restrictions on hire purchase, the volume of new credit extended will often leap to a level which can be sustained for only two or three months before falling back to a more easily sustained long-term level. Mechanically applied, the techniques used in this investigation might describe such a surge and retreat as cyclical, but this would be contrary to the conclusions which would be drawn by any contemporary observer.

The cumulated series of total hire purchase debt outstanding (M428) displays an unusual pattern with, on average, lengthy lags at peaks and equally lengthy leads at troughs. Again it seemed possible that the effects of

[1] The corresponding series on 'M1' is not given because the run of data was too short to match with certainty the 1964–5 production peaks, leaving too small a number of observations.

inflation had tended to advance upturns and that, in 'real' terms, the series had a more definite lagging tendency, but once more tests on an appropriately deflated series did not bear out the supposition.

The series on total business failures (M474) dates only from 1960, but it is a particularly consistent indicator at both peaks and troughs and looks a useful addition to those series commonly used for short-term forecasting.

The final batch of series considered are four measuring interest rates: Two (M449 and M453) are chosen to represent short-term money rates; respectively the Treasury bill discount rate (monthly average of discount rates for 91 day bills made at the weekly tender), and the rate on three months (minimum term) deposits with Local Authorities. A number of other rates could also be used, but these two appear to be the most commonly used by analysts to represent general trends in short-term rates. The Treasury bill rate alone might be used, except that at some periods it has been 'managed'; hence the Local Authority rate may more truly represent market forces. Both were, like other interest rates, much influenced in the past by changes in Bank Rate. From 1972 Bank Rate has been replaced by the Bank of England's minimum lending rate, which is normally ½ per cent higher than the average rate of discount for Treasury bills established at the most recent tender. Both series lag production cycle turns by a few months on average at both peaks and troughs (the lengthy average lag shown by M453 at peaks seems to be something of a statistical aberration caused by a double peak in 1956 and 1957). Of the two, a graphical inspection suggests that the Local Authority rate is the more convenient for cyclical analysis, although tending to lag a month or so behind the other series.

Two indicators are also listed to measure long-term interest rates. The first (M465), representing yields on government securities, is the gross flat yield on 2½ per cent Consolidated stock (commonly known as 2½ per cent Consols). The second series (M468) is the FT–Actuaries index of the redemption yield on company debenture and loan stocks with an average term to maturity of about twenty years. As it happens, turning-points in the two series generally occur close together and, although the FT–Actuaries index is slightly less irregular, the better known Consols series would be the one normally used. Both series lag by a few months at troughs and have what appears to be a remarkably stable lag of about a year and a half at peaks.

All the interest-rate series conform to the expected pattern, continuing to rise for some months (the long-term series a good deal longer) after the downturn, and likewise continuing to decline for a few months after the upturn, although here the demand for finance as the expansion gathers pace leads to a quicker turn round in interest rates.

An interesting exercise is to take these series and invert them, matching troughs in the interest rates against peaks in the production cycle, and vice versa. Analysed in this manner, the series become leading instead of lagging indicators; indeed the long-term rates particularly turn out to be leading indicators of high quality as measured by their scores and standard deviations.

One explanation of cyclical movement in an economy is on the lines that certain 'lagging' variables (for example, stock levels and unit costs) prevent a swing into the next phase of the cycle until those variables themselves have moved into the next phase of their specific cycle. In this sense the lagging variable analysed on a positive basis could be considered as leading the cycle if treated as an inverted series. Clearly one needs to be careful with this sort of reasoning, which could lead to the mechanical conversion of any lagging indicator into a leading indicator for the next succeeding cyclical turn. Although inverted interest rates could be given an economic rationale as leading series (for example via the effects of interest-rate changes on housing starts, and also the effect of capital costs on profit-margins), the more logical approach here is to take them as lagging the production cycle.

FOREIGN TRADE SERIES

Some material is available on export orders and anticipations. Thus, for the engineering industry there are monthly indices of net new export orders and export orders on hand, as well as of deliveries to the export sector. Unfortunately, and as was also the case for total new orders, the series for net new export orders was so irregular that it had to be excluded from the analysis. Export orders on hand (M479) are however summarised in table 9.7. The notable feature of the series is the extremely long average lag at production downturns – so it would seem that well-stocked order books are no guarantee of continuing prosperity either for the engineering industry or for the economy as a whole. Another series is for the production of cars for export (M482), downturns in which on average lead downturns in the production cycle by a few months.

Three series measuring in different ways the 'balance of trade' are listed at the top of table 9.7. All three are analysed as inverted series. They are the two quarterly series (Q455 and Q472), measuring the visible trade balance and the current trade balance, and the monthly series for the visible balance (M493). The two quarterly balances extend back only to 1958, but the monthly series to 1955, making use for the earlier period of the 'crude trade gap', simply exports f.o.b. less imports c.i.f. All three series can be classed as leading indicators at both peaks and troughs. The quarterly series do not score particularly well, but the monthly series, despite its extreme irregularity (it requires seven months for cyclical dominance, see appendix C) must clearly be amongst the more useful leading indicators.

Returning to separate consideration of export and import series, the volume index for total exports (M495) is in general a lagging indicator,

Table 9.7. *Foreign trade series as indicators for production*

Series no.	Median lead (−) or lag (+) P	T	P & T	Standard deviation P	T	Timing class[a] P	T	P & T	Basic score[b] P	T	P & T	Total score[c] P	T	P & T
		(months)		(months)										
Trade balance at current prices (inverted)														
Q455	−2·0	−6·0	−4·0	10·1	4·2	–	–	–	24	31	27	39	46	42
Q472	−2·0	−6·0	−4·0	10·1	4·2	–	–	–	15	22	18	30	37	33
M493	−4·0	−8·5	−6·5	8·3	4·4	–	–	–	33	52	43	45	64	55
Export orders														
M479	+14·0	+0·5	+8·0	7·1	4·4	+	U	+	35	28	31	50	43	46
M482	−7·0	+2·0	−4·0	5·0	10·3	–	+	–	46	31	39	64	49	57
Volume of exports and imports														
M495	+6·0	+3·0	+4·0	9·6	7·6	+	U	+	22	24	23	28	30	29
M524	−5·5	−8·0	−8·0	8·5	3·3	U	–	–	20	37	28	26	43	34
Export and import unit values, annual rate of increase														
M580	+2·0	−3·0	−0·5	10·4	15·4	+	–	U	8	8	8	23	23	23
M581	+10·0	−0·5	0·0	11·6	10·3	+	C	U	26	26	26	41	41	41
M582	−12·0	−6·5	−8·0	5·4	3·7	–	–	–	34	40	37	52	58	55
M583	−8·0	−1·5	−2·0	5·4	1·1	–	C	–	27	47	37	45	65	55
Prices in international trade, annual rate of increase														
Q487	+0·5	−9·5	−2·5	8·9	9·1	U	–	–	17	17	17	26	26	26
Q485	+3·0	+1·0	+2·5	7·6	8·1	+	+	+	37	29	33	49	41	45

Notes: see *a* to *c* of table 9.1.

whereas the volume index of basic materials imported (M524) is a leading indicator, at least at troughs. Neither series scores particularly highly.

The cyclical movements in the indicators measuring annual rates of increase in export and import unit values tend to match roughly those in the volume indices. That is, export unit values are more likely to lag the cycle and import unit values to lead. Strangely the total series (M581 and M582) perform somewhat better than do series measuring price movements in those components which would normally be expected to be the most significant – exports of manufactured goods (M580) and imports of basic materials (M583). Both export unit value series however show high variability, whereas the series measuring the rate of increase in import unit values appears more reliable and quite a high-scoring leading indicator.

The final two series deal with prices in world trade. (Series measuring world economic activity were also tested but were insufficiently closely related to the British cycle to be reported here.) The quarterly series measuring annual rates of change in export prices for world primary commodities (Q487) does not look particularly useful, except that it again confirms the tendency for input prices to lead the general cycle. The annual rate of change in world export unit values (Q485) moves more consistently, showing a short lag.

SUMMARY TABLES

From the information set out in tables 9.1 to 9.7, it is clear that many of the series tested are poor indicators of the production cycle (although not necessarily of other target variables). In other instances two or more series are so closely related as to duplicate almost exactly one another's timing patterns. Clearly a short list is needed, eliminating those series which are either low-scoring or provide very little additional information. Such a short list, made up of 43 series plus the target variable itself, is given in table 9.8. In selecting these series, the score given to the series is naturally a prime consideration, but is not the only factor considered.

In setting out table 9.8 the indicators are sorted into timing classes and ranked according to their total scores. This procedure can sometimes give a considerable advantage to monthly series which are speedily available for publication. Thus the basic score is also given, and the rank of the series when ordered by that score.

There are a few general points about the table.

(i) Some series have low scores because of the shortness of the period covered (for example Q11 and M382). Conversely a few of the results are likely to be statistical 'freaks', with the relationships established for the past proving a poor guide for the future.

(ii) Only for a few of the shortlisted series (seven in all) was it necessary to remove a trend component.

(iii) The series listed as coincident indicators are only approximately coincident, and may on average lead or lag by a month or so. Even so, there is a comparative paucity of 'coincident' indicators – partly because of the greater span over which the average timing difference can range for leading or lagging indicators.

The employment and unemployment series, sometimes classified as coincident indicators, for example in the United States, are here classified as lagging. This is because the analysis in the United States was in terms of peaks and troughs in the original values of the series (in the index of production in particular), whereas the material in these tables represents a matching with peaks and troughs in detrended production data. As argued earlier, it is in any case inappropriate to attempt to detrend the unemployment data, while the employment series would require a different approach to detrending from that used for the production series.

Finally, table 9.9 sets out the median leads and lags for the shortlisted indicators, and also the adjustments required for the effects of publication and recognition lags. That is, in this table we recognise that there is a time-lag between the occurrence of a cyclical turning-point and its recognition, and make an attempt to measure the size of this lag. The lag is made up of two components:

Table 9.8. *Shortlisted indicators for production ranked within each timing relationship*

By total score

	Rank	Series no.	Score
Leading indicators	1	M384	68
	2	M557	66
	3	M313	63
	4	Q309	62
	5	Q305	60
	6	M482	57
	7	M493, M582	55
	9	M206	53
	10	Q366	50
	11	Q163*	48
	12	Q7, M10, M15, M287	47
	16	M474	46
	17	Q11	45
	18	M409, M267	44
	20	M382	37
Coincident indicators	**1**	**M116***	**100**
	2	M120*, M1, M25	65
	5	Q231*	60
	6	M583	55
	7	Q157	52
	8	M8	51
	9	Q230*	49
	10	M60	47
	11	M9	44
Lagging indicators	1	M70	69
	2	Q59, M560	68
	4	M49	67
	5	Q259	66
	6	Q247, M37, M468	64
	9	M181	63
	10	Q214*	62
	11	M48	60
	12	M378	59
	13	Q212*	55

By basic score

	Rank	Series no.	Score
Leading indicators	1	M493	43
	2	M557, Q305	42
	4	M384, Q309, Q366, Q7	41
	8	M482, Q163*	39
	10	M10, M15	38
	12	M582, M474	37
	14	M313	36
	15	M206	35
	16	M409	32
	17	M287	26
	18	M382	25
	19	Q11	24
	20	M267	23
Coincident indicators	**1**	**M116***	**70**
	2	Q231*	51
	3	M120*	50
	4	M8	48
	5	M1	44
	6	Q157, Q230*	40
	8	M25	38
	9	M583	37
	10	M60, M9	35
Lagging indicators	1	Q259	54
	2	Q214*	53
	3	M49, Q247	52
	5	Q59	50
	6	Q212*	46
	7	M48	45
	8	M70	42
	9	M560	41
	10	M181	39
	11	M378	38
	12	M37, M468	37

Notes: (i) Scores are as defined on pp. 121–4 for peaks and troughs combined.
(ii) **M116*** is the series for the target variable, production.

Table 9.9. *Leads and lags of shortlisted indicators for production adjusted for reporting and recognition lags*

Months

	Series no.	Median lead or lag P	Median lead or lag T	Reporting lag	MCD statistic	Recognition lag	Adjusted medians P	Adjusted medians T
Leading indicators	M384	−5·0	−7·0	0	2	1	−4·0	−6·0
	M557	−2·0	−5·0	0	2	1	−1·0	−4·0
	M313	−4·0	−7·0	0	2	1	−3·0	−6·0
	Q309	−3·0	−5·0	0	2	3	0·0	−2·0
	Q305	−6·0	−7·0	0	3	3	−3·0	−4·0
	M482	−7·0	+2·0	0	4	2	−5·0	+4·0
	M493	−4·0	−8·5	0	7	3	−1·0	−5·5
	M582	−12·0	−6·5	1	2	1	−10·0	−4·5
	M206	−2·0	−15·0	0	4	2	0·0	−13·0
	Q366	−10·0	−3·5	3	3	3	−4·0	+2·5
	Q163*	−2·0	−8·0	1	3	3	+2·0	−4·0
	Q7	−12·0	−3·0	2	4	5	−5·0	+4·0
	M10	−6·5	−1·5	1	3	1	−4·5	+0·5
	M15	−6·0	−1·0	1	3	1	−4·0	+1·0
	M287	−2·0	−5·0	0	3	1	−1·0	−4·0
	M474	−10·5	−4·0	1	5	2	−7·5	−1·0
	Q11	−3·0	−6·0	1	2	3	+1·0	−2·0
	M409	−6·0	−9·5	1	4	2	−3·0	−6·5
	M267	−2·0	−21·0	0	3	1	−1·0	−20·0
	M382	−13·0	−14·5	1	2	1	−11·0	−12·5
Coincident indicators	**M116***	**0·0**	**0·0**	**1**	**3**	**1**	**+2·0**	**+2·0**
	M120*	0·0	0·0	1	3	1	+2·0	+2·0
	M1	0·0	−1·0	0	3	1	+1·0	0·0
	M25	+3·0	0·0	0	1	0	+3·0	0·0
	Q231*	−7·0	+1·5	3	3	3	−1·0	+7·5
	M583	−8·0	−1·5	1	2	1	−6·0	+0·5
	Q157	+2·0	0·0	2	3	3	+7·0	+5·0
	M8	+0·5	−1·5	1	5	2	+3·5	+1·5
	Q230*	−2·0	+0·5	2	3	3	+3·0	+5·5
	M60	−1·0	+1·5	1	2	1	+1·0	+3·5
	M9	+0·5	−1·0	1	3	1	+2·5	+1·0
Lagging indicators	M70	+6·0	+2·0	0	1	0	+6·0	+2·0
	Q59	+7·0	+5·0	0	1	2	+9·0	+7·0
	M560	+12·0	+5·0	0	1	0	+12·0	+5·0
	M49	+6·0	+7·0	1	1	0	+7·0	+8·0
	Q259	+22·0	+15·0	3	4	4	+29·0	+22·0
	Q247	+19·0	+5·5	3	2	3	+25·0	+11·5
	M37	+3·0	+2·0	0	1	0	+3·0	+2·0
	M468	+18·0	+8·0	0	2	1	+19·0	+9·0
	M181	+10·0	+9·0	0	2	1	+11·0	+10·0
	Q214*	+15·5	+8·0	2	3	3	+20·5	+13·0
	M48	+6·0	+4·0	1	1	0	+7·0	+5·0
	M378	+11·0	+5·0	0	3	1	+12·0	+6·0
	Q212*	+8·0	+4·5	3	3	3	+14·0	+10·5

Notes: (i) As shown the adjustment to the target variable itself (**M116***) is 1+1 = 2 months, so that the other adjustments in this table are overstated by that amount.
(ii) Leads are shown as negative and lags as positive.

(i) The reporting or publication lag, being the time required for the statistical agency concerned to collect and publish the data.[1]

(ii) The recognition lag, being the period needed, in addition to the reporting lag, to recognise that a true turning-point has in fact occurred. Generally, the more irregular the series, the longer the recognition lag. (The caution induced by false alarms or sub-cycles in the past is a complication, which for simplicity is ignored.) To give an approximate measure of the size of the recognition lag, we make use of the Shiskin MCD statistic as defined in appendix C.[2]

In real-life situations one or two qualifications are needed to these measures of lags. For instance, if near-certainty is required that a turning-point has been reached, the recognition lag is likely to be a good deal longer than the measure described above. Conversely the reporting lags given in the table are probably overstated in a number of cases, as they are based in general on publication dates, and quite frequently the information can be obtained from the appropriate statistical agency prior to publication.

One final point to be remembered is that the target variable is also subject to lags in reporting and turning-point recognition, and if these lags are substantial they will exceed those in the shortlisted indicators. A corollary is that one of the more important uses of leading or coincident indicators may be to 'forecast the present', that is to estimate the current position of the target variable.

[1] The lag is taken as 0 if data on month M are reported by the end of month M+1, 1 if by the end of month M+2, etc.

[2] Suppose the MCD statistic equals three months. Then a three-month moving average applied to the series should eliminate sufficient of the irregular movement for the remaining month-to-month movement in the smoothed series to be predominantly cyclical. Turning-points are more easily recognisable. The cost, however, is the loss of one month's currency in the indicator series; that is, the recognition lag is one month. More generally, if the MCD statistic is x months, the recognition lag is taken as $x/2$ if x is even, and $(x-1)/2$ if x is odd. For quarterly series the measure of smoothness of the series is converted to a monthly basis in the same manner as when scoring the series (see appendix A). Also there is an additional two months' lag in turning-point recognition, in comparison with an equivalent monthly series, to be added to the recognition lag for a quarterly series.

R. Long has shown in an interesting paper that in practice only about one-third of turns signalled by MCD-smoothed series were in fact true turning-points, as against the predicted half or more. Presumably this results from cyclical movements being weaker than average in the neighbourhood of cyclical turning-points, and irregular movements possibly stronger than usual. ('Forecasting specific turning points', *Journal of the American Statistical Association*, vol. 65, June 1970, pp. 520–31.)

CHAPTER 10

INDICATORS OF CYCLICAL TURNS IN INVESTMENT

In this chapter turning-points in monthly and quarterly time-series are related to the reference turns in the target variable investment, the full definition of which is gross domestic fixed capital formation, at constant (1970) prices, in the private sector, excluding dwellings, or, more concisely, private non-residential fixed investment. The reference series was detrended, so that its chronology is a growth-cycle chronology. Manufacturing fixed investment, a major component of total private sector investment, could alternatively have been used as the target variable, and cyclical movements in that series are rather more easily located, but the greater generality of the private sector series more than compensates for this.

Quarterly data on capital formation extend no further back than 1955, so that for many indicator series fewer turning-points are matched against the reference turning-points than for the other target variables. That is, the estimated average leads and lags are based on a smaller number of observations and are therefore rather more susceptible to sampling error; also the indicator series tend to have lower scores than for the other target variables. Secondly, the investment cycle lags on average a considerable time behind the production cycle (as established in Part II). It follows that leading and coincident indicators of the production cycle are almost automatically leading indicators of investment. But, of course, much of the information provided by these series simply duplicates that which would be obtained by an examination of the cyclical behaviour of the index of production. This is frequently apparent from a comparison of the standard deviations shown by a specific indicator series against production and then investment. In general a series shows a greater variance when compared with investment, reflecting two components, the original variance about the production cycle, plus the variance of the timing relationship between production and investment.

Even so, some series appear more closely connected to movements in investment than in production, and for other series it seems worthwhile to try and establish the direct relationship as well as that via the production cycle. We therefore examine the indicators under the same classification as used for matching the series against production. As features peculiar to individual indicators have generally been discussed already in chapter 9, and also fewer series are analysed, the discussion in this chapter is much more condensed.

LABOUR-MARKET SERIES

A selection of labour-market indicators is shown in table 10.1. There is little to say about the results apart from the observation that labour-market series are, not surprisingly, poor indicators of movements in investment. A comparison with the corresponding tables in chapters 9 and 11 shows that these series are more closely related to either the production cycle or the cycle in unemployment.

Table 10.1. *Labour-market series as indicators for investment*

Series	Median lead (−) or lag (+)			Standard deviation		Timing class[a]			Basic score[b]			Total score[c]		
no.	P	T	P & T	P	T	P	T	P & T	P	T	P & T	P	T	P & T
	(months)			(months)										
Vacancies														
M25	−9·0	−5·5	−7·5	11·9	2·4	–	–	–	25	48	37	52	75	64
M37	−7·0	−4·5	−5·5	11·3	2·9	–	–	–	25	33	29	52	60	56
Employment														
Q25	+7·0	−3·5	+1·0	6·9	5·6	+	–	U	25	26	25	37	38	37
Wholly unemployed by industry (inverted)[d]														
M70	−4·0	−2·5	−4·0	9·3	4·9	–	U	U	26	31	28	53	58	55
M90	−2·5	−2·5	−2·5	9·2	4·9	–	U	–	26	31	28	47	52	49
M91	−2·5	−3·5	−2·5	9·6	2·1	–	–	–	23	32	27	44	53	48
M92	−7·0	+1·5	−5·0	10·1	6·5	–	U	–	18	22	20	36	40	38

[a] U = unclassified; C = coincident; – = leading; + = lagging.
[b] Total for items (i) to (iii) on p. 10.
[c] Total for items (i) to (v) on pp. 10–11.
[d] Excluding school-leavers and adult students.

OUTPUT, CONSUMPTION AND INCOME SERIES

The first few series in table 10.2 either measure gross domestic product detrended (Q230* and Q231*) or are indices of output, again detrended (M116* and M120*). All these series have fairly similar characteristics, leading in general at both peaks and troughs, usually with longer leads at peaks. The best of these series is the detrended output index for all production industries (M116*) – that is the reference series for the production cycle. It scores well as a leading indicator and is stable about the average, notably at troughs.

The series measuring cyclical movements in steel production and consumption (M147, Q156 and Q157), or in metal manufacturing in general (Q92), have only weak timing relationships with the investment cycle, consistently scoring lower than when matched against the production cycle. Production of vehicles (M154) and vehicle registrations (M206) also score better against production. One series in the table, however, M160 measuring pro-

Table 10.2. *Output, consumption and income series as indicators for investment*

Series no.	Median lead (−) or lag (+)			Standard deviation		Timing class[a]			Basic score[b]			Total score[c]		
	P	T	P & T	P	T	P	T	P & T	P	T	P & T	P	T	P & T
	(months)			(months)										
GDP at constant prices														
Q230*	−18·0	−6·0	−6·0	7·1	4·5	–	–	–	43	36	39	52	45	48
Q231*	−9·0	−3·0	−6·0	4·2	3·0	–	U	–	46	37	42	55	46	51
Output and productivity														
M116*	−8·0	−4·5	−4·5	7·1	2·1	–	–	–	43	49	46	58	64	61
M120*	−11·0	−5·0	−7·5	5·2	3·2	–	–	–	42	44	43	57	59	58
Q92	+3·0	−4·5	−1·5	7·3	2·5	U	–	U	22	28	25	34	40	37
Production of steel, bricks and cars														
M147	+2·5	−6·0	−2·5	8·2	3·7	U	–	–	16	22	19	34	40	37
M160	−8·0	−9·0	−8·5	7·0	7·6	–	–	–	37	36	37	55	54	55
M154	−12·5	−19·5	−15·5	6·1	6·6	–	–	–	23	23	23	41	41	41
Consumption of steel and new car registrations														
Q156	−6·0	−7·5	−7·5	4·7	4·4	–	–	–	24	25	24	39	40	39
Q157	−7·5	−4·5	−4·5	6·2	2·5	–	–	–	22	27	25	34	39	37
M206	−17·0	−22·5	−19·0	8·3	7·8	–	–	–	20	35	28	38	53	46
Consumers' expenditure at constant prices														
Q163*	−18·0	−9·0	−15·0	8·6	5·0	–	–	–	41	45	43	50	54	52

Notes: see notes *a* to *c* of table 10.1.

duction of bricks, does score reasonably well as a leading indicator of investment and a good deal better than when matched against the production cycle.

INVESTMENT AND INVESTMENT ORDERS SERIES

The series for contractors' new orders (table 10.3) have highly variable leads against the investment cycle, as they had also against production. However, the total new orders series (Q173) does have some value as a leading indicator.

Both the private sector housing indicators – housing starts (M267) and housing completions (M287) – are more useful indicators here than when measured against production. Again it is the completions series which appears to be the better, although its high variability at troughs must make it somewhat unreliable for predicting investment upturns.

The series derived from the CBI survey all score particularly well, and in general have long leads. The optimism balance (Q305) shows, not unexpectedly, that investment decisions are strongly related to business confidence. Three of the CBI series (Q307 to Q309) are taken directly from questions addressed to survey respondents as to their investment intentions over the next year; whether they intend to increase or decrease investment in

Table 10.3. *Investment, orders and anticipation series as indicators for investment*

Series no.	Median lead (−) or lag (+) P	T	P & T	Standard deviation P	T	Timing class[a] P	T	P & T	Basic score[b] P	T	P & T	Total score[c] P	T	P & T
	(months)			(months)										
Contractors' new orders at 1970 prices														
Q173	−9·0	−24·0	−22·5	11·6	7·9	–	–	–	37	40	39	49	52	51
Q176	−9·0	−21·0	−21·0	12·6	5·7	–	–	–	15	31	23	27	43	35
Q180	−3·0	−9·0	−7·5	2·8	2·4	–	–	–	34	35	34	43	44	43
Private housing														
M267	−9·5	−21·5	−16·0	7·0	7·2	–	–	–	26	26	26	47	47	47
M287	−4·5	−7·0	−6·5	6·2	11·0	–	–	–	42	37	40	63	58	61
CBI survey														
Q305	−17·0	−12·0	−14·5	6·6	3·9	–	–	–	39	42	40	57	60	58
Q306	−1·0	−3·0	−2·5	8·2	4·5	U	–	–	27	42	35	51	66	59
Q307	−5·0	−10·0	−8·5	5·2	2·1	–	–	–	43	47	45	64	68	66
Q308	−5·0	−11·0	−10·5	5·2	0·8	–	–	–	43	49	46	64	70	67
Q309	−8·0	−11·0	−11·0	5·1	0·0	–	–	–	43	49	47	64	70	68
GDFCF at 1970 prices														
Q209	−1·5	−12·0	−9·0	6·8	9·0	C	–	–	32	44	38	41	53	47
Q214	+6·0	0·0	0·0	6·8	3·9	+	C	C	32	35	34	41	44	43
Q214*	0·0	+1·5	0·0	6·5	3·7	C	C	C	36	40	38	45	49	47
Capital expenditure by manufacturing sector at 1970 prices														
Q223	0·0	+3·0	0·0	1·3	3·9	C	+	C	43	25	34	52	34	43
Q224	−6·0	−16·5	−12·0	5·8	4·4	–	–	–	19	35	27	28	44	36
Q225	+7·5	0·0	+1·5	6·2	3·9	+	C	C	23	26	25	32	35	34
Q225*	+7·5	+1·5	+3·0	5·4	3·7	+	C	+	33	36	34	42	45	43

Notes: see notes *a* to *c* of table 10.1.

buildings, in plant and machinery, and in the total of these two. All three series score approximately equally and all show long leads with not too much variability about the average, and so should be very useful for forecasting cyclical turns in investment, particularly now that the surveys are conducted four times a year.

Quarterly capital formation in private dwellings (Q209) has a timing pattern not dissimilar to that for private housing completions, with generally lengthy but variable leads at investment upturns. The remaining principal investment aggregates shown (both for capital formation in the manufacturing sector) are, however, usually coincident with the investment chronology, particularly once the trend component is removed (Q214*).

STOCK SERIES

The series measuring stock-levels (table 10.4) are the only major group which fairly consistently lag rather than lead the investment cycle. Even so,

Table 10.4. *Stock series as indicators for investment*

Series no.	Median lead (−) or lag (+) P	T	P & T	Standard deviation P	T	Timing class[a] P	T	P & T	Basic score[b] P	T	P & T	Total score[c] P	T	P & T
	(months)			(months)										
Stock-levels at constant prices														
Q247	+11·5	+2·5	+4·0	7·2	2·5	+	+	+	46	37	41	58	49	53
Q264	+11·5	+2·5	+7·0	7·5	7·5	+	U	+	22	22	22	37	37	37
Q267	+13·0	+7·0	+8·5	9·6	5·0	+	+	+	15	34	24	30	49	39
Stock-ratios at constant prices														
Q254	+19·0	+13·0	+13·0	7·0	2·8	+	+	+	45	46	46	57	58	58
Q258	+19·0	+7·0	+19·0	1·3	3·7	+	+	+	57	50	53	69	62	65
Q259	+19·0	+13·0	+13·0	7·0	5·7	+	+	+	53	51	52	65	63	64
Changes in stocks at constant prices														
Q269	−9·5	−2·0	−5·0	6·2	4·7	−	U	−	45	32	39	48	35	42
Q270	−8·0	+1·0	−2·0	2·4	3·9	−	U	−	42	29	35	48	35	41
Q275	−11·0	−6·5	−8·0	9·9	3·4	−	−	−	22	44	33	28	50	39
Q276	+4·0	+1·0	+4·0	12·2	3·9	U	U	U	22	29	26	28	35	32
Q286	−8·0	−9·5	−8·0	2·1	7·5	−	−	−	48	27	38	57	36	47

Notes: see notes *a* to *c* of table 10.1.

the tabulated scores and standard deviations suggest that almost all the series are more closely related to the production cycle than to investment.

This is true also of those series measuring changes in stocks and work in progress, except for finished steel stock-changes (Q286), which is the most potentially useful leading indicator in the group.

PRICES, COSTS AND PROFITS SERIES

The FT index of industrial share prices (M313 in table 10.5) scores particularly highly as a leading indicator for fixed investment, although this is partly due to its smoothness and prompt availability, and the basic score ranks comparatively lower. Price–cost ratios for the manufacturing sector (M382) are another series with a lengthy lead, but lower scores than most other series in the table.

Examining the quarterly series which measure aggregate profits in the company sector, we find that, as was also the case for the production cycle, the original series of quarterly profits (Q345) requires detrending to give a stable timing relationship with the reference cycle. The detrending can be by means of extracting a mathematically fitted exponential trend (as in Q345*), or, more satisfactorily, by taking quarterly profits as a proportion of gross domestic product (Q366). In either case, the indicator leads by over a year at peaks and has a substantial lead at troughs, with individual leads comparatively stable about these averages. This is a valuable result for forecasting,

Table 10.5. *Prices, costs and profits series as indicators for investment*

Series no.	Median lead (−) or lag (+) P	T	P & T	Standard deviation P	T	Timing class[a] P	T	P & T	Basic score[b] P	T	P & T	Total score[c] P	T	P & T
	(months)			(months)										
Share prices														
M313	−6·0	−13·0	−10·5	6·2	2·9	–	–	–	41	45	43	68	72	70
Price–cost ratio														
M382	−14·5	−19·0	−14·5	1·5	7·0	–	–	–	30	24	27	42	36	39
Company profits														
Q345	−12·0	−18·0	−15·0	7·5	13·0	–	–	–	24	21	23	33	30	32
Q345*	−15·0	−15·0	−15·0	2·4	6·7	–	–	–	45	43	44	54	52	53
Q366	−15·0	−7·5	−12·0	2·4	6·4	–	–	–	50	49	49	59	58	58

Notes: see notes *a* to *c* of table 10.1.

even remembering the high variability and estimation error attached to profits series and the additional lag in recognition as a result of the series being quarterly.

MONEY AND CREDIT SERIES

Several of the series listed in table 10.6, for example the hire purchase series (M409 and M428) and currency in circulation (M400), appear more appropriately related to production than to investment. However the monthly series of business failures and the interest-rate indicators are more closely

Table 10.6. *Money, credit and interest-rate series as indicators for investment*

Series no.	Median lead (−) or lag (+) P	T	P & T	Standard deviation P	T	Timing class[a] P	T	P & T	Basic score[b] P	T	P & T	Total score[c] P	T	P & T
	(months)			(months)										
Change in money supply														
M400	−14·0	−5·0	−9·0	7·4	4·7	–	–	–	34	37	36	49	52	51
Hire purchase and other instalment credit														
M409	−17·0	−14·5	−17·0	7·5	11·1	–	–	–	43	43	43	55	55	55
M428	0·0	−18·0	−8·0	8·2	10·3	U	–	–	17	29	23	38	50	44
Total business failures (inverted)														
M474	−12·0	−9·0	−11·0	1·0	9·5	–	–	–	41	38	40	50	47	49
Interest rates														
M449	−2·0	−5·0	−3·0	4·7	3·3	–	–	–	28	30	29	55	57	56
M453	+1·0	−1·5	+1·0	2·6	2·7	+	C	C	45	31	38	69	55	62
M465	+12·0	−3·0	+2·0	6·9	4·6	+	U	+	22	25	23	49	52	50
M468	+8·5	−2·5	+4·0	6·1	8·0	+	U	+	38	21	30	65	47	57

Notes: see notes *a* to *c* of table 10.1.

allied to the investment cycle. Business failures on an inverted basis (M474) lead the investment cycle by almost a year on average, and the indicator seems particularly stable at downturns, though possibly this is because of the comparative shortness of the period covered (only from 1960). The two series for short-term interest rates, the Treasury bill discount rate (M449) and the rate on three months deposits with Local Authorities (M453), are clearly both closely related to the investment cycle, with the latter being coincident or nearly coincident with the reference cycle turning-points.

SUMMARY TABLES

Weeding out the less useful series from the earlier tables, we are left with a number selected for the short list as indicators for investment. Normally the higher-scoring series are selected, but an occasional comparatively low-scoring series, such as private housing starts (M267), has been retained purely because of its theoretical economic significance, while some high-scoring series are excluded because they largely duplicate other, and better, indicators.

Apart from a few fixed investment and stock-level indicators, almost all

Table 10.7. *Shortlisted indicators for investment ranked within each timing relationship*

	By total score			By basic score		
	Rank	Series no.	Score	Rank	Series no.	Score
Leading indicators	1	M313	70	1	Q366	49
	2	Q309	68	2	Q309	47
	3	M25	64	3	M116*	46
	4	M116*	61	4	M313	43
		M287			M409	
	6	Q366	58		Q163*	
		Q305		7	M287	40
	8	M409	55		Q305	
		M160			M474	
	10	Q163*	52	10	Q173	39
	11	Q173	51		Q230*	
	12	M474	49	12	M25	37
	13	Q230*	48		M160	
	14	M267	47	14	M267	26
Coincident indicators	**1**	**Q212***	**100**	**1**	**Q212***	**70**
	2	M453	62	2	M453	38
	3	Q214*	47		Q214*	

Notes: (i) Scores are as defined on pp. 121–4 for peaks and troughs combined.
(ii) **Q212*** is the series for the target variable, investment.

Table 10.8. *Leads and lags of shortlisted indicators for investment adjusted for reporting and recognition lags*

Months

	Series no.	Median lead or lag P	Median lead or lag T	Reporting lag	MCD statistic	Recognition lag	Adjusted medians P	Adjusted medians T
Leading indicators	M313	−6·0	−13·0	0	2	1	−5·0	−12·0
	Q309	−8·0	−11·0	0	2	3	−5·0	−8·0
	M25	−9·0	−5·5	0	1	0	−9·0	−5·5
	M116*	−8·0	−4·5	1	3	1	−6·0	−2·5
	M287	−4·5	−7·0	0	3	1	−3·5	−6·0
	Q366	−15·0	−7·5	3	3	3	−9·0	−1·5
	Q305	−17·0	−12·0	0	3	3	−14·0	−9·0
	M409	−17·0	−14·5	1	4	2	−14·0	−11·5
	M160	−8·0	−9·0	0	4	2	−6·0	−7·0
	Q163*	−18·0	−9·0	1	3	3	−14·0	−5·0
	Q173	−9·0	−24·0	1	3	3	−5·0	−20·0
	M474	−12·0	−9·0	1	5	2	−9·0	−6·0
	Q230*	−18·0	−6·0	2	3	3	−13·0	−1·0
	M267	−9·5	−21·5	0	3	1	−8·5	−20·5
Coincident indicators	**Q212***	**0·0**	**0·0**	**3**	**3**	**3**	**+6·0**	**+6·0**
	M453	+1·0	−1·5	0	3	1	+2·0	−0·5
	Q214*	0·0	+1·5	3	3	3	+6·0	+7·5

Notes: (i) As shown, the corresponding adjustment to the target variable itself (**Q212***) is 3+3 = 6 months, so that the other adjustments in this table are overstated by that amount.

(ii) Leads are shown as negative and lags as positive.

the shortlisted series are leading indicators when matched against investment. Thus table 10.7, ranking indicators by their scores, shows a selection of leading indicators, plus only two coincident series in addition to the target variable itself. Table 10.8, where median leads and lags are adjusted for reporting and recognition lags (see chapter 9 for a more detailed discussion), likewise consists almost entirely of leading series.

The most noticeable characteristic of these leading indicators is the length of their average leads when matched against the investment cycle. A good number of median leads exceed a year, and this takes no account of the generally greater delay in recognising a turning-point in investment than in the individual indicators. Many of the series have individual leads varying widely about the average, a drawback when they are used in forecasting. This shows also when the series are combined together in a summary index, a point taken up in chapters 12 and 14 below.

CHAPTER 11

INDICATORS OF CYCLICAL TURNS IN UNEMPLOYMENT

LABOUR-MARKET SERIES

A large number of monthly and quarterly labour-market time-series are available for comparison against turning-points in unemployment (a good number of these have already been tested against production in chapter 9). For convenience the series are split into four categories: marginal employment adjustments, vacancies, employment and unemployment. All the series listed have been seasonally adjusted, many especially for this project by the Department of Employment, whose help is gratefully acknowledged.

Marginal employment adjustments

Under this heading (table 11.1) come all those labour-market series reflecting changes in labour input or in the demand for labour at the margin. For example, series measuring the numbers working short-time or temporarily stopped (M1 and M10), the numbers on overtime (M5) and average hours being worked (M15 and the following series) all fall within this category. It seems reasonable to expect beforehand that many of these series will exhibit clear-cut and consistent timing relationships with unemployment, and normally too these series could be expected to show some lead over unemployment turning-points. This is on the reasonable assumption that initially employers adjust labour input by altering average hours worked, or increasing overtime or short-time, before committing themselves to increasing or decreasing numbers employed. The series are unlikely to have very long leads over unemployment (although net quarterly engagements (Q7) are an exception), but nevertheless may be of value for forecasting and certainly are of some analytical interest.

The series measuring engagement and discharge rates (Q1, Q4 and Q7) have been computed for four-weekly periods once a quarter since the third quarter of 1948. The figures are derived from a monthly sample of substantial size – since 1956 some 25,000 manufacturing establishments, with complete coverage of all those with 100 employees or more. The series for both engagements (Q1) and net engagements (Q7) have average leads of substantial length, particularly at peaks. This suggests that these are indicators of potentially high forecasting value, but qualified by the fact that the series are quarterly, so that there is a reporting lag of at least two months when compared with a corresponding monthly series. Also the series are

Table 11.1 *Marginal employment adjustment series as indicators for unemployment*

Series no.	Median lead (−) or lag (+)			Standard deviation		Timing class[a]			Basic score[b]			Total score[c]		
	P	T	P & T	P	T	P	T	P & T	P	T	P & T	P	T	P & T
	(months)			(months)										
Labour turnover in manufacturing														
Q1	−7·0	−3·5	−6·0	4·1	6·5	—	—	—	52	45	49	58	51	55
Q4	−4·0	−1·0	−1·0	6·2	4·3	—	C	C	36	50	43	42	56	49
Q7	−18·0	−6·0	−9·5	5·9	6·2	—	—	—	49	49	49	55	55	55
Temporarily stopped and short-time (inverted)														
M1	−3·0	−2·5	−3·0	5·0	6·5	—	—	—	36	39	37	57	60	58
M10	−8·5	−3·0	−5·5	3·7	7·5	—	—	—	50	31	41	59	40	50
Overtime in manufacturing														
M5	−2·5	−2·5	−2·5	2·7	6·5	—	—	—	37	47	42	49	59	54
M7	−3·0	−2·5	−2·5	2·3	6·5	—	—	—	52	47	49	61	56	58
M8	−9·5	−3·0	−6·0	4·2	4·5	—	—	—	39	39	39	42	42	42
Average hours in manufacturing														
M15	−13·0	−2·5	−5·0	7·4	7·6	—	—	—	33	22	27	42	31	36
M16	−13·0	−0·5	−4·0	4·8	2·1	—	C	—	32	25	28	41	34	37
M17	−13·0	−5·0	−6·0	7·8	7·1	—	—	—	35	26	30	44	35	39
M18	−13·0	−4·0	−10·0	5·1	3·6	—	—	—	38	44	41	47	53	50
M20	−13·0	−1·0	−9·0	7·4	8·5	—	—	—	29	17	23	41	29	35
M21	−1·0	−5·0	−4·0	3·3	7·1	C	—	—	40	36	38	49	45	47

[a] U = unclassified; C = coincident; − = leading; + = lagging.
[b] Total for items (i) to (iii) on p. 10.
[c] Total for items (i) to (v) on pp. 10–11.

fairly irregular, and this is reflected in the comparatively small difference between their basic and total scores. But even so, the leads are long enough to suggest that these series should occupy a more prominent place in the forecaster's bag of tools, and also could be sufficient reason for further statistical development of the series.

A perhaps surprising result at first sight is the 'positive' relationship between the rate of discharges (Q4) and the business cycle, indicating that discharges increase with prosperity and decline in recession. The series includes voluntary as well as involuntary discharges, and the positive relationship to the general cycle results from cyclical changes in labour turnover, the increase in voluntary discharges during expansion being more than sufficient to outweigh any reduction in involuntary discharges. Conversely, in the course of a contraction voluntary discharges contract more rapidly than involuntary discharges expand.

A desirable statistical development would be the separation of voluntary from involuntary discharges and their publication as separate series. This is done in the United States for example, and the 'voluntary quits' series there has useful analytical properties. The United States series for total separations, corresponding to the British quarterly discharge rate, seems to have a different mix of voluntary and involuntary discharges from the British series, and as a result does not always conform well to the cycle.[1]

Examining next the series for numbers temporarily stopped (M1) and for numbers on short-time in manufacturing (M10) – both are seen to be leading indicators with respect to cyclical turning-points in unemployment. Both, however, have also been matched against the production cycle (in chapter 9) and the temporarily stopped series in particular seems to be more appropriately regarded, after comparing scores and standard deviations, as a coincident indicator for the production cycle rather than a leading indicator of unemployment.

The overtime series (M5, M7 and M8) were obtained by linking earlier quarterly data with the monthly series dating from 1961. The sharp drops in normal hours in 1960 and 1965 had some impact on the series, but would tend to delay the peaks in the series in both years. That is, the impact on these series would be much the same as on unemployment, the target against which the series are being compared, and so would probably not affect very much the timing relationships involved. The series display fairly consistent leads, with the series for total hours overtime (M7) the most consistent.

The interesting feature of the average hours series, showing cyclical leads and lags in average hours worked in all of manufacturing (M15), as well as for the principal industry groupings (the food, drink and tobacco group is omitted as being altogether too irregular for useful analysis), is the sizeable difference between the very long average leads shown at cyclical peaks and the fairly short average leads at troughs. This contrasts quite sharply with United States experience. There the average hours series is one of the shortlisted leading indicators, showing a median lead of six months at troughs and four months at peaks.[2]

The asymmetry in average leads for the United Kingdom series is found on investigation to be the result of the quite sharp reductions in the normal working week which took place in 1960 and 1965–6. The Department of Employment's indices of normal hours reveal a drop of nearly 4 per cent in the manufacturing sector from January 1960 to January 1961, and an identical percentage drop between October 1964 and April 1966. The effect of these changes appears to have been to leave the location of the peaks in the average hours series not much altered, but to have retarded the peaks in the unemployment series, so leading to the long average leads at peaks.

If an adjustment is made to the series, such as for instance dividing the average hours series by the normal hours index to give the series M21, then

[1] This is discussed in a little more detail in O'Dea, 'The cyclical timing of labor market indicators in Britain and the United States'.

[2] Peaks and troughs in the general cycle, see Moore and Shiskin, *Indicators of Business Expansions and Contractions.*

the adjusted series is much more closely aligned to the unemployment cycle. The table shows the adjusted series to be approximately coincident at peaks, with little variability about the average.

Unfilled vacancies

Statistics of unfilled vacancies (table 11.2) are obtained from notifications by employers to local branches of the Department of Employment. In no sense can they be regarded as a complete count of jobs available, but movements in the series can be regarded as approximately paralleling movements in the true, but unknown, number of vacancies available. Clearly the series is one of the more important indicators of demand pressures in the labour market (these points were discussed in more detail in chapter 6).

Table 11.2. *Vacancy series as indicators for unemployment*

Series no.	Median lead (−) or lag (+)			Standard deviation		Timing class[a]			Basic score[b]			Total score[c]		
	P	T	P & T	P	T	P	T	P & T	P	T	P & T	P	T	P & T
	(months)			(months)										
M25	−4·0	−2·0	−3·0	2·6	3·9	–	C	–	45	48	46	72	75	73
M26	−1·0	−2·0	−2·0	4·1	3·9	U	–	–	33	45	39	60	72	66
M27	−5·0	−2·5	−3·0	2·9	3·9	–	C	–	44	48	46	71	75	73
M37	−3·0	0·0	−1·0	2·4	4·0	–	C	C	45	48	46	72	75	73
Q11	−9·0	−11·5	−11·0	6·0	4·5	–	–	–	18	20	19	39	41	40

Notes: see notes to table 11.1.

The total series (M25) shows stable leads at both peaks and troughs, although short enough at troughs to be labelled an approximately coincident indicator. At both peaks and troughs the series scores well on the basic criteria and, taking into account the smoothness of the indicator and its immediacy of publication, the series has a very high total score. The standard deviations, when compared with the corresponding values in chapter 9, show that the series is more closely associated with the unemployment cycle than the production cycle (except at the 1967–8 trough, where the turn in unemployment showed an unusually long lag). Vacancies was one of the series listed as of potential value for forecasting peaks in the production cycle, but from this result looks a more appropriate forecasting tool for movements in unemployment. The average leads shown by the series are not, it will be noted, particularly long, but are nevertheless sufficient to give, on average, some two to three months forewarning that a turn in unemployment is about to occur. Separate details are given for the male and female components of the total series (M26 and M27 respectively). Essentially they reproduce the results for the total series, although with the male series rather more variable at cyclical peaks.

The ratio of vacancies to unemployment (M37) is expected to be dominated by the vacancies component at cyclical peaks and by the unemployment component at troughs (that is by the component which is not flattening out near its 'floor' value). This is confirmed by the average leads shown in the table, the lead at peaks being approximately that shown by the vacancies series, while at cyclical troughs the series on average coincides with turning-points in unemployment. Again the series is a particularly high-scoring indicator, although for forecasting purposes (as against giving a particularly clear picture of cyclical movements) it contributes nothing additional to that already given by unfilled vacancies.

The final series in this group (Q11) is one compiled by a commercial agency (Management Selection Limited) showing the number of advertisements for executive positions appearing in a selected sample of leading newspapers each quarter. The series dates back only to 1963, perhaps a factor in its rather low scores. A comparison with the corresponding figures in chapter 9 suggests that the series is more appropriately considered as an indicator of the production cycle.

Employment series

Employment in the manufacturing sector (table 11.3) can be measured either by the number of persons working, or by the total number of hours worked. Series measuring the latter, for all manufacturing and for industry groups within manufacturing, are the first group of employment indicators to be analysed.

Outside the manufacturing sector there are no measures of hours worked, but a number of series measuring numbers employed. In decreasing order of generality they are: economy-wide series; series covering all production, or total manufacturing; and employment by industry group.

Examining first the series for total hours worked in the manufacturing sector (M60) and its major industrial subdivisions (excluding the food-manufacturing group, where the total hours series is highly erratic), all are found to display a reasonably clear cyclical pattern. However, the series for the engineering sector (M61) conforms more consistently, judging by its scores, than the series for vehicles (M62) and textiles (M63). The general pattern is for a lengthy average lead at peaks, but for approximate coincidence at troughs. But this timing pattern, both for the individual industrial sectors and for the total manufacturing series, is of course affected by the reductions in normal hours during the 1960s. As discussed above, these reductions have probably affected the timing relationships at peaks sufficiently for them not to be a reliable guide to the future. A more useful estimate of the average lead or lag should therefore be obtained by eliminating the effects of the reductions in normal hours. This has been attempted here for total manufacturing, but not the industrial sub-groups,

Table 11.3. *Employment series as indicators for unemployment*

Series no.	Median lead (−) or lag (+) P	T	P & T	Standard deviation P	T	Timing class[a] P	T	P & T	Basic score[b] P	T	P & T	Total score[c] P	T	P & T
	(months)			(months)										
Total weekly hours in manufacturing														
M60	−12·0	−0·5	−1·0	4·0	0·5	–	C	–	37	45	41	49	57	53
M61	−1·0	−1·0	−1·0	4·8	0·4	C	C	C	28	48	38	40	60	50
M62	−13·0	−0·5	−4·0	9·9	8·3	–	C	–	32	24	28	38	30	34
M63	−13·0	−1·0	−4·5	7·3	2·2	–	U	–	29	24	27	41	36	39
M65	−5·0	−1·0	−4·5	4·0	3·3	–	–	–	40	30	35	52	42	47
M66	+1·0	−0·5	0·0	0·5	0·5	C	C	C	48	52	50	60	64	62
Employment economy-wide														
Q16	+8·0	−1·0	+1·0	5·0	1·6	+	C	U	41	45	43	53	57	55
Q17	+6·5	−1·0	+1·0	6·2	2·7	+	C	U	39	37	38	51	49	50
Q18	+9·0	−2·0	+4·0	2·9	3·5	+	C	+	57	47	52	69	59	64
Q25	+7·0	0·0	+0·5	6·0	1·5	+	C	C	43	57	50	55	69	62
Q19	+7·0	−6·0	+2·5	6·0	3·9	+	U	U	26	28	27	38	40	39
Q22	+7·0	−2·0	+4·0	0·9	2·9	+	U	U	39	36	38	51	48	50
Employment by industry group														
M48	0·0	+1·0	+0·5	5·8	3·0	U	C	C	37	47	42	52	62	57
M49	+2·0	0·0	+1·0	3·0	4·5	C	C	C	44	36	40	59	51	55
M50	+2·0	+4·0	+3·0	8·2	4·3	+	+	+	26	38	32	41	53	47
M51	+7·0	+1·0	+2·0	5·4	3·0	+	C	+	38	30	34	53	45	49
M52	−2·5	0·0	0·0	8·7	2·7	U	C	U	24	31	27	39	46	42
M53	−1·0	−1·0	−1·0	9·7	6·0	U	–	–	29	41	35	44	56	50
M54	+10·0	−1·0	−1·0	7·6	2·6	U	C	U	29	35	32	38	44	41
Q34	+2·0	−1·0	+0·5	8·6	4·2	U	C	U	29	34	31	44	49	46
Q35	+12·0	+5·0	+8·5	3·4	4·9	+	+	+	45	33	39	60	48	54
Q36	−7·0	+2·0	+0·5	16·1	2·4	U	+	U	15	24	19	30	39	34
Q37	−10·5	+0·5	−2·0	10·5	4·5	U	U	U	15	22	18	30	37	33
Q46	+7·0	−5·0	−3·5	11·6	2·1	U	–	U	14	23	19	26	35	31

Notes: see notes to table 11.1.

by dividing the original total hours index by the Department of Employment's index of normal hours. The resulting series (M66) is approximately coincident at both peaks and troughs, and the values of the standard deviations show the relationship to be a particularly stable one. The close correspondence of the adjusted series with the turns in unemployment is a more reasonable relationship to expect than that shown by the unadjusted series.

All the remaining employment indicators measure numbers of persons rather than hours worked. The first group consists of those quarterly series measuring employment for the whole economy (that is including services and administration, as well as manufacturing and the other 'index of production' industries). Taking the series for employees in employment, Q16, as the base, the other series listed are total in civil employment, including also employers and the self-employed (Q25); the total working population, including also the wholly unemployed and the forces (Q22); total employees, employees in employment plus the wholly unemployed (Q19).

A change caused by economic factors in the number of persons employed does not usually result in a change of equal magnitude (in the opposite direction) in the number of wholly unemployed. There are many individuals marginal to the labour force who drop out but do not register as unemployed in recession, and who rejoin the labour force during periods of expansion. Married women are an important component of this marginal labour force, a factor presumably responsible for the greater cyclical sensitivity of the female employment series (Q18) as listed in the table. It follows that the series of total employees and working population, despite including the wholly unemployed, still show cyclical movements. However, the cycles are damped and sometimes omitted entirely, and these two series do not score as well as those measuring employees in employment and the total in civil employment.

The characteristic feature of the economy-wide employment series is the average lag of several months shown at cyclical peaks, as against the approximate coincidence at troughs. These timing relationships, however, may be not so much an intrinsic part of the cyclical relationship between employment and unemployment as a result of the strong upward trend in the employment series over much of the postwar period until the mid-1960s. The difference of some months between peak and trough averages is most likely a consequence of the trend-component shifting turning-point locations.

More recently, since about 1966, the upward trend has given way to a downward trend; the reasons for this change are uncertain. Certainly on demographic grounds a levelling-off in the labour force over the last few years was to be expected and indeed was predicted, but a substantial fall in total employment was not predicted. Various grounds have since been advanced for the fall, but until such time as the trend-determining factors can be identified and eliminated with more certainty, the estimated timing relationships between employment and unemployment can be used only with a good deal of caution.

If a single series were to be selected as representative of the group, the best candidate would seem, from the tabulated scores, to be the total in civil employment (Q25). However the series differs from the total of employees in employment (Q16) only by the numbers of employers and self-employed, which itself is an approximate estimate, altering only very slowly. Thus the employees series is the more appropriate employment indicator to represent changes in employment in the economy as a whole.

The two monthly series showing the number of employees in the production industries and in manufacturing industry (M48 and M49) are much more restricted in coverage than the quarterly series just considered. However they are available much more speedily and also at monthly rather than quarterly intervals. They are composite series, built basically from monthly series extending back to the mid-1950s (with breaks due to changes in industrial classification), with turning-point dates in the early 1950s obtained from analogous quarterly series.[1] Both are approximately coincident on average with troughs in unemployment (inverted). At peaks the manufacturing series shows a short average lag, while the index of production series is roughly coincident on average.

An interesting point is that neither monthly series shows the lengthy average lag at cyclical peaks which characterised the quarterly employment series. The main reason for this difference appears to be that the quarterly series include services, administration and agriculture, whereas the monthly series cover only the 'productive' sectors. Growth in employment in the services sector (defining this as being all those industries outside the scope of the index of production) has been more rapid, at least over the last decade, than in the production industries.[2] This would strengthen the upward trend and hence tend to retard cyclical downturns.

The final group of series, measuring employment in individual industry groups, requires little comment. They are, like the employment series with broader coverage, generally coincident at cyclical troughs. At peaks, the pattern is more diverse; some series lag on average, while others cannot be allocated to any particular timing class. None of this group of indicators scores very well.

Unemployment series

Three groups of series are examined under this heading: unemployment classified by sex, by industry group, and by duration of unemployment. Another group of unemployment series – wholly unemployed by region – was also examined, but is not reported on here. It showed very much the same type of timing behaviour as the industry group series listed in table

[1] The seasonally adjusted indices currently published monthly by the Department of Employment are very nearly equivalent to the two series listed in the table, although there is sometimes some loss of accuracy in rounding off from actual numbers to index number form.

[2] The total number of employees in employment increased by approximately 1.4 million (from 21 million to 22.4 million) over the period 1951 to 1961, but between 1961 and 1971 it fell by 350,000, with the actual change of direction fairly marked in 1966. In the earlier period the number of employees in the 'service' (i.e. non-index of production) industries grew only slightly faster than the number in the 'production' industries, and the proportion of employees in services remained roughly constant at about 49 per cent. From 1961 to 1971, however, the number employed in services continued to grow, whereas the production industries showed an absolute decline. The result was to send the proportion of employees in the service or non-index industries up to 53 per cent by 1971. These figures are taken from *British Labour Statistics: Historical Abstract* and the *Department of Employment Gazette*. The percentages are for the 1958-based industrial classification, the 1951 and 1971 data being made approximately comparable to the 1961 data by taking ratios over breaks in the series.

Table 11.4. *Unemployment series as indicators for unemployment*

Series no.	Median lead (−) or lag (+) P	T	P & T	Standard deviation P	T	Timing class[a] P	T	P & T	Basic score[b] P	T	P & T	Total score[c] P	T	P & T
	(months)			(months)										
Wholly unemployed (inverted)[d]														
M71	0·0	0·0	0·0	0·4	0·4	C	C	C	54	54	54	81	81	81
M72	−1·0	+1·0	+1·0	1·9	5·3	C	C	C	55	46	51	82	73	78
M73	+1·0	+1·0	+1·0	1·6	1·9	C	C	C	46	50	48	70	74	72
Wholly unemployed by industry (inverted)[d]														
M90	0·0	0·0	0·0	1·6	1·1	C	C	C	55	57	56	76	78	77
M91	0·0	0·0	0·0	1·6	3·4	C	C	C	55	48	52	76	69	73
M92	0·0	+0·5	0·0	2·1	2·9	C	C	C	35	39	37	53	57	55
M93	0·0	0·0	0·0	2·9	4·9	C	C	C	37	42	40	52	57	55
M94	+2·0	0·0	+2·0	1·1	3·2	+	C	C	39	29	34	57	47	52
M95	0·0	0·0	0·0	1·9	3·0	C	C	C	48	42	45	69	63	66
M96	0·0	+2·5	+2·0	2·9	4·2	C	+	C	44	36	40	62	54	58
M97	+2·0	0·0	+1·0	2·2	2·4	C	C	C	47	37	42	68	58	63
Wholly unemployed by duration (inverted)[e]														
M78	−2·0	−6·0	−4·0	3·0	5·1	–	–	–	34	49	42	49	64	57
M99	−1·0	−3·5	−2·0	1·9	2·4	C	–	–	42	52	47	57	67	62
M100	−1·0	−3·5	−2·0	1·9	2·7	C	–	–	42	46	44	57	61	59
Q58	+2·0	+1·0	+1·0	1·8	2·0	C	C	C	52	47	50	67	62	65
Q59	+2·0	+1·0	+1·0	1·7	2·7	+	C	C	43	35	39	61	53	57
Q60	+5·0	+7·0	+7·0	2·9	4·5	+	+	+	47	39	43	65	57	61
Q74	+11·0	+13·0	+12·0	6·3	4·0	+	+	+	49	51	50	64	66	65

[d] Excluding school-leavers and adult students.
[e] Including school-leavers and adult students.
See also notes to table 11.1.

11.4, that is, approximately coincident with total unemployment, with the occasional divergence probably attributable to sampling error rather than to any systematic effect.

Male and female unemployment (M71 and M72 respectively), when analysed separately, vary very little in their turning-point locations from total unemployment, although turning-point locations in the female series are a bit more variable, as might be expected. Practice varies internationally as to whether it is more appropriate to use the total number unemployed or the unemployment rate as the best measure of the level of unemployment. The number of wholly unemployed is used in this paper, but the alternative, the unemployment rate (M73), is analysed too. This series is, naturally, an approximately coincident indicator, but it seems that the rounding to a percentage figure is sufficient to delay recognition of the turns by a month on average.

The eight series classifying wholly unemployed by industry group are all approximately coincident with total unemployment, assuming that the average lags shown in a couple of instances are not of particular statistical significance. A number of the listed series score quite highly as coincident indicators, but this does not of course imply that they are particularly useful for analysis or for assessing the current state of the economy, except that a turn in the total number of wholly unemployed which is not matched by turns in most of the component unemployment series is probably an irregular fluctuation of no cyclical significance.

The final group are those series classifying unemployed persons by the length of time they have been registered as unemployed. These differ in composition from the other unemployment series so far considered, as they include both unemployed school-leavers and unemployed adult students, which are excluded from all the wholly unemployed series. The difference in coverage is important for short-duration unemployment, and the greater irregularity which results is quite noticeable in graphs of the series, particularly at Easter and in the summer holiday period.

Quarterly statistics on unemployment by duration are available from 1948, and monthly statistics, although only for the shorter durations up to eight weeks, from June 1963. Thus the results given for the short-duration series (M78, M99 and M100) are obtained from a 'spliced' series, combining the earlier quarterly series with the more recent monthly data. Another point is that the short-duration series as originally published (in categories 2–4 weeks and 4–8 weeks) are here cumulated, after seasonal adjustment, giving the cumulated totals unemployed under four weeks (M99) and under eight weeks (M100). The series are smoother and more easily interpreted when this is done.

All three short-duration series on average lead turns in unemployment. Although the average lead is only a month or two at cyclical peaks, at cyclical troughs the average is three to six months. These leads, coupled with the low standard deviations about the average values, suggest that the series will be useful for giving forewarning of turns in unemployment, even if their potential usefulness is lessened by the irregularities caused by fluctuations in the numbers of school-leavers and adult students on the register.

The longer-duration quarterly series (Q58, Q59 and Q60) on average all lag behind total wholly unemployed, although for the two series of shorter duration the lags are sufficiently small for them to be classified as coincident. The third series, unemployed for more than 52 weeks, lags by several months. A characteristic of this series, incidentally, is its extreme smoothness and its failure to pick up cyclical fluctuations in unemployment of less than normal amplitude – for instance the 1968–9 downturn is not shown.

To summarise, table 11.4 shows leads for the short-duration unemployment series (under eight weeks) gradually swinging to lags on average for the longer-duration series. This sequence is one which would be automatically assumed if one considered only new additions to the unemployment register. Peaks and troughs in the numbers of newly unemployed would move in sequence through the various duration classes, with a more immediate and greater proportionate impact on the series for under two weeks than on, say, under four weeks. The picture becomes more complex when exits from the register are also taken into account. An increase in the demand for labour will push up the number of exits from the register for all durations, concurrently with the decrease in the numbers of newly unemployed coming on to the register. Conceivably, if the separation rate from the register at the longer durations were to be more sensitive to prevailing economic conditions than the separation rate at shorter durations, peaks and troughs could occur first in the longer-duration series. In practice, however, we expect those who have been some months on the register to have greater difficulty in finding new employment, and expect also that these difficulties are not affected much one way or another by changes in the demand for labour. Such statistical evidence as is available bears out these expectations.[1] Combined with the earlier impact on the short-duration series of new entrants to the register, this evidence is sufficient to explain the observed sequence.

The last indicator given in the table (Q74) measures the average time which has been spent on the register of unemployed by those still there at each quarterly count. (The open-ended group, 52 weeks and above, are assumed to have spent on average 78 weeks on the register, while all other durations are taken at their mid-points.) The series, analysed like all the unemployment series in 'inverted' form (that is matching a trough in the series to a peak in general economic conditions, and vice versa), has a consistent lag of approximately a year on average. The series, in this or slightly different form, is sometimes used as a measure of demand pressures in the labour market, but the magnitude of the average lag given here suggests this is an inappropriate use.

NON-LABOUR-MARKET SERIES

Only a selected few of the large number of non-labour-market indicators tested against the target variables of production and investment in the two previous chapters were matched against the unemployment cycle. The results are given in tables 11.5, 11.6 and 11.7. Most cyclical indicators can reasonably be expected to be more closely allied to changes in production or investment rather than to changes in unemployment, with the exception of course of those series measuring labour-market changes. Thus the only indicators tested here are those which either have rated very highly when

[1] See R. F. Fowler, *Duration of Unemployment on the Register of Wholly Unemployed*, London, HMSO, 1968, which shows that the turnover rate is much higher for those who have been only a short time on the unemployment register, and also that these turnover rates are apparently more sensitive to changes in the level of total unemployment than those for longer-duration unemployed.

Table 11.5. *Output and consumption series as indicators for unemployment*

Series no.	Median lead (−) or lag (+) P	T	P & T	Standard deviation P	T	Timing class[a] P	T	P & T	Basic score[b] P	T	P & T	Total score[c] P	T	P & T
	(months)			(months)										
Output and productivity														
M114*	−9·0	−6·0	−6·0	5·4	6·3	–	–	–	47	48	47	56	57	56
M115*	−9·5	−3·0	−6·0	5·3	6·7	–	–	–	40	40	40	49	49	49
M116*	−6·0	−2·0	−3·0	5·8	3·2	–	–	–	31	50	41	46	65	56
Production of commodities														
M154	−12·0	−12·0	−12·0	5·6	9·8	–	–	–	32	27	30	50	45	48
M160	−7·0	−12·0	−9·5	8·6	7·7	–	–	–	22	30	26	40	48	44
Consumption														
Q163*	−13·0	−9·0	−13·0	3·3	6·0	–	–	–	49	47	48	58	56	57
M206	−11·0	−18·0	−15·0	5·1	4·9	–	–	–	44	44	44	62	62	62

Notes: see notes to table 11.1.

Table 11.6. *Investment, orders and anticipation series as indicators for unemployment*

Series no.	Median lead (−) or lag (+) P	T	P & T	Standard deviation P	T	Timing class[a] P	T	P & T	Basic score[b] P	T	P & T	Total score[c] P	T	P & T
	(months)			(months)										
Private housing														
M267	−14·0	−24·0	−17·0	9·7	5·7	–	–	–	28	42	35	49	63	56
M287	−14·0	−13·0	−13·5	11·8	8·7	–	–	–	32	43	37	53	64	58
CBI survey														
Q305	−18·0	−14·0	−15·5	10·2	4·2	–	–	–	34	41	38	52	59	56
GDFCF at 1970 prices														
Q212*	+4·0	+2·5	+4·0	9·3	4·9	+	U	+	12	17	14	21	26	23
Q214*	+9·5	+6·5	+6·5	11·5	6·4	+	+	+	32	36	34	41	45	43

Notes: see notes to table 11.1.

matched against the other target variables, or those for which economic theory suggests some connection with changes in unemployment.

The detrended production index for all production industries, M116*, examined in table 11.5, is the series chosen to determine the production cycle chronology, and can be seen to be a reasonably high-scoring leading indicator. Two other detrended labour productivity series are examined (M114* and M115*); they also score reasonably well, showing lengthy average leads over the turning-points in unemployment.

Three particularly sensitive series measuring the production or consump-

Table 11.7. *Prices, costs, profits and credit series as indicators for unemployment*

Series no.	Median lead (−) or lag (+)			Standard deviation		Timing class[a]			Basic score[b]			Total score[c]		
	P	T	P & T	P	T	P	T	P & T	P	T	P & T	P	T	P & T
	(months)			(months)										
Share prices														
M313	−4·0	−9·0	−8·0	6·4	4·4	–	–	–	33	46	39	60	73	66
Price–cost ratio														
M382	−19·0	−20·0	−20·0	6·0	1·0	–	–	–	25	31	28	37	43	40
Profits														
Q366	−13·0	−8·5	−10·0	7·7	3·7	–	–	–	35	44	40	44	53	49
Credit														
M409	−17·0	−15·5	−17·0	1·7	9·1	–	–	–	49	45	47	61	57	59
M474	−16·5	−14·0	−14·0	6·5	7·8	–	–	–	21	27	24	30	36	33

Notes: see notes to table 11.1.

tion of individual commodities are also listed. Production of bricks (M160) scores less well than the others and, checking back to the previous chapter, is more closely related to movements in investment than in unemployment. Of the two indicators measuring vehicle production and new car registrations (M154 and M206), the latter scores particularly well and has very lengthy average leads. New car registrations (Q163*) are one facet of total consumers' expenditure, and can also be seen to be a high-scoring indicator with very lengthy average leads. The principal difficulty is in identifying precisely the economic linkages between these indicators and changes in unemployment.

A similar problem holds for the first three series listed in table 11.6; private housing starts and completions, and the optimism balance from the CBI survey. All three indicators show lengthy average leads against unemployment and all score quite well despite fairly high variability about the average leads. Nevertheless all three seem more logically connected with changes in investment and, apart from housing starts, score a little better when matched against the investment series.

The last two indicators in table 11.6, fixed investment in the private sector (Q212*) and in manufacturing (Q214*), are lagging series. The relationships with cyclical movements in unemployment are obviously fairly tenuous.

Three indicators measuring prices and profits are listed in table 11.7. The series for the ratio of output prices to unit labour costs in the manufacturing sector (M382) scores only moderately well. The other two series, however, the FT ordinary share price index (M313) and the ratio of profits

Table 11.8. *Shortlisted indicators for unemployment ranked within each timing classification*

	By total score			By basic score		
	Rank	Series no.	Score	Rank	Series no.	Score
Leading indicators	1	M25	73	1	{M7, Q1, Q7}	49
	2	M313	66	4	Q163*	48
	3	{M99, M206}	62	5	{M99, M409}	47
	5	M409	59	7	M25	46
	6	M7	58	8	M206	44
	7	{Q163*, M78}	57	9	M78	42
	9	M116*	56	10	{M116*, M10}	41
	10	{Q1, Q7}	55	12	Q366	40
	12	M10	50	13	{M313, M8}	39
	13	Q366	49	15	M21	38
	14	M21	47			
	15	M8	42			
Coincident indicators	**1**	**M70**	**100**	**1**	**M70**	**70**
	2	M90	77	2	M90	56
	3	{M91, M37}	73	3	M91	52
	5	Q58	65	4	{Q58, M66}	50
	6	M66	62	6	M37	46
	7	Q4	49	7	Q4	43
Lagging indicators	1	Q74	65	1	Q74	50
	2	Q60	61	2	Q60	43

Notes: (i) Scores are as defined on pp. 121–4 for peaks and troughs combined.
(ii) **M70** is the series for the target variable, unemployment.

to gross domestic product (Q366) are clearly both useful leading indicators of turning-points in unemployment. The average leads are lengthy, even after allowing for the substantial reporting lag for the second of these two indicators.

The last two indicators considered, in table 11.7, are again series which proved to be high-scoring when matched against production and investment in the preceding two chapters. However the series for business failures (M474) here has only a weak cyclical relationship with unemployment. The series measuring the increase in hire purchase debt (M409) is, however, clearly an indicator with high potential for forecasting turns in unemployment, although, as with some of the other indicators considered in this section, the linkages involved ideally require further analysis.

SUMMARY TABLES

As in the two previous chapters, we now select from the series set out in tables 11.1 to 11.7 the 'best' indicators of the unemployment cycle. The series excluded from the short list are rejected either because in their timing class they are comparatively low-scoring, or else because the information they convey largely duplicates that of another indicator.

A total of 24 series are listed in table 11.8, with over half of them leading indicators when matched against the unemployment cycle. Most of the series have already appeared on the summary lists for the production and investment cycles, but a few additional labour-market series appear here. Some specific details worth noting are:

(i) The series for both average hours (M21) and total hours (M66) in

Table 11.9. *Leads and lags of shortlisted indicators for unemployment adjusted for reporting and recognition lags*

	Series no.	Median lead or lag		Reporting lag	MCD statistic	Recognition lag	Adjusted medians	
		P	T				P	T
Leading indicators	M25	−4·0	−2·0	0	1	0	−4·0	−2·0
	M313	−4·0	−9·0	0	2	1	−3·0	−8·0
	M99	−1·0	−3·5	0	3	1	0·0	−2·5
	M206	−11·0	−18·0	0	4	2	−9·0	−16·0
	M409	−17·0	−15·5	1	4	2	−14·0	−12·5
	M7	−3·0	−2·5	1	3	1	−1·0	−0·5
	Q163*	−13·0	−9·0	1	3	3	−9·0	−5·0
	M78	−2·0	−6·0	0	3	1	−1·0	−5·0
	M116*	−6·0	−2·0	1	3	1	−4·0	0·0
	Q1	−7·0	−3·5	2	4	5	0·0	+3·5
	Q7	−18·0	−6·0	2	4	5	−11·0	+1·0
	M10	−8·5	−3·0	1	3	1	−6·5	−1·0
	Q366	−13·0	−8·5	3	3	3	−7·0	−2·5
	M21	−1·0	−5·0	1	3	1	+1·0	−3·0
	M8	−9·5	−3·0	1	5	2	−6·5	0·0
Coincident indicators	**M70**	**0·0**	**0·0**	**0**	**1**	**0**	**0·0**	**0·0**
	M90	0·0	0·0	1	1	0	+1·0	+1·0
	M91	0·0	0·0	1	1	0	+1·0	+1·0
	M37	−3·0	0·0	0	1	0	−3·0	0·0
	Q58	+2·0	+1·0	0	2	3	+5·0	+4·0
	M66	+1·0	−0·5	1	2	1	+3·0	+1·5
	Q4	−4·0	−1·0	2	4	5	+3·0	+6·0
Lagging indicators	Q74	+11·0	+13·0	0	2	3	+14·0	+16·0
	Q60	+5·0	+7·0	0	1	2	+7·0	+9·0

Notes: (i) As shown the corresponding adjustment to the target variable itself (**M70**) is 0+0 = 0 months; the other adjustments in this table are not overstated.

(ii) Leads are shown as negative and lags as positive.

manufacturing industry are adjusted for changes in normal hours. The adjustment was intended, as explained earlier in this paper, to give the probable timing relationship between hours worked and unemployment on the assumption of no change in normal hours. Assuming this attempt has been successful, then the average leads or lags established for the adjusted series can be taken to apply to the unadjusted series in future, provided of course that there are no further major reductions in normal hours.

(ii) Apart from six of the leading indicators, all the selected series are labour-market indicators. The non-labour-market series have generally lengthy leads compared with the labour-market indicators but also are more variable about their average leads.

(iii) The fact that changes in the level of unemployment come comparatively late in the general economic cycle is the cause of the shortness of the list of lagging indicators. Likewise, to get a reasonable list of coincident indicators it is necessary to have a high proportion of series measuring unemployment, with a good deal of duplication in coverage.

In table 11.9, we see how the median leads (or lags) computed from past experience are affected by the delays in reporting data and in recognising turning-points which apply when trying to assess the current situation. Particularly affected by these lags are the series for quarterly engagements and discharges (Q1, Q4 and Q7), and also the quarterly profits ratio (Q366). This results in a significant reduction of the forecasting value of, in particular, the series for quarterly labour turnover.

CHAPTER 12

SUMMARISING THE INFORMATION: DIFFUSION AND COMPOSITE INDICES

In the past three chapters the potential usefulness of a considerable number of cyclical indicators has been evaluated by various tests. The tests lead to the elimination from subsequent analysis of a good number of series, leaving only those higher-ranked indicators listed in the summary tables at the end of each chapter. But even these indicators are still a considerable number, as shown by table 12.1. Naturally there is a good deal of overlap between the three target variables, but in all there are about 60 shortlisted indicators, about 75 per cent of which have been matched against the production cycle. The fairly high proportion which are labour-market series is a result of concentration upon such series when analysing the cycle in unemployment.

Given this number of indicators it is clearly difficult to arrive at any overall assessment of the current situation unless there is some statistical measure which collates and summarises the information presented by the individual indicators. Two such measures are described and computed in this chapter. They are:[1]

(i) diffusion indices, measuring the extent to which movements, either upwards or downwards, are diffused amongst the component indicators making up the index;

(ii) composite indices, which are a weighted amalgam of the series, with adjustments to avoid the dominance of the index by any individual series. A composite index thus has the theoretical advantage over a diffusion index of measuring the strength as well as the direction of the cyclical movement.

For both types of index, the first step is normally to classify the indicators into one of the three timing classes – leading, roughly coincident, or lagging – and then to construct separate indices for each timing class. Both indices are alike also in weighting the indicators together in an objective manner. In the case of diffusion indices the indicators are given equal weights; in constructing composite indices more complicated combinations are possible and it is necessary to discuss not only the construction of the index but also the derivation of the weights.

The series used for the construction of both types of index were first

[1] Further material on the construction of diffusion and composite indices can be found in Moore and Shiskin, *Indicators of Business Expansions and Contractions*, particularly pp. 83ff, and Julius Shiskin, *Signals of Recession and Recovery*, New York, NBER, 1961. In the latter Shiskin uses the term 'amplitude-adjusted general indices' to define those series here labelled composite indices. A more recent publication, *Canadian Business Cycle Composite Indicators*, Toronto, W. A. Beckett Associates Ltd., 1973, describes the construction of composite indices for the Canadian economy. The methods are closely modelled on the Shiskin approach.

Table 12.1. *Economic categories and timing classification of shortlisted indicators*

Numbers of series

	Target variable			
	Production	Investment	Unemployment	Total
Labour-market	14	1	18	26
Output, consumption and income	8	4	3	9
Fixed investment[a]	6	7	0	7
Stocks (levels and changes)	2	0	0	2
Prices, costs and profits	7	2	2	7
Money and credit	3	3	1	4
Foreign trade	4	0	0	4
All categories	44	17	24	59
of which: leading	20	14	15	
coincident	11	3	7	
lagging	13	0	2	

[a] Includes series for orders and anticipations.

smoothed by simple moving averages with equal weights. The length of the moving average was taken as equal to the MCD statistic (or the equivalent QCD statistic for quarterly series), that is any inter-period movements in the smoothed series should predominantly represent cyclical rather than irregular movements, leading eventually to a smoother index that could be more easily interpreted.

DIFFUSION INDICES

Diffusion indices collate together information on the direction of movements – either up or down – of the individual indicators. The size of the change in an individual series is discarded as irrelevant.

During the expansionary phase of the cycle, most of the available indicators could be expected to be moving upwards (contra-cyclical indicators such as unemployment having been inverted) although there would generally be at least one or two series moving in the opposite direction. As the group of indicators approach a cyclical downturn, the normal pattern would be for one or two particularly sensitive series to turn downwards first, followed shortly by a few more, until the month-to-month movement of the bulk of the series was downwards. The exact timing of the cyclical downturn is derived by computing each month the excess of series expanding over series contracting (no change being taken as half each way). This excess expressed as a percentage constitutes the diffusion index and cyclical downturns or upturns are signalled by those points where the index crosses the zero line.

In practice the signals are often unclear as, despite preliminary smoothing of the series, the indices are generally fairly erratic unless a substantial number of series is included. One method of overcoming this is to use a cumulated diffusion index, obtained by cumulating the excess of series expanding over those contracting from period to period, starting from some arbitrary base-date. This has the advantage also that cyclical peaks and troughs in the economy are signalled by corresponding peaks and troughs in the cumulated index, that is analysis and interpretation of the combination of series is exactly the same as for individual series.

COMPOSITE INDICES

Composite indices allow for the magnitude of movements in the indicator series as well as their direction and hence provide a possible bridge by which indicators can be used to forecast magnitudes as well as turning-points. Another difference from diffusion indices is in the weighting together of the individual indicator series. The advantage of giving equal weights to the component series is that the diffusion index can then be described in a simple, easily understandable way. Once, however, the size of the inter-period change in a series is taken into consideration, there is no particular advantage in giving all the series equal weight. In fact the more logical procedure is to combine the series together giving greater weight to the better indicators. In judging what weight should be given to an indicator, the important factors are the performance of the indicators in the past and also the general statistical quality and economic significance of the series. Both aspects are covered by the scoring system outlined earlier in this paper (and detailed in appendix A) and used there as a means of selecting and ranking the indicator series. That is, appropriate weights for combining together the evidence of a number of indicators would be the scores measuring the overall quality of those indicators. This still leaves some choice as to which of the scores should be used; for example, in some situations it might be preferable to use the scores at peaks or troughs separately rather than the combined scores, and sometimes too the basic score might be preferable to the total score. However the weights used for the indices charted in this chapter are the total scores for peaks and troughs combined.

Given an objective weighting system, there are still problems to meet in combining the indicators into one series. The obvious difficulty of differences in units of measurement is met easily enough by converting all the series into index numbers on the same base-date. But there remains the objection that some series have cyclical fluctuations of much larger amplitude proportionally than others (for example, vacancies as compared with, say, production) and so will 'swamp' the movements of the less sensitive series. This problem is met by converting each indicator into an amplitude-adjusted index; that is the average monthly or quarterly change in the cyclical component of the series is computed over a number of cycles and then divided into the series. The amplitude-adjusted series in index form are finally combined together to give the overall composite indices.[1]

Composite indices, like diffusion indices, are less irregular and more readily understood if presented in cumulated form and all the indices presented subsequently in this paper, whether diffusion or composite, are cumulated.

COMPOSITE AND DIFFUSION INDICES FOR THE TARGET VARIABLES

The charts present various diffusion and composite indices for the three target variables. Chart 12.1 shows three diffusion indices related to the production cycle, representing groups of leading, coincident and lagging series; the series making up the indices are those listed in table 9.8. Chart 12.2 presents composite indices for the same three groups of indicators, and charts 12.3 and 12.4 present similar diffusion and composite indices for investment and unemployment constructed from the series listed in tables 10.7 and 11.8. However, lagging indices have not been attempted for these two variables, nor a coincident index for investment, because of the insufficient number of suitable indicators.

Table 12.2 sets out the leads and lags of the composite and diffusion indices at turning-points in their respective target variables. The median leads and lags are computed in the standard manner and given in table 12.3. As a rough approximation one would expect these average leads or lags to be approximately equal to the appropriately weighted averages of the median leads and lags for the individual indicators included in the indices.[2] To show this the equally weighted mean of the median values for the individual series, corresponding to the diffusion index, is also given in the table.

Before discussing the conclusions to be drawn, it needs to be clearly understood that the selection of series for inclusion in the indices was in part determined by subjective considerations, such as the ease of obtaining up-to-date values and the number of series representing a particular sector of economic activity. It follows that any results described in this chapter should be regarded as provisional rather than final, and that the

[1] The procedure described here differs in some details from Shiskin's approach. Here, absolute rather than percentage changes are used as the measure of cyclical amplitude, which permits the inclusion of series taking both positive and negative values. Also a refinement used by Shiskin but not in this paper is to adjust the final composite index so that its own inter-period change in amplitude also averages unity (as well as each component of the index having this property). The advantage is that a current movement in the index can be immediately seen as being larger or smaller than the average cyclical change.

[2] Only approximately because the series cover different ranges; the number of series in the indices is much less in the early 1950s than in 1970.

Chart 12.1 *Diffusion indices for production*

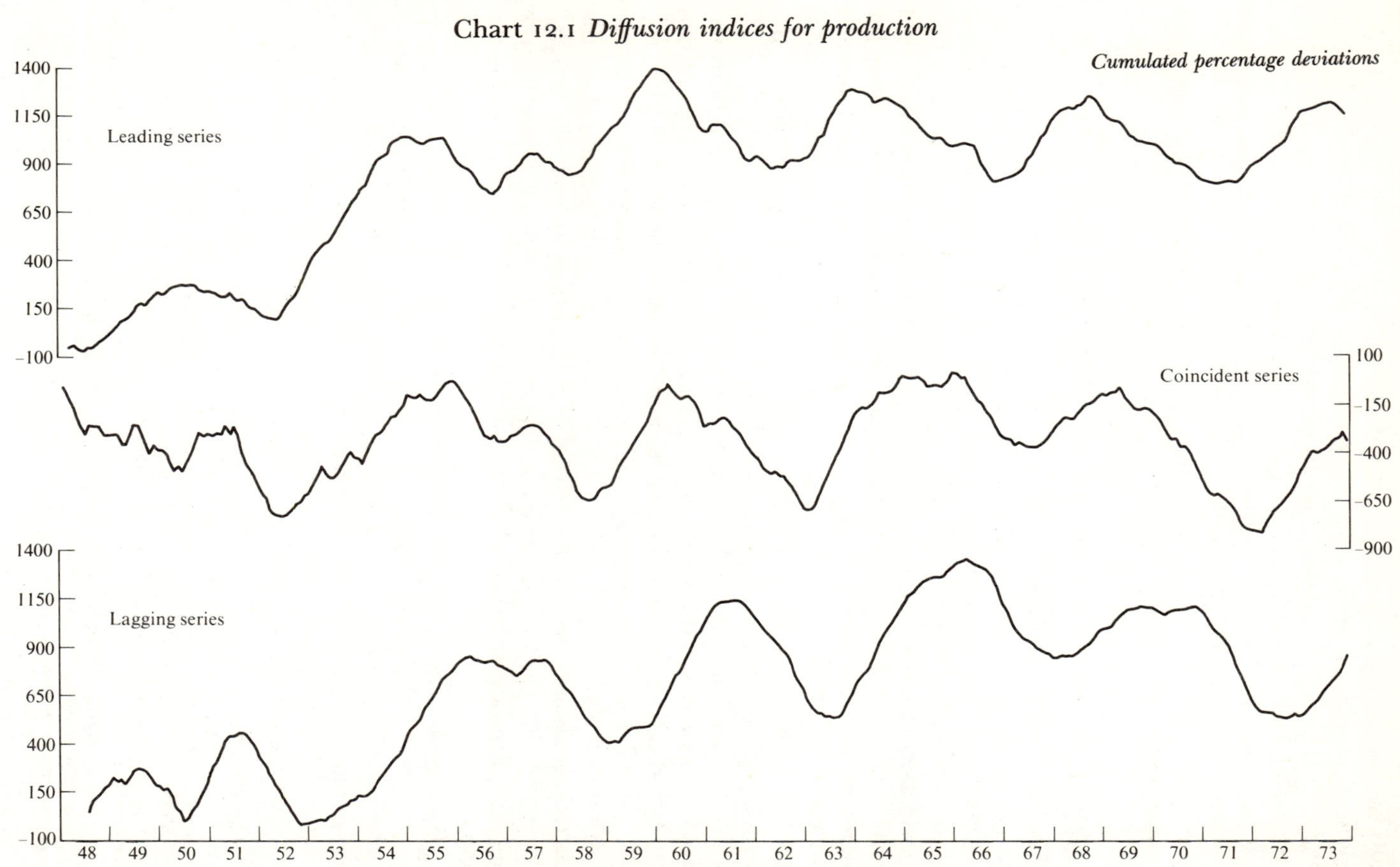

Chart 12.2. *Composite indices for production*

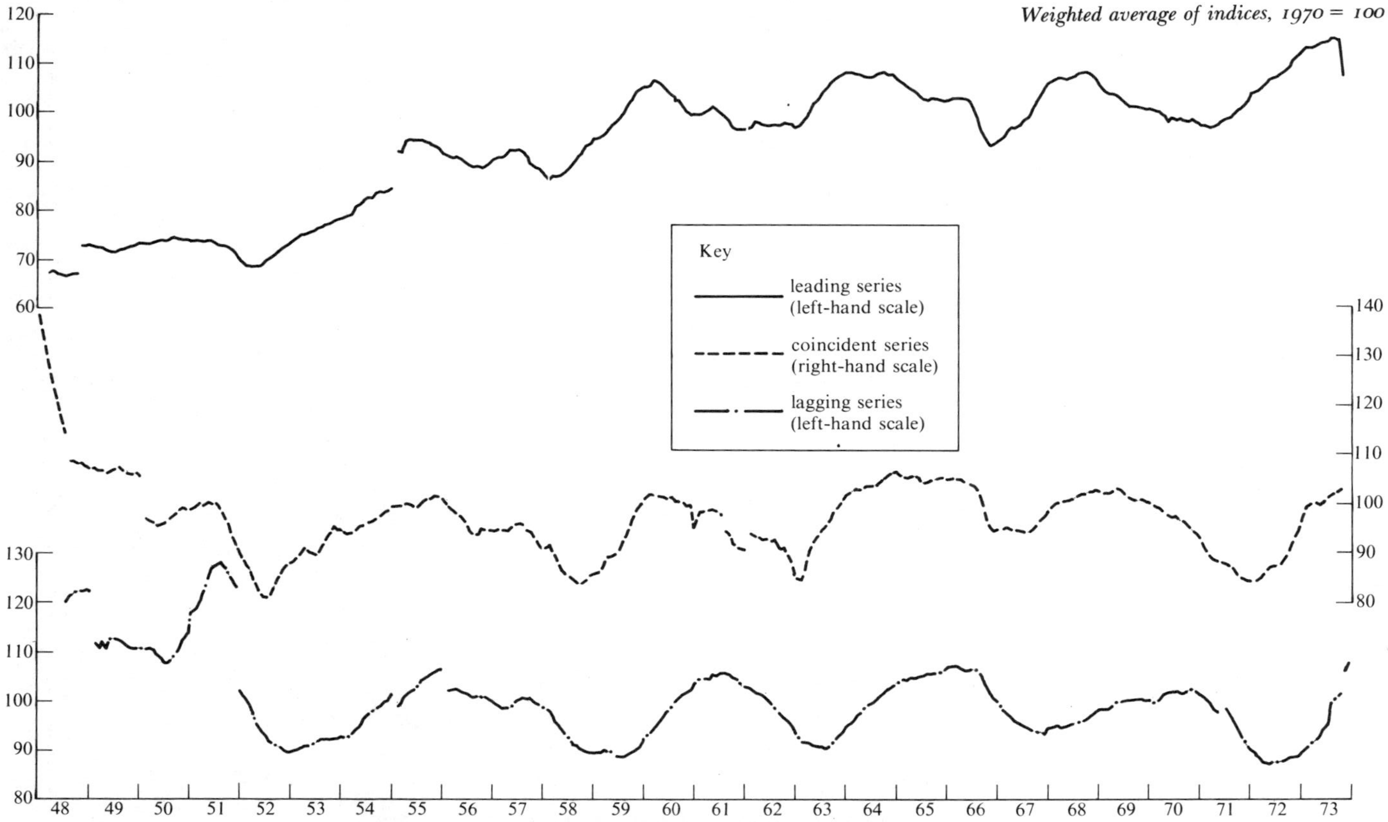

Note: Breaks in the graphs are points at which further series were included in the indices.

Chart 12.3. *Diffusion indices for investment and unemployment*

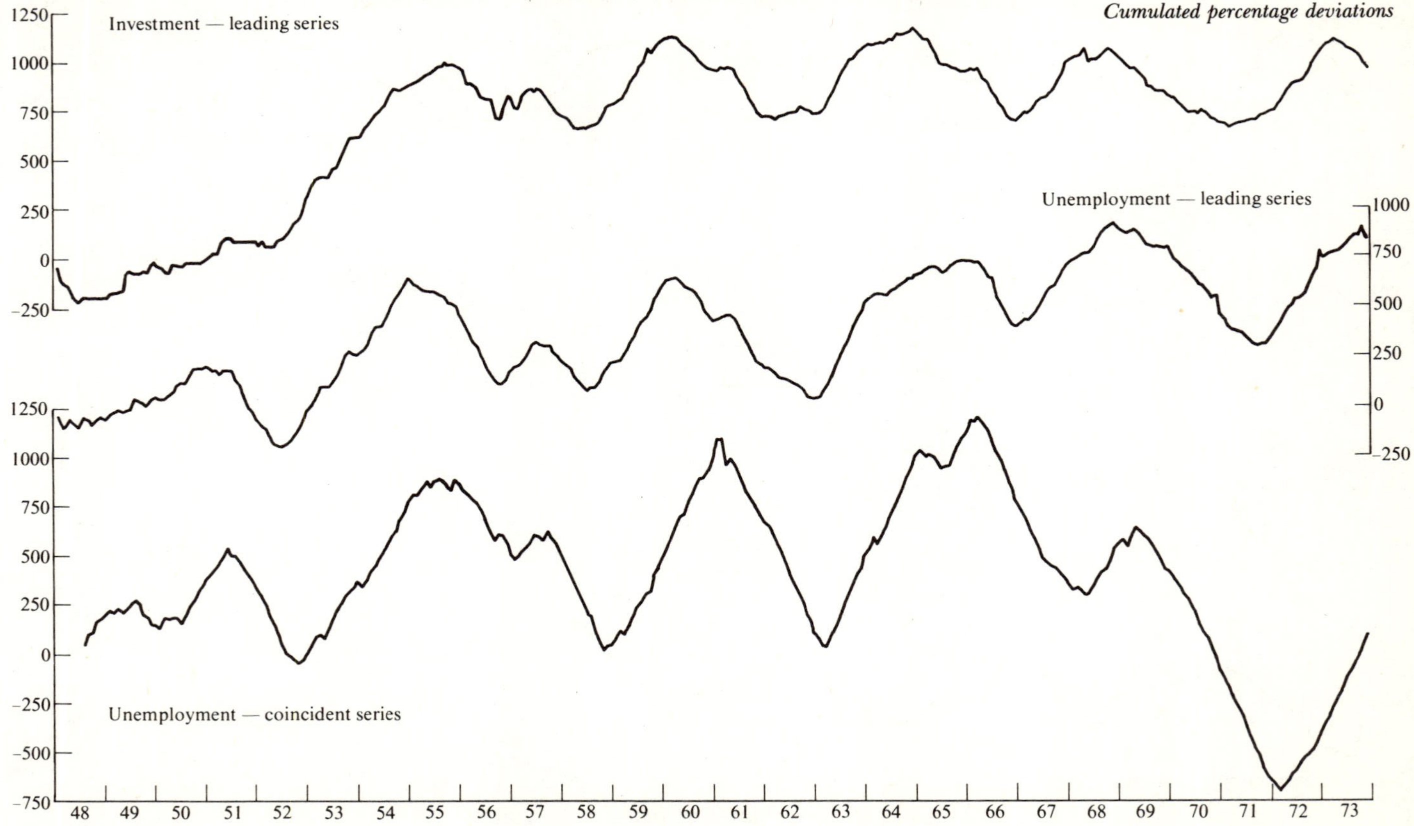

Cumulated percentage deviations

Investment — leading series

Unemployment — leading series

Unemployment — coincident series

1250
1000
750
500
250
0
−250
−500
−750

48 49 50 51 52 53 54 55 56 57 58 59 60 61 62 63 64 65 66 67 68 69 70 71 72 73

Chart 12.4. *Composite indices for investment and unemployment*

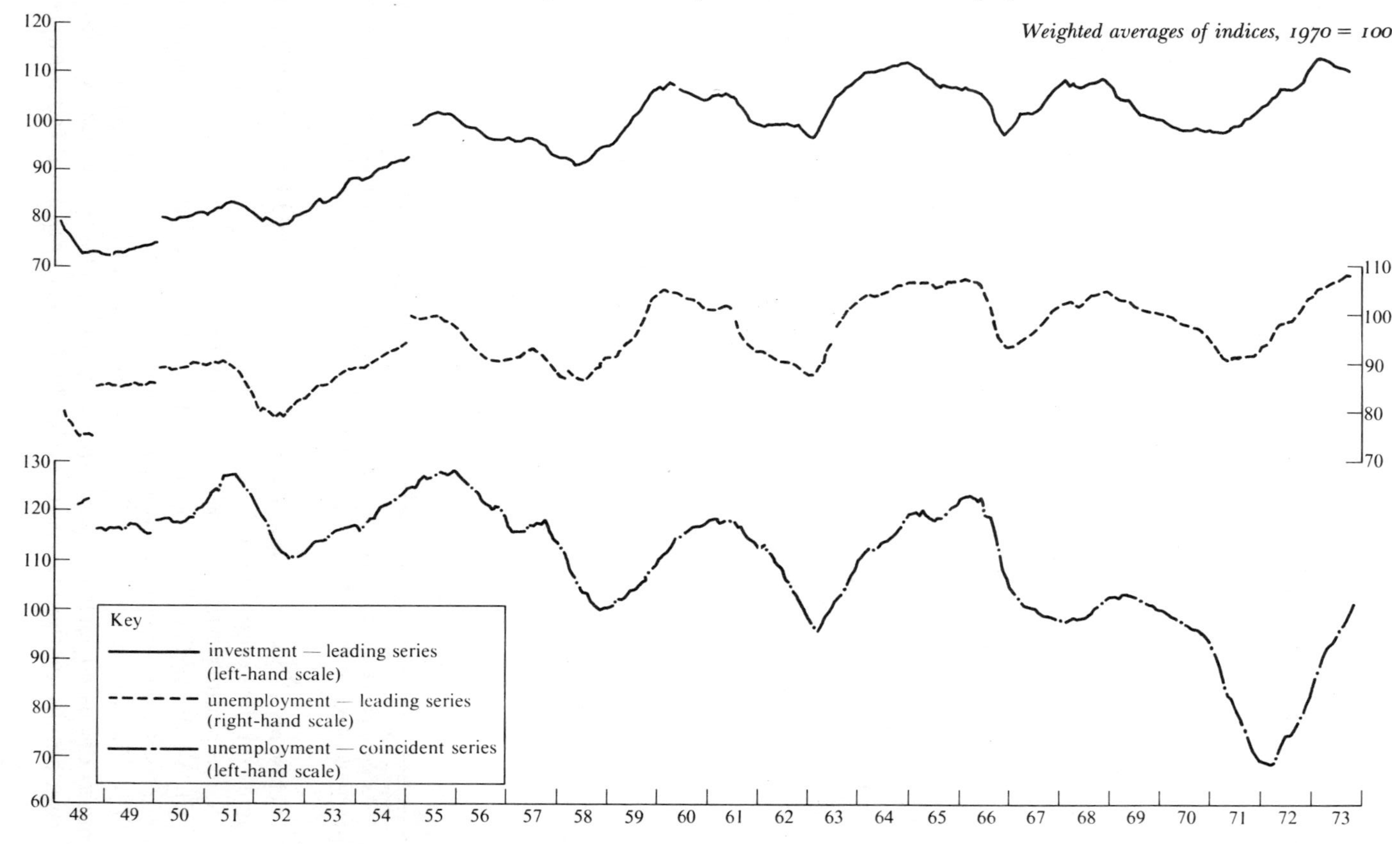

Note: Breaks in the graphs are points at which further series were included in the indices.

Table 12.2. *Leads and lags in diffusion and composite indices against the target variables*

Months

	Target dates P	Target dates T	Leading series: Diffusion index	Leading series: Composite index	Coincident series: Diffusion index	Coincident series: Composite index	Lagging series: Diffusion index	Lagging series: Composite index
Production	51/2		−5	−5	+5	+3	+7	+6
		52/7	−2	−3	0	0	+4	+6
	55/12		−11	−6	0	−1	+4	+4
		58/9	−5[a]	−7	0	0	+7	+4
	60/3		−2	0	+1	−1	+18	+17
		63/1	−8	0	+1	+1	+7	+7
	65/1		−12	−12	+13	0	+15	+13
		67/8	−9	−9	0	−1	+5	+3
	69/6		−8	−9	−1	−1	+4	+17
		72/2	−9	−11	+1	0	+7	+3
Investment	57/2		−16	−18				
		58/11	−4	−6				
	61/8		−16	−17				
		63/8	−16	−6				
	65/2		−1	−2				
		67/11	−10	−12				
	69/8		−9	−9				
		72/8	−17	−17				
Unemployment		50/7			−5	0		
	51/8		−7	−3	−2	−2		
		52/11	−4	−4	0	0		
	55/12		−11	−4	0	0		
		58/11	−4	−4	0	0		
	61/3		−11	−13	0	−1		
		63/3	−2	−2	0	0		
	66/2		−2	0	+2	0		
		68/6	−17	−18	−1	−4		
	69/5		−5	−6	0	0		
		72/3	−5	−10	0	0		

[a] As shown in chart 12.1, an earlier trough occurred in 56/10, but it is assumed that by 1958 this would have been recognised as a false signal.

conclusions reported below should ideally be checked by further experiments on the composition of the indices.

Some points particularly worth noting are that:

(i) All the indices have peaks and troughs in a one-to-one correspondence with the reference cycle turning-points.

(ii) The indices also show the presence of the various sub-cyclical movements discussed earlier. In the coincident indices these are clearly of much lesser amplitude than the main cycles, both for the diffusion and composite

Table 12.3. *Average leads or lags in diffusion and composite indices compared with individual indicators*

Months

	Individual indicators (averages)		Diffusion index (median values)		Composite index (median values)	
	P	T	P	T	P	T
Production						
Leading series	−5·9	−6·8	−8·0	−8·0	−6·0	−7·0
Coincident series	−1·1	−0·1	+1·0	0·0	−1·0	0·0
Lagging series	+11·0	+6·2	+7·0	+7·0	+13·0	+4·0
Investment						
Leading series	−11·4	−11·0	−12·5	−13·0	−13·0	−9·0
Unemployment						
Leading series	−7·9	−6·4	−7·0	−4·0	−4·0	−4·0
Coincident series	−0·6	−0·1	0·0	0·0	0·0	0·0

indices. Sometimes, however, the sub-cyclical effect is of sufficient magnitude to shift the turning-point location. For example, the diffusion index of coincident indicators for the production cycle has a peak early in 1966, whereas the corresponding composite index peaks early in 1965.

(iii) The composite indices have a number of breaks. This results from the method of constructing them: the individual amplitude-adjusted series are in effect indices 'pivoting' on the index base-date (taken in all cases as the first month or quarter of 1970). The number of series in the index varies from period to period, and the breaks show the dates when additional indicators were added.

(iv) There seems to be a tendency for the diffusion indices to lead the corresponding composite indices. Possibly this reflects the different weighting patterns rather than any inherent property of the indices. *A priori*, the reverse pattern would be expected, on the assumption that at downturns, for example, the slackening growth-rate just prior to the peak would show up more quickly in the composite index than in the diffusion index, which reflects merely the fact of continuing increases even if miniscule.

(v) Both diffusion and composite indices for coincident series match turns in their respective target variables closely.

(vi) Finally, and most important in a forecasting context, the indices for leading series have in general substantial average leads at both upturns and downturns. This point is expanded in the next chapter.

It is noteworthy that there are no noticeable peak–trough differentials in the average leads displayed by the indices. Such differentials can sometimes arise from the presence of a trend in the indices.[1]

[1] In the United States, a 'reverse trend adjustment' is made, that is a trend component is added to the index of leading series, so that the composite indices for the three timing classes have

REPORTING AND RECOGNITION LAGS

The indices charted and tabulated above are on an 'historical' or 'date of occurrence' basis. That is, a reading for a particular series is treated as though it were observable immediately upon occurrence, whereas it may not in practice have been available until some time afterwards. This is the reason for the charts of the indices, computed in February 1974, terminating about October 1973. (If indices were being constructed regularly, one would expect to gain a month or so on this.) From that date onwards, the number of series available each month diminishes rapidly, and so, consequently, does the reliability of the indices.

An alternative would be to construct indices on a 'lagged' or 'date of reporting' basis, attributing each observation to the month during which it is reported. This is dubious conceptually, but does result in the latest reading of the combined indices containing almost all the series and so being less liable to subsequent change. Such indices were computed but are not shown here. Most of the comments already made apply equally to them, although they lag behind the corresponding original index on average in the range of two to four months. This lag gives an approximate idea of the time lost in either predicting or identifying cyclical turning-points as a result of reporting and recognition lags.

approximately the same trend component and an improved timing relationship at both peaks and troughs (see Julius Shiskin, 'Reverse trend adjustment of leading indicators', *Review of Economics and Statistics*, vol. 49, February 1967).

Part IV

FORECASTING WITH INDICATORS

CHAPTER 13

FORECASTING TECHNIQUES

So far this paper has been solely an analysis of the historical relationships between indicators and the reference cycle chronologies for production and the other target variables. Throughout, however, a major objective of the research has been to investigate the forecasting potential of indicators, and to illustrate how forecasters might make use of the information provided by indicator series.

We turn therefore to an examination of the forecasting potential of leading indicators. After some introductory remarks on the nature of forecasting in general, and leading indicator forecasting in particular, we look first at the forecasting tools which can be constructed from indicators, and then (in the next chapter) at the performance of these tools. The nature of the tools will already be apparent from the discussion in the preceding chapter on diffusion and composite indices, and the charts there of such indices. In the final section of this chapter, we describe a 'forecasting kit' based on these tools, as well as on the individual indicator series, which would give a practising forecaster sufficient information from which to make forecasts based on cyclical indicators.

GENERAL ISSUES

There are three questions which can appropriately be asked of any forecasting procedure:

(i) What is being forecast?

(ii) How accurate will the forecasting procedure be on average?

(iii) What is the cost of making the forecast? (Or equivalently, how quickly and easily can the forecast be made?) This is becoming less important all the time as computer terminals and computerised models of the economy become more and more readily accessible, but it is still an important factor in some situations.

General answers can be given to these questions as they apply to leading indicator forecasting even prior to the detailed discussion about the forecasting tools to be used and the accuracy of the resulting forecasts.

First, forecasts based on leading indicators are forecasts not of actual magnitudes of the target variables, but only of whether or not there will be a cyclical turning-point in its path in the near future.[1] This is a serious limitation, but one which results naturally from the concentration on timing relationships at turning-points; also it should not be forgotten that cyclical turning-points are intrinsically more interesting than other parts of the cycle. A second characteristic of leading indicator forecasts is that they are very much short-term, normally extending only a few months into the future, at most perhaps a year.

The second question, about the accuracy of leading indicator forecasts, is covered in much more detail in the next chapter, but one point worth noting is that the time-span covered by a prediction of the type 'There will/will not be a cyclical turn in the economy in the near future' is often not defined. A useful rule in assessing forecasting accuracy in such instances would be to assume that the 'near future' covered the next six months.

Finally, an important advantage of leading indicator forecasting is its comparatively low cost to a person not having facilities for more elaborate methods. This assumes that the latest readings of the indicators are presented regularly and promptly in some official publication, together with a record of their past performances.

The ease of forecasting with leading indicators has a drawback – that the forecasts can be made without a proper understanding of the relationship between the different variables, or of the effect of recent changes in the economic structure not reflected in the historical record, or of the probable effects of forthcoming events and policy changes. This brings out the greatest weakness of forecasts based solely on leading indicators, namely their unconditional nature. That is, the evidence of the indicators will commonly take no account of changes in either official policy or general economic conditions which are known to be about to occur. In this respect, of course, forecasting with leading indicators does not differ from forecasting with, say, econometric models, where the initial 'mechanical' forecast from the model will normally be modified to allow for known or probable future developments. Where however econometric models and other analytic type forecasts do have an advantage over leading indicators (in addition to their generally longer range) is in the specification of relationships between the major economic variables. This both makes it easier to assess the effect of coming changes, and also ensures consistency between the different variables being forecast. Indicator forecasts on the other hand

[1] It should be noted however that Geoffrey Moore in 'Forecasting short-term economic change', *Journal of the American Statistical Association*, vol. 64, March 1969, pp. 1–22, obtained some interesting results in predicting year-to-year changes in gross national product from changes in a composite index of leading indicators.

are under no such constraint, either between the different indicators or between the different target variables being forecast.

A FORECASTING KIT

If in practice it is advisable to weave the forecasts produced by leading indicators together with information from other sources, it is still of interest to consider the 'pure' indicator forecast, and the techniques by which such forecasts can be obtained. In this section, the material required to make a soundly based indicator forecast is described in the form of a forecasting kit providing the information that would be required.

The basic data for the forecast will naturally be the latest observations of those leading indicators or approximately coincident indicators which have been selected as specially relevant to forecasting the cyclical path of the specified target variable. It may seem strange that the evidence provided by the coincident indicators should be taken into consideration in addition to that of the leading series. However the coincident series are useful for providing a continuing check on the signals of the leading indicators. Possibly too, if there are considerable lags in identifying a cyclical turn in the target variable (a situation most likely to occur when fixed investment is the variable being forecast), then the use of coincident indicators in estimating the current situation is effectively no different in practice from making a forecast.

Given the basic data, the forecaster has a choice between two different approaches:

(i) The indicators can be weighted together subjectively; that is, the analyst considers together the evidence, generally conflicting to greater or lesser degree, of a number of selected indicators and subjectively decides on the likely outcome in terms of turning-points in the target variable. Clearly such a forecasting procedure is highly intuitive and close to the original type of 'judgemental' forecast. Even so, provided the procedure for selecting the indicators is soundly based and details of their past performance are available to the forecaster, his predictions could well be reasonably accurate.

or (ii) The indicators can be weighted together objectively; that is, the information provided by the selected individual indicators is combined into a composite series. The procedures for doing this were described in detail in the preceding chapter. The forecaster has a choice between diffusion indices, where the directions of movements in the individual series are combined together with each indicator being given equal weight, or composite indices, where both the direction and size of the movement are taken into account, and the weights, at least in this paper, are based on the quality of the indicator.

The information required by the forecaster if he is to make a good forecast is not too dissimilar for either approach. In one case he requires information on past performance for the individual indicators, in the other for the combined series. Given a list of selected indicators, the basic information needed for each (and also for the diffusion and composite indices) is the latest value recorded for the series and a graphical display, preferably covering more than one complete cycle, of how the value relates to the previous cyclical path of the indicator. If the indicator is irregular, there should also be available a suitably smoothed graph of the series.

To proceed from this basic information to making a forecast, the analyst requires, in addition, the following background information for each individual series (whether for peaks or for troughs depends on the current phase of the cycle):

(a) the timing class in which the indicator falls, based on past experience;

(b) the consistency of timing of the indicators; that is, of the total turns in the target variable covered, the number of matching turns in the indicator series which actually lie in the specified timing class;

(c) the average lead or lag, measured by the median value, shown by the indicator at previous target variable turning-points (alternatively, the arithmetic mean lead or lag could be used, but the median value is preferred as being less influenced by extreme values);

(d) measures of the variability of individual leads or lags about the average value; either the range between the two extreme values, or the standard deviation about the mean lead or lag;

(e) the number of extra turning-points in the indicator, additional to those turns which can be matched against a reference turn in the target variable (for a leading indicator the number of extra turns will correspond closely to the number of 'false alarms' it gives);

(f) finally, the weight or score given an indicator for the purpose, first, of providing a single summary measure of the quality of the series and, secondly, for weighting it together with other indicators to form a composite series.

Combining the latest set of observations, on both the individual series and on the combined indices, together with the information provided under headings (a) to (f) above, we have a complete 'forecasting kit', from which it should be possible to make forecasts of reasonable quality, assuming that is that the forecaster has sound judgement and that relationships estimated from past data will be reasonably stable in future.

The data listed here as necessary for soundly based forecasts are given for individual indicators in appendix B where not already available in the text tables of chapters 9–11. As an illustration for one indicator, M313, the Financial Times ordinary industrial share price index, which is one of the highest-ranked series when matched against the production cycle, the information is as follows:

(a) it is unclassified at peaks, but leads at troughs (table 9.5);

(b) it led at all five production cycle troughs covered in the postwar period, but was less consistent at peaks, leading at only three of the five peaks covered (appendix table B.1);

(c) the median lead at peaks was four months and at troughs seven months (table 9.5). The corresponding mean values were a lag of nearly one month at peaks – the result of a lengthy lag at one peak – and a lead of seven months at troughs (table B.1);

(d) individual leads and lags covered a range of nineteen months relative to reference cycle peaks, and ten months at troughs (table B.1). The greater variability at peaks is apparent also in the standard deviation about the mean value shown in table 9.5;

(e) the index had six 'extra turns' in total (table B.1); that is, as a leading indicator, the series is rather prone to giving false alarms;

(f) the basic score is low at peaks, moderately good at troughs; the total scores show an improvement relative to other series as a consequence of the prompt availability of the series, and the total score at troughs is particularly high (table 9.5).

To conclude, the information needed for indicator forecasts has been outlined in general terms, and illustrated by specific figures for one particular indicator. The material in appendix B and the text tables consists of the corresponding data for all the series which, from the analysis in this paper, appear to be useful indicators of cyclical movement in the three selected target variables. The series include most of those which would customarily be examined when making an assessment of the current situation and of likely developments in the near future, and contain also some useful additional time-series to those normally examined.

The possession of this information does not, it need scarcely be added, guarantee accurate forecasts, but without it forecasting would certainly be more difficult. The assessment of forecasting performance which follows in the next chapter is, for the British economy, made on an *ex post* basis, and so it is difficult to assess accurately the improvement in predictive accuracy resulting from the possession of background information of the type just discussed. It is probable, however, that the improvement is significant.

CHAPTER 14

ASSESSMENT OF FORECASTING PERFORMANCE

There are two parts to the assessment in this chapter of the forecasting use of leading indicators. The first is an analysis of how accurate leading indicator forecasts of the British business cycle would have been in recent years. The forecasts are primarily concerned with the cycle in production, but brief examination is also made for the other target variables. The analysis is intended to give a general rather than a closely detailed assessment of forecasting performance. In view of the known drawbacks of an *ex post* analysis, and remembering also that the analysis is based on values of the series as they are now recorded rather than as published at the time, it did not seem profitable to expend a great deal of energy on constructing more than a few hypothetical forecasts.

In the second part, experience elsewhere with the technique is discussed. The only material readily available is from the United States. From our point of view it has the drawbacks that the forecasts are in terms of a general cycle and also that the predictions are of turning-points in absolute terms rather than relative to a long-term growth-rate, so that the results are not completely comparable with those for Britain. Nevertheless it does give some guidance to the effectiveness of the technique in practice.

INDICATOR FORECASTS OF TURNING-POINTS IN THE PRODUCTION CYCLE IN BRITAIN

Forecasts based on individual indicators

Before the record of diffusion and composite indices is examined, a first test is to analyse the performance of individual leading indicators. Rather than test the series at every postwar turning-point only the last two turns are taken, although the later of these cannot yet be precisely located. The first of the two is the clearly marked upturn in production occurring in the first quarter of 1972, the second the downturn occurring late in 1973. For convenience this peak is taken as October 1973, although eventually this might be found to be two or three months out. The difficulty in dating it is that unusually severe exogeneous disturbances – the Middle East war and the coal-mining dispute – came into play about the time of the downturn.

Table 14.1 shows, for each of the twenty leading indicators, the dates of the upturn and downturn (in the smoothed series) corresponding to the upturn in production in early 1972 and the downturn in late 1973. These dates for the upturns show quite substantial leads in general, but they do not allow for

Table 14.1. *Turning-points in leading indicators matching the latest trough and peak in production*[a]

Series no.	Median lead T	Median lead P	Turning-point[b] T	Turning-point[b] P	Recognition lead[c] T	Recognition lead[c] P
	(months)				(months)	
M384	−7·0	−5·0	70/12	72/4	−14	−18
M557	−5·0	−2·0	70/12		−14	n.a.
M313	−7·0	−4·0	71/2	72/4	−14	−18
Q309	−5·0	−3·0	71/9	73/9	−3	+1
Q305	−7·0	−6·0	71/8	73/6	−4	−2
M482	+2·0	−7·0	skipped		n.a.	n.a.
M493	−8·5	−4·0	71/7		−5	n.a.
M582	−6·5	−12·0	71/1		−12	n.a.
M206	−15·0	−2·0	69/12	73/1	−25	−8
Q366	−3·5	−10·0	71/8	73/5	−1	0
Q163*	−8·0	−2·0	71/2	73/2	−9	−5
Q7	−3·0	−12·0	71/8		0	n.a.
M10	−1·5	−6·5	71/11		−2	n.a.
M15	−1·0	−6·0	71/11		−2	n.a.
M287	−5·0	−2·0	69/11	73/1	−27	−9
M474	−4·0	−10·5	70/6	73/2	−18	−6
Q11	−6·0	−3·0	71/8	73/8	−3	+1
M409	−9·5	−6·0	69/3	73/1	−33	−7
M267	−21·0	−2·0	70/2	73/1	−24	−9
M382	−14·5	−13·0	70/7	73/2	−18	−7

[a] Taken as 72/2 and (more doubtfully) 73/10 respectively.
[b] In MCD smoothed series.
[c] The lead remaining after deduction of reporting and recognition lags (see table 9.9).

the delays in recognition which occur in a real-life forecasting situation. The recognition leads shown in the last two columns of the table attempt to allow for this by deducting from the original lead given by each indicator that length of time which must elapse before the turn is recognised. This is taken as the sum of the reporting and recognition lags as defined and measured for each series in table 9.9. To provide a basis of comparison, the median values in the first two columns show the sort of lead (although not adjusted for recognition and reporting lags) a forecaster would be expecting from previous experience.

Clearly most of the indicators in the table gave ample warning of the coming upturn. Only two of the twenty series had not given a recognisable signal prior to the actual upturn (although 'recognisable' is of course here defined in a rather special way). In the case of the cyclical downturn in production occurring late in 1973, the generally shorter average leads mean that reporting and recognition lags are of greater significance than at upturns. Presumably this factor is responsible for the downturn not yet being apparent in a considerable number of the series. However, ten of the series can be seen to have signalled, prior to the event, the downturn late in the year. The stock exchange series (M384 and M313), and also those series dealing with various aspects of consumption, seem on this occasion to have turned down a good deal earlier than on average.

Forecasts based on diffusion indices and composite indices

Looking back to the material in tables 12.2 and 12.3 and also charts 12.1 and 12.2, we find that from 1951 onwards the diffusion index of twenty leading indicators for production led by eight months on average at both peaks and troughs. The composite index shows a very similar pattern, except that at production downturns its average lead is rather shorter at two months, and on six occasions coincided with, rather than leading, the cyclical turn. With these exceptions, the leads of the composite index appear more stable; also the composite index is conceptually a more attractive means, although more complex, of combining the individual indicators.

The average leads tabulated for both indices do not make allowance for reporting and recognition lags, and so would probably overstate the leads to be expected in a practical forecasting situation by at least a couple of months. This still leaves a useful lead at most individual turns, but implies that neither of the two indices can be relied on to give a forewarning at every cyclical turning-point. It appears that this was the case in late 1973, with the two leading indices both peaking in September – too soon before the downturn to be of use in forecasting.

The material in chapter 12 on diffusion and composite indices for the other two target variables shows a similar picture. The indices give lengthy average leads for investment, although with high variability. The leading indices for unemployment have much shorter average leads.

These results for the diffusion and composite indices generalise those given in table 14.1 for the individual series, and again show that leading indicators can be useful in some situations, much less so in others. Although they frequently provide a forewarning of a coming cyclical turn, this is not invariably the case. On occasion, the best they do is to signal the turn about the time that it is actually occurring.

UNITED STATES EXPERIENCE WITH LEADING INDICATOR FORECASTING

United States literature on forecasting with leading indicators is substantial. Indeed, the volume of material is rather large to be easily digestible and in this section we concentrate only on the more recent and important appraisals of forecasting performance. A useful reference to much of the earlier literature, and also a good general review of the subject, is a paper by Daly, together with the subsequent conference discussion.[1] Here we rely principally on the material presented in three recent American publications;[2] that by Fels and Hinshaw is a review of *ex ante* forecasting performance in general, with some material on leading indicator forecasts, while those by Hymans and by Stekler and Schepsman concentrate more specifically on leading indicator forecasts, but in *ex post* terms.

Two general points are worth making here. The first is that, when testing a list of selected leading indicators one by one, it is quite usual to find that nearly all the series have performed unsatisfactorily on some occasions and hence to conclude that only a very limited number are of any forecasting value, so that the whole approach should be discounted.[3] This, however, misses the point that the interpretation of movements in any individual series is very much influenced, if only subjectively, by what is happening at the same time to other indicators. Thus, the behaviour of the group of series as a whole, as well as of the individual indicators, is of importance, and one of the principal justifications of composite series is that the aberrations which appear from time to time in any one series will cancel out or be reduced in significance.[4]

The second general point is that those experienced in the use of indicator analysis are cautious in their claims about leading indicator forecasting. If there is a general view, it would appear to be that not much warning is given of coming peaks or troughs, but that indicators certainly do help to recognise cyclical turns about the time that they occur.[5]

[1] D. J. Daly, 'Forecasting with statistical indicators' in Bert G. Hickman (ed.), *Econometric Models of Cyclical Behavior*, vol. II, New York, Columbia University Press, 1972.

[2] Rendigs Fels and C. Elton Hinshaw, *Forecasting and Recognizing Business Cycle Turning Points*, New York, NBER, 1968; H. O. Stekler and Martin Schepsman, 'Forecasting with an index of leading series', *Journal of the American Statistical Association*, vol. 68, June 1973, pp. 291–6; Saul R. Hymans, *On the Use of Leading Indicators to Predict Cyclical Turning Points*, Washington (DC), Brookings Institution, 1973, pp. 339–84 (including discussion).

[3] For instance, M. K. Evans, *Macroeconomic Activity: theory, forecasting and control: an econometric approach*, London, Harper and Row, 1969, uses this method of assessment.

[4] Hymans, *On the Use of Leading Indicators*, gives a line of argument which he believes would represent the views of most proponents of leading indicator forecasting, and which is of particular interest in this context. Briefly, it runs as follows: a number of series can be identified whose turning-points generally precede turning-points in overall economic activity; this does not imply direct causality, only that the forces leading to upturns or downturns are generally transmitted through certain of those processes identified as leading. However, the order in which the series signal a coming turn, and the strength of the signals, will depend on the real cause of the turn and the process by which that cause acts to induce the turn. It follows that the gathering together of a number of 'potentially duplicative' series can be justified as allowing for the different possible causes of turning-points, and checking the different routes by which those causes can take effect.

[5] See for example the discussion on Hymans' paper, with the comments by Julius Shiskin especially relevant.

Ex ante *forecasts – the record*

While an indicator may show quite lengthy leads when the historical data are analysed, the leads which eventuate in real life are generally much shorter. The problem is the lapse of time before a turning-point in the leading series is recognised as more than a temporary fluctuation. In consequence, an appraisal of forecasting performance on an *ex post* basis is likely to lead to an over-optimistic assessment of the usefulness of leading indicator forecasts.

One way round this is to apply a set of rules to past data, on the basis of which it is assumed that a forecaster at the time would have predicted either no change or a cyclical turn.[1] Unfortunately such rules are always somewhat artificial in their construction and it is generally possible to find instances where a forecaster would probably not, in practice, have adhered to the rules. Ideally, the material needed for an appraisal of forecasting performance is a record of *ex ante* forecasts. Unfortunately little such material is available, and those forecasts which are recorded make use of other material in addition to leading indicators.

Such material as there is has been analysed by Fels and Hinshaw.[2] They examined the postwar record in forecasting turning-points of a number (ten in all) of analysts or groups of analysts. Two of the publications surveyed were known to rely heavily on the use of business cycle indicators. They found, with qualifications regarding the size of the sample and the number of turning-points covered, that those forecasters using indicators were possibly more accurate at forecasting downturns, less accurate at predicting upturns, and on average not more accurate than their fellows relying more on other approaches. However, these findings were highly tentative, particularly as none of the forecasters relied exclusively on one method. That is, the price paid for being able to use *ex ante* material to assess the forecasting accuracy of leading indicator techniques is uncertainty about the relative roles of indicators and of other information in making the forecasts.

[1] Such rules can be along two main lines of approach:

(i) smoothing the series with a moving average of predetermined length (normally equal to, or longer than, the MCD statistic) and taking all turns in the smoothed series as signalling a coming turn in the target variable. There is a trade-off between the increased lag resulting from a longer moving average, and the reduction in false alarms resulting from the greater smoothness of the series (see Long, 'Forecasting specific turning points', for further discussion);

(ii) requiring a change in direction to be confirmed by a given number of further movements in the same direction or by remaining a given number of months below (or above) the previous peak (or trough) value. Again there is a trade-off between speed of recognition and increased certainty.

A problem with either approach is the procedure to follow for a false signal, and this is one of the respects where forecasts constructed according to rule after the event probably differ most from *ex ante* forecasts. (The other major cause of difference is the information available from other sources to the *ex ante* forecaster.)

[2] *Forecasting and Recognizing Business Cycle Turning Points.*

Ex post examinations of forecasting performance

The two most significant recent assessments are those already cited by Stekler and Schepsman, and by Hymans.[1] Both concentrate on the composite index of twelve leading series published monthly in *Business Conditions Digest*, although Stekler and Schepsman match the index against turns in the Federal Reserve Board's index of production (which corresponds to the index of production used as a target variable in this paper, although not in detrended form), whereas Hymans retains the National Bureau's general cycle turning-points.

Stekler and Schepsman found that the composite index leads peaks in the production cycle by a mean value of two months, and troughs by four months. However sizeable lags have to be added before predictions based on turns in the index reach a reasonable level of reliability, and their conclusion was that the index was 'not a very reliable indicator of peaks, but is more reliable in the vicinity of troughs'. Another result of some interest was that the index was unambiguously superior on every criterion to a first-difference approach, using the rate of change in the production index.

Hymans' paper[2] is particularly interesting, endeavouring, in addition to examining past performance of the composite index, to assess the relative contributions of the components of the index by the techniques of spectral analysis, and also to construct an improved index based on this assessment. He noted first the fact remarked already that, because of lags in recognition, there is 'a distinct tendency for the hindsight leads to exceed the foresight leads'. Also he finds it a serious indictment that, under certain fairly reasonable rules, nearly half of the peak predictions were false. This is in accordance with the widely heard criticism that leading indicators, individually and generally, are over-prone to incorrectly predicting coming downturns. (Although the force of this criticism could be considerably softened if Ilse Mintz's arguments in favour of a new chronology for the United States based on 'growth cycles' were to be accepted.) On the credit side the composite index is more reliable in its signalling of coming troughs.

The remainder of Hymans' paper is particularly interesting to those seeking a concrete illustration of how spectral analysis might be used to improve short-term economic forecasting, and usefully illustrates also how the technique can be used to identify those individual indicators where the cyclical component most strongly dominates the short-term irregular components. An alternative index constructed using spectral techniques does give substantially fewer false alarms, but unfortunately at the cost of a deterioration in lead-time. Overall, the paper heavily underscores the

[1] 'Forecasting with an index of leading series'; *On the Use of Leading Indicators.*

[2] Ibid.

conclusions of earlier studies about excessive false signalling, notably of coming downturns.

The conclusions of these two *ex post* analyses contradict Fels' work[1] on one point. Fels found a tendency for those using indicator methods to be more accurate at forecasting downturns, whereas both of the more recent papers found the greatest unreliability to occur at downturns. This latter conclusion is in agreement also with the result established in this paper for the production cycle, namely that forecasts of cyclical downturns are likely on past experience to be a good deal less timely than forecasts of upturns. In saying this it must be remembered also that the forecasts in this paper were in terms of growth-cycle turning-points, equivalent to removing a trend from the variable being forecast. Were the American forecasts to be on a similar basis, bringing reference peak dates forward but retarding trough dates, their predictions of upturns would be expected to improve even further in terms of timeliness relative to predictions of downturns. However, this does not exclude the possibility of forecasts of downturns becoming more reliable, with false signals on the old cyclical basis being seen now to match a retardation in growth relative to the long-term trend.

CONCLUSIONS

The usefulness of leading indicators for forecasting has been examined in this chapter from two approaches: the first being an assessment of how indicator-based forecasts would probably have performed over recent British economic cycles, and the second an examination of United States material on the performance of leading indicator analysis in that country. The conclusions for the two countries are not too dissimilar, remembering that the tests on the British indicators were exploratory in nature and a good deal less sophisticated than some of the United States analyses reported.

A first conclusion is that the indicator series in composite form have signalled all the major postwar recessions and recoveries. On the other hand the leading series, both individually and in composite form, display a tendency to give occasional false alarms (to quote Paul Samuelson, 'Stock prices have accurately predicted nine of the last five recessions!'). In America these appear in the form of signals of downturns which do not then eventuate. In Britain, on the other hand, it seems to be the upturn which is more often falsely signalled (in 1962 and 1966), although the growth-cycle approach used for the British analysis may have something to do with this.

Experience in both countries suggests that, if used in isolation, leading indicators do have fairly definite limitations as forecasting tools. The

[1] *Forecasting and Recognizing Business Cycle Turning Points.*

principal point is that quite long leads historically become much shorter in real life, where it may be some time before a turn in an indicator is recognised and accepted as a true signal. Another drawback is that the content of a forecast is in general limited to the question of whether there will or will not be a turning-point.

These deficiencies should not be overstated, nor should it be forgotten that other forecasting techniques fall a good way short of complete accuracy. And, despite the criticisms made above, the forecaster does appear to gain some useful information from indicator analysis, if only in knowing better where he stands at the moment he makes his forecast. The analysis in this chapter has largely been on the hypothesis that the forecasts are based solely on the evidence of indicators. If this artificial restriction were to be lifted, more optimistic conclusions would probably be reached.

Combining the evidence from leading and coincident indicators with the initial forecasts from some formal model of the economy, one would expect on average more accurate forecasts than from either approach separately. This would be more particularly the case for the simpler linear models, where the indicator data would help overcome their known deficiencies in turning-point prediction. In conclusion, British economic analysts would be expected to find, as have a large number of their American colleagues, that indicators have a useful role either supplementing or serving as an independent check on other methods.

Part V

CHAPTER 15

CONCLUSION

Three things have been done in this paper. Reference chronologies of peaks and troughs in the postwar cycle were identified for production, investment and unemployment. Next, those economic time-series which show cyclical movement and the stablest linkages with the reference chronologies were identified, classed as leading, coincident or lagging, and tabulated. A statistical test on the cyclical behaviour of these series (the details are reported in appendix A) showed that most of them perform significantly better than could be expected of purely random series. Finally, the use of this material for forecasting cyclical turns was discussed and illustrated.

Many of the results given are capable of further development. For instance, they could be compared with those obtained from a standard regression model or cross-spectral analyses. Perhaps the technique of principal components analysis is applicable, particularly if trying to identify a general reference cycle for the economy as a whole. Individual indicators too might be improved in quality and additional useful series discovered. The presentation of long runs of data and graphs of the indicators in a form suitable for cyclical indicator analysis would in itself be a considerable help. (In fact the Central Statistical Office does intend to experiment with such publication in *Economic Trends*, probably starting in early 1975.) On the forecasting side there is clearly a great deal of potential for development. Not the least important of the possible applications is the use of the series identified as leading to give better estimates of the current values of certain important economic variables.

Even at this stage, the results are sufficiently far developed to be useful to those interested in cyclical analysis. The reference chronologies will provide a framework for discussion of the postwar cycle. The material tabulated on individual indicators suggests areas where further research might be productive. Finally, and most important, the tabulated relationships between individual indicators and the target variables can reasonably be expected to lead to better assessments of the current situation and more accurate predictions of the near future.

APPENDIX A

THE SCORING SYSTEM

The system is modelled on that used by the National Bureau,[1] although some adaptation is required to make it fit the British context. In particular, much of the information used in the National Bureau's scoring system under the heading 'statistical adequacy' is not readily available for British series. Other changes made to the system are designed to prevent short-duration series, for example those starting in 1960, from being too harshly penalised. Another modification is the omission from the scoring system of any allowance for the amplitude of cycles in the series.[2]

The system used here for assessing the indicators has the five main headings which were listed with their weights in chapter 2 (page 11). The maximum score attainable under any of the main headings is 100. Negative scores under any sub-heading are taken as zero.

DETAILS OF THE SYSTEM

Economic significance (weight 15 per cent)

(i) Broad series (economy-wide; total of production industries; main national income aggregates): score 75

(ii) Intermediate series (manufacturing, other large industry group aggregates): score 50

(iii) Narrow series (individual industries or products, e.g. production of bricks): score 25

This is obviously a fairly subjective classification. The score is based only on the coverage of the series, and does not give weight to any supposed theoretical significance a particular process might have.

[1] As given in Moore and Shiskin, *Indicators of Business Expansions and Contractions*, app. A. Some points are also taken from Bush and Cohen, *The Indicator Approach to the Identification of Business Cycles.*

[2] Under the NBER system amplitude is measured by finding the average value of the series over each cycle (on both a peak to peak and a trough to trough basis) and computing the peak and trough values as percentage relatives of these averages. The average change per month without regard to sign between these peak and trough values over all the cycles is then taken as the amplitude. This measure is designed to give some objectivity to the assessment of how clearly the cycles stand out from other components of the indicator series, but it cannot be used for series with a significant number of negative values. Also some series with easily observable and regular cycles, but whose amplitude is low in relation to the total value of the series, score poorly; this applies to a number of the employment series. These reasons, and the necessity for a fairly significant expenditure of computer time, led to the amplitude measure being omitted from the scoring system discussed here.

Cyclical conformity (weight 25 per cent)

(i) Conformity probability:[1] score 300 $(0{\cdot}2-P_c)$, where P_c is the combined conformity probability for both expansions and contractions (maximum 60)

(ii) Extra turns: score 80 $(0{\cdot}5-E/T)$, where E is the number of extra turns and T the total number of business cycle turns covered by the series (maximum 40)

The ideal indicator should, when shifted to allow for average lead or lag, expand during every expansion of the reference cycle and contract during every contraction (vice versa for inverted series). The conformity probability measures how closely a particular series approaches the ideal.

The simplest measure would be to take the proportion of total reference cycle expansions and contractions which the series correctly matches. However the drawback to this is its failure to allow for the number of turns covered by the series. A series expanding during four out of five general cycle expansions receives the same value as another series covering ten expansions and expanding during eight. The former result however would be more likely to occur purely by chance than the latter. The conformity probability overcomes this problem; based on the assumption that a random series would be equally likely to expand or contract during each reference cycle expansion, it is the probability that such a random series would conform as well or better than the indicator series being examined. For instance, if the indicator expands during four out of a total of five expansions, the conformity probability is the probability that a random series ($p = 0{\cdot}5$) would match four expansions or all five expansions, that is, 0·187. In other words, the smaller the probability value, the better the series conforms.

Timing stability (weight 30 per cent)

(i) Timing probability:[2] score 200 $(0{\cdot}3-P)$, where P represents the timing probability associated with the series falling within the timing class (leading, lagging, or roughly coincident) which seems most suitable (maximum 60)

(ii) Dispersion: score 4 $(10-\sigma)$, where σ is the standard deviation of the leads and lags at peaks or troughs (maximum 40)

The score under this heading is calculated separately for peaks and for troughs, and then averaged to give the score for peaks and troughs together.

[1] This is based on the binomial distribution, which strictly should be used only if the probability of success is the same for each trial and if each trial is independent of the other trials. The present application almost certainly departs from these requirements. However this is not too important if one regards the results not as exact measures of statistical significance, but as a means of ranking the indicator series.

[2] This too is based on the binomial probability distribution and the same proviso applies as to the conformity probability.

An indicator series should fall consistently within one of the three timing classes – leading, coincident (including roughly coincident, with a lead or lag of 3 months or less, and so overlapping leading and lagging indicators), and lagging. However, most series occasionally fall outside their usual timing classification. The probability of a particular turn falling within one of the timing classes is taken to be 0·5.[1] The timing probability then measures, approximately, the likelihood of achieving as good a result as the indicator series, or better. Again the smaller the probability, the better the indicator.

Dispersion is measured by the standard deviation (in months) of the leads or lags about the mean lead or lag (not the median).

Smoothness (weight 15 per cent)

Monthly series:

MCD (months)	1	2	3	4	5	6+
Score	100	80	60	40	20	0

Quarterly series:

$\bar{I}/\bar{C}$	Under 0·33	0·33–0·66	0·67–0·99	1·00–1·33	1·34–1·66	1·67+
Score	100	80	60	40	20	0

Smoothness is scored by using the well-known Shiskin MCD (months for cyclical dominance) statistic, which gives the number of months required for the cyclical component of the inter-period change to dominate, on average, the change in the irregular component of the series (all changes measured without regard to sign). A smooth series will have an MCD of one month, one of average smoothness an MCD of perhaps two to three months, and a very irregular series five months or more. The quarterly analogue used here, $\bar{I}/\bar{C}$, is simply the ratio of the irregular movement to the cyclical movement over one quarter (measured without regard to sign).[2] The MCD statistic is not a completely reliable measure of smoothness. For instance, a strong upward trend in a series will tend to reduce the MCD statistic (by increasing the mean change in the cyclical movement). An article in *Economic Trends* discusses some of these points.[3]

Currency (weight 15 per cent)

Monthly series (maximum 100)

Available with lag of 1 month: score 80
2 months: score 40
over 2 months: score 0

[1] This is an approximation and a slightly more sophisticated procedure would be to examine all the series in this paper and obtain a more accurate distribution.

[2] For a rather more detailed description of these measures see appendix C.

[3] Central Statistical Office, 'Measuring variability in economic time series', *Economic Trends*, no. 226, August 1972, pp. v-viii.

Additional data available more
frequently than monthly: score 20
Quarterly series (maximum 60)
Available in month following quarter
(or other period covered by data): score 60
Available in second month following
quarter (or other period covered by data): score 20
Available later: score 0

AN APPRAISAL OF THE SYSTEM

First, to give a feel for the system, table A.1 sets out for the most common cases the points lost for various 'defects' in a series.

Tests on random series

It is quite easy to construct artificial series which, at least to casual inspection, seem to be cyclical in nature and resemble rather closely many of the indicator series examined in this paper. For instance simple 'random walk' series, obtained by cumulating a sequence of independent random deviates (zero mean and constant variance) will display an approximately cyclical pattern, with cycle durations which may be of about the same average length as those found for actual business cycles.

Normally such series should be found on close examination to match the general reference cycle poorly, except of course for the occasional 'fluke' matching, and therefore should score poorly on the testing system outlined above. It follows that actual economic series of a random walk type (as is sometimes claimed for stock prices and other time-series where speculation is a factor) should also score poorly and, if the scoring system is properly designed, should have scores lower than those indicator series which conform to the cycle.

The question is then, does the scoring system discriminate adequately between random series and business cycle indicators? To check this, ten random walk series were constructed in the form of monthly series covering the period 1948 to 1971. These were then matched to the unemployment cycle turning-points on both a positive and an inverse basis, giving in effect twenty series. (No attempt was made to detrend the series prior to matching. In most cases there was no obvious trend apparent.) These series were then rated under the relevant scoring criteria, that is conformity and extra turns, and timing probability and dispersion.[1]

Table A.2 sets out the scores obtained under various headings. The final column is an attempt to approximate to a 'basic score' for each of the

[1] Scores for smoothness were not computed. It may, however, be of interest to know that the MCD statistic was two months for three series and three months for the remaining seven.

Table A.1. *Scoring significance of defects in an indicator series*

	Points lost from maximum	Weight	Effect on total score
Economic significance			
Broad coverage	25	0·15	4
Intermediate coverage	50		8
Narrow coverage	75		11
Cyclical conformity			
(a) Conformity probability			
10 phases, 0 missed	0	0·25	0
10 phases, 1 missed	2		0
10 phases, 2 missed	11		3
5 phases, 0 missed	6		2
5 phases, 1 missed	37		9
5 phases, 2 missed	40		10
Short series, starting 1960	6		2
(b) Extra turns			
10 turns, 2 extra	16	0·15	4
10 turns, 4 extra	32		8
5 turns, 2 extra	32		8
Timing stability[a]			
(a) Timing probability			
5 turns, 0 failures	6×½	0·30	1
5 turns, 1 failure	37×½		6
5 turns, 2 failures	60×½		9
3 turns, 0 failures	25×½		4
3 turns, 1 failure	60×½		9
Short series, starting 1960	25		8
(b) Dispersion			
Standard deviation 5 months	20×½	0·30	3
Smoothness			
MCD statistic 3 months	40	0·15	6
Currency			
By end of month M+2			
Monthly	40	0·15	6
Quarterly	60		9

[a] Factor of ½ represents averaging of peaks and troughs.

random walks (averaged over peaks and troughs), and is obtained by weighting together the general conformity and consistency of timing scores in the correct proportions (25:30) and then adding a contribution under the heading 'economic significance' on the assumption that the series was of intermediate significance.

This table shows clearly enough that, while on average the series do not score particularly well, there are a proportion which do do quite well. One thing that is clear, however, is that in comparison to the tests for conformity

Table A.2. *Scores given to ten random walk series as indicators for unemployment*

Series no.	Cyclical conformity: Conformity probability	Cyclical conformity: Extra turns	Cyclical conformity: Total	Consistency of timing: Timing probability P	Timing probability T	Timing probability P & T	Dispersion P	Dispersion T	Dispersion P & T	Total P	Total T	Total P & T	Basic score[a] P & T
(Max. score)	(60)	(40)	(100)		(60)			(40)			(100)		(70)
Positive basis													
1	59	24	83	54	0	27	24	0	12	78	0	39	40
2	54	24	78	23	23	23	0	15	8	23	38	30	36
3	0	24	24	0	0	0	16	0	8	16	0	8	16
4	0	8	8	0	0	0	0	26	13	0	26	13	14
5	54	8	62	23	0	12	2	23	12	25	23	24	31
6	54	24	78	0	0	0	12	0	6	12	0	6	29
7	0	24	24	0	0	0	0	14	7	0	14	7	16
8	54	40	94	23	0	12	0	2	1	23	2	12	35
9	33	24	57	0	0	0	0	18	9	0	18	9	25
10	0	24	24	0	0	0	2	0	1	2	0	1	14
Mean	31	22	53	12	2	7	6	10	8	18	12	15	26
Inverted basis													
1	33	40	73	54	54	54	0	14	7	54	68	61	45
2	0	24	24	54	54	54	18	2	10	72	56	64	33
3	33	40	73	0	0	0	2	0	1	2	0	1	27
4	0	40	40	0	0	0	0	0	0	0	0	0	18
5	33	8	41	54	23	38	3	0	1	57	23	40	30
6	0	24	24	54	23	38	18	0	9	72	23	48	28
7	33	40	73	0	0	0	0	0	0	0	0	0	26
8	0	24	24	23	0	12	6	12	9	29	12	20	20
9	0	8	8	0	0	0	0	0	0	0	0	0	10
10	0	24	24	0	0	0	0	0	0	0	0	0	14
Mean	13	27	40	24	15	20	5	3	4	29	18	23	25
Overall mean	22	24	46	18	8	14	6	6	6	24	15	19	25

[a] The weighted sum of the total scores for cyclical conformity and consistency of timing (with weights 0·25 and 0·30 respectively) plus an assumed score for economic significance taking the series to have intermediate coverage.

and extra turns, the series score poorly on timing probability (the overall average is 14 out of a possible 60), and very poorly on dispersion (averaging 6 out of 40). The reverse implication is that if an indicator series shows high dispersion about its mean lead or lag, there must be a suspicion that the series is essentially a random process being forced to conform to the reference cycle. Of course the test here was made on just one type of random process, namely simple random walks derived by cumulating independent random normal deviates, but a similar conclusion seems likely enough for other random processes.

A possible conclusion from these tests is that the weight given to such factors as conformity and extra turns should be reduced relative to other scoring criteria. This makes sense if the only object of the scoring system is to distinguish cyclically influenced series from random processes, but of course this is not the case. The system is primarily intended to rank the indicators in order of merit, and for this purpose the number of extra turns, for example, is certainly relevant.

To proceed further we need to examine the corresponding performance of some actual series.

Comparison of actual indicators with random walk scores

The basic score given in the final column of table A.2 is designed to permit comparison between the random walk series and the results established for actual indicators in the body of this paper (chapters 9–11). Ranking the random series in order, two of the twenty series, that is 10 per cent, are found to have a score exceeding 38, 25 per cent exceeding 32, and so on.

That is, a purely random series (when cumulated) would normally score below these values, but with an occasional value exceeding them. It follows that an actual indicator series should be expected to score in general better than one or other of these values if it is to be assumed that the timing relationship between the indicator and the reference cycle is not simply a matter of chance.

Table A.3 tests the indicators tabulated in this paper, finding the proportions in the various groups which exceed (or equal) the median of the random walk scores, the upper quartile and the uppermost decile. The test

Table A.3. *Scores for the indicators compared with random walk scores*

Percentages

	Proportion of series with basic score greater than		
	26·5	32	38
20 random walk series	50	25	10
Indicators for production			
All 117 tabulated series	73	65	41
20 shortlisted leading indicators	80	80	55
11 shortlisted coincident indicators	100	100	73
13 shortlisted lagging indicators	100	100	85
44 shortlisted indicators	91	91	68
Indicators for investment			
All 60 tabulated indicators	73	58	42
14 shortlisted leading indicators	93	93	79
Indicators for unemployment			
All 78 tabulated indicators	90	77	63
15 shortlisted leading indicators	100	100	100
7 shortlisted coincident indicators	100	100	100
22 shortlisted indicators	100	100	100

is, incidentally, severer than might at first be apparent, as the random walk series are scored over the longest obtainable reference chronology – that for unemployment dating back to 1948 (though not including the latest trough). A good number of the individual indicators, however, extend over a much shorter period and this, as illustrated in table A.1 above, can cause a quite considerable reduction in the score attributed to a series. Series such as changes in money supply (from 1963) and, among the shortlisted indicators, those measuring for instance the number of business failures or price–cost ratios, are examples of series which could well score better if data were available for a longer period.

The important deduction from table A.3 is that the indicators in general score considerably better than the artificially constructed test series. The difference is even more marked, naturally enough, for the shortlisted indicators for the three target variables. Our conclusion is that the scoring system would seem to distinguish reasonably well between genuine economic relationships and those arising purely by chance.

APPENDIX B

FURTHER CYCLICAL CHARACTERISTICS OF THE SHORTLISTED INDICATORS

Table B.1. *Leading indicators for production*

Series no.	Reference turns covered		Matching turns[a]		Mean lead (−) or lag (+)		Range[b]				Extra turns[c]
	P	T	P	T	P	T	P		T		
					(months)		(months)				
Labour-market series (table 9.1)[d]											
Q7	5	5	4	4	−10·0	−3·4	−19	+5	−9	+1	2
M10	4	4	4	3	−6·0	−2·5	−10	−1	−9	+2	6
M15	3	4	3	3	−5·7	−2·2	−10	−1	−9	+2	2
Q11	2	2	2	2	−3·0	−6·0	−4	−2	−6	−6	4
Consumption series (table 9.2)											
M206	5	5	3	5	−3·8	−16·2	−16	+2	−27	−8	6
Q163*	5	5	4	4	−6·4	−6·4	−16	0	−12	+1	4
Investment, orders and anticipation series (table 9.3)											
M267	5	5	4	5	−4·4	−17·4	−18	+15	−25	−9	4
M287	5	5	3	4	−1·2	−9·6	−15	+13	−26	0	2
Q305	3	3	3	3	−9·0	−8·3	−16	−5	−12	−6	2
Q309	3	3	2	3	−3·3	−5·7	−7	0	−8	−4	0
Prices, costs and profits series (table 9.5)											
M313	5	5	3	5	+0·8	−7·0	−5	+14	−11	−1	6
M384	5	5	4	5	−5·0	−7·8	−13	+2	−14	−2	6
M557	5	5	4	5	−1·2	−6·0	−4	+2	−14	−2	8
M382	2	2	2	2	−13·0	−14·5	−14	−12	−20	−9	4
Q366	3	4	3	3	−8·3	−4·5	−14	−1	−11	0	2
Money and credit series (table 9.6)											
M409	3	4	3	4	−8·3	−14·0	−15	−4	−31	−6	2
M474	2	3	2	3	−10·5	−9·3	−11	−10	−22	−2	0
Foreign trade series (table 9.7)											
M493	4	4	3	4	−5·7	−9·7	−19	+4	−17	−5	2
M482	5	5	5	4	−8·8	−1·6	−16	−2	−22	+6	2
M582	3	4	3	4	−8·7	−6·7	−13	−1	−12	−2	8

[a] Turns by the indicator in the correct timing class.
[b] Greatest lead or smallest lag to smallest lead or greatest lag.
[c] Both peaks and troughs, equally divided.
[d] Text tables given are those where the other cyclical characteristics of the indicators can be found.

Table B.2. *Coincident indicators for production*

Series no.	Reference turns covered P	Reference turns covered T	Matching turns[a] P	Matching turns[a] T	Mean lead (−) or lag (+) P	Mean lead (−) or lag (+) T	Range[b] P	Range[b] T	Extra turns[c]
					(months)		(months)		
Labour-market series (table 9.1)[d]									
M1	5	5	5	4	−0·4	−2·2	−2 +2	−9 +1	8
M8	4	4	2	4	−1·3	−0·8	−10 +4	−2 +2	0
M9	4	4	2	3	+1·7	−2·0	−5 +11	−7 +1	2
M25	5	5	3	4	+3·0	+0·2	−6 +15	−2 +4	4
M60	3	4	2	3	−1·7	+3·2	−5 +1	0 +10	2
Output and consumption series (table 9.2)									
M120*	5	5	5	5	+0·2	−0·4	−1 +2	−3 +1	8
Q230*	3	4	3	2	−6·3	.	−16 −1	−6 +5	2
Q231*	3	4	3	4	−5·3	+1·5	−8 −1	0 −3	2
Q157	5	5	5	4	+1·4	−0·4	−1 +3	−5 +2	6
Foreign trade series (table 9·7)									
M583	3	4	2	4	−6·3	−1·5	−12 +1	−3 0	6

Notes: see notes to table B.1.

Table B.3. *Lagging indicators for production*

Series no.	Reference turns covered P	Reference turns covered T	Matching turns[a] P	Matching turns[a] T	Mean lead (−) or lag (+) P	Mean lead (−) or lag (+) T	Range[b] P	Range[b] T	Extra turns[c]
					(months)		(months)		
Labour-market series (table 9.1)[d]									
M37	5	5	3	4	+4·0	+1·0	−6 +15	−2 +4	4
M48	5	5	4	5	+7·0	+4·8	−5 +23	+1 +11	2
M49	5	5	5	5	+8·0	+5·6	+2 +15	+1 +10	2
M70	5	5	3	5	+6·0	+3·8	−1 +13	+1 +10	4
Q59	5	5	5	5	+8·2	+4·2	+3 +15	+2 +6	4
Income series (table 9.2)									
M181	5	5	5	3	+11·0	+7·0	+3 +19	−4 +16	4
Investment series (table 9.3)									
Q212*	4	4	4	4	+8·5	+4·5	+1 +17	+2 +7	4
Q214*	4	4	4	4	+12·2	+7·5	+1 +17	+3 +11	0
Stock series (table 9.4)									
Q247	4	4	4	4	+19·2	+6·3	+18 +21	+4 +10	0
Q259	4	3	4	3	+24·5	+13·0	+21 +33	+8 +16	0
Prices series (table 9.5)									
M378	5	5	5	5	+13·8	+10·0	+3 +26	+1 +21	4
M560	5	5	5	4	+12·4	+4·2	+3 +25	−2 +9	6
Interest-rate series (table 9·6)									
M468	5	5	5	3	+17·4	+9·6	+12 +21	−4 +29	2

Notes: see notes to table B.1.

Table B.4. *Leading indicators for investment*

Series no.	Reference turns covered P	Reference turns covered T	Matching turns[a] P	Matching turns[a] T	Mean lead (−) or lag (+) P (months)	Mean lead (−) or lag (+) T (months)	Range[b] P (months)		Range[b] T (months)		Extra turns[c]
Labour-market series (table 10.1)[d]											
M25	4	4	3	4	−5·5	−5·2	−18	+14	−8	−2	4
Output and consumption series (table 10.2)											
M116*	4	4	4	4	−8·5	−4·5	−17	−1	−7	−2	6
Q230*	3	4	3	3	−13·0	−4·5	−18	−3	−9	+3	2
M160	4	4	4	4	−9·2	−12·2	−20	−1	−25	−6	2
Q163*	4	4	4	4	−16·5	−10·5	−27	−3	−18	−6	4
Investment, orders and anticipation series (table 10.3)											
Q173	3	3	3	3	−14·0	−28·0	−30	−3	−39	−21	2
M267	4	4	4	4	−9·5	−21·0	−17	−2	−29	−12	4
M287	4	4	4	4	−6·7	−13·0	−17	−1	−32	−6	2
Q305	3	3	3	3	−15·7	−13·7	−23	−7	−19	−10	2
Q309	3	3	3	3	−10·0	−11·0	−17	−5	−11	−11	0
Prices and profits series (table 10.5)											
M313	4	4	4	4	−8·5	−13·0	−19	−3	−17	−9	4
Q366	3	4	3	4	−15·0	−9·0	−18	−12	−18	−3	2
Credit series (table 10.6)											
M409	3	4	3	4	−15·0	−18·5	−23	−5	−37	−8	2
M474	2	3	2	3	−12·0	−14·7	−13	−11	−28	−7	0

Notes: see notes to table B.1.

Table B.5. *Coincident indicators for investment*

Series no.	Reference turns covered P	Reference turns covered T	Matching turns[a] P	Matching turns[a] T	Mean lead (−) or lag (+) P (months)	Mean lead (−) or lag (+) T (months)	Range[b] P (months)		Range[b] T (months)		Extra turns[c]
Investment series (table 10.3)[d]											
Q214*	4	4	3	3	+3·8	+3·0	0	+15	0	+9	0
Interest-rate series (table 10·6)											
M453	4	4	4	3	+2·5	−1·0	+1	+7	−4	+3	4

Notes: see notes to table B.1.

Table B.6. *Leading indicators for unemployment*

Series no.	Reference turns covered P	Reference turns covered T	Matching turns[a] P	Matching turns[a] T	Mean lead (−) or lag (+) P	Mean lead (−) or lag (+) T	Range[b] P		Range[b] T		Extra turns[c]
					(months)		(months)				
Marginal employment adjustment series (table 11.1)[d]											
Q1	5	6	5	5	−8·2	−5·3	−15	−3	−16	+3	2
Q7	5	5	5	5	−16·0	−7·2	−24	−7	−19	−1	2
M10	4	4	4	3	−8·2	−6·3	−13	−3	−19	0	2
M7	4	4	4	4	−3·5	−5·8	−7	−1	−17	−1	2
M8	4	4	3	3	−7·3	−4·5	−10	0	−12	0	0
M21	3	4	2	3	−1·0	−7·2	−5	+3	−19	0	0
Vacancy series (table 11.2)											
M25	5	6	4	5	−3·0	−2·8	−5	+2	−11	+1	4
Unemployment series (table 11.4)											
M78	5	6	3	6	−2·8	−6·8	−8	0	−17	−2	4
M99	5	6	4	6	−1·6	−4·0	−5	0	−7	−1	4
Output and consumption series (table 11.5)											
M116*	5	5	3	5	−6·0	−3·8	−13	+1	−10	−1	6
Q163*	5	6	5	6	−12·4	−9·3	−15	−6	−19	−1	8
M206	5	5	5	5	−9·8	−20·0	−15	−2	−28	−14	6
Prices, profits and credit series (table 11.7)											
M313	5	6	4	6	−5·2	−10·3	−17	+2	−19	−5	6
Q366	3	4	3	4	−16·3	−8·2	−27	−9	−13	−3	2
M409	3	4	3	4	−16·3	−17·7	−18	−14	−32	−8	2

Notes: see notes to table B.1.

Table B.7. *Coincident indicators for unemployment*

Series no.	Reference turns covered P	Reference turns covered T	Matching turns[a] P	Matching turns[a] T	Mean lead (−) or lag (+) P	Mean lead (−) or lag (+) T	Range[b] P		Range[b] T		Extra turns[c]
					(months)		(months)				
Marginal employment adjustment series (table 11.1)[d]											
Q4	5	6	3	5	−4·6	−1·8	−15	+3	−11	+3	0
Vacancy series (table 11·2)											
M37	5	6	4	5	−2·0	−2·3	−5	+2	−11	0	4
Employment series (table 11.3)											
M66	3	4	3	4	+0·7	−0·5	0	+1	−1	0	2
Unemployment series (table 11·4)											
Q58	5	6	5	5	+1·0	−0·3	−2	+3	−4	+1	4
M90	5	6	5	6	+0·2	−0·5	−2	+3	−3	0	4
M91	5	6	5	5	+0·4	−1·8	−2	+3	−9	+1	4

Notes: see notes to table B.1.

Table B.8. *Lagging indicators for unemployment*

Series no.	Reference turns covered		Matching turns[a]		Mean lead (−) or lag (+)		Range[b]				Extra turns[c]
	P	T	P	T	P	T	P		T		
					(months)		(months)				
Employment series (table 11.3)[d]											
M49	5	5	4	3	+2·0	+1·8	−2	+7	−3	+9	2
Unemployment series (table 11.4)											
Q60	5	6	4	4	+5·3	+6·6	+2	+9	−1	+13	0
Q74	5	5	5	5	+12·6	+13·2	+6	+23	+8	+19	2

Notes: see notes to table B.1.

APPENDIX C

MCD STATISTICS AND RELATED MEASURES

If a seasonally adjusted series is defined as having two components – cyclical (plus trend), C, and irregular, I – the irregular component is obtained by dividing the cyclical component (estimated as a smooth, flexible, moving average of the series) into the original seasonally adjusted series. MCD (months for cyclical dominance) statistics provide an estimate of the appropriate time-span over which to observe cyclical movements in a monthly series. They are small for smooth series and large for irregular series. They are derived by computing separately percentage changes for the irregular component and the cyclical component over spans of 1, 2, 3, etc. months up to 8 months. Then MCD is the shortest span in months for which the average percentage change (without regard to sign) in the cyclical component is larger than the average percentage change (without regard to sign) in the irregular component and remains so (that is, it is the shortest span for which $\bar{I}/\bar{C}$ is consistently less than one).[1] A similar statistic, QCD, can be computed for quarterly series, but it is too coarse a measure for scoring purposes. In such cases therefore $\bar{I}/\bar{C}$ was used instead (see appendix A).

The values of these measures for the shortlisted indicators are shown in tables C.1 and C.2.

Table C.1. *Measures of smoothness for shortlisted quarterly indicators*

Series no.	Period covered	$\bar{I}$	$\bar{C}$	$\bar{I}/\bar{C}$	QCD	$\bar{I}/\bar{C}$ for 1 quarter
Q1	48/III to 72/II	2·89	1·56	1·85	2	1·04
Q4	48/III to 72/II	2·16	1·10	1·97	2	1·20
Q7	48/III to 72/II	0·05	0·03	1·88	2	1·04
Q11	63/I to 73/1	3·94	2·54	1·55	1	0·53
Q58	48/III to 72/II	4·28	2·93	1·46	1	0·43
Q59	48/III to 72/II	4·12	3·00	1·37	1	0·26
Q60	48/III to 72/II	2·31	1·70	1·36	1	0·17
Q74	48/III to 72/II	1·40	0·93	1·51	1	0·47
Q157	50/I to 72/IV	1·16	0·70	1·67	1	0·72
Q163*	49/I to 72/IV	0·38	0·21	1·76	1	0·88
Q173	60/I to 72/II	4·15	2·58	1·61	1	0·74
Q212*	58/I to 72/IV	1·29	0·69	1·87	1	0·98
Q214*	55/I to 72/IV	1·54	0·92	1·67	1	0·74
Q230*	58/I to 72/II	0·29	0·18	1·62	1	0·71
Q231*	58/I to 72/II	0·34	0·19	1·83	1	1·00
Q247	60/I to 72/IV	0·42	0·30	1·44	1	0·37
Q259	58/I to 72/IV	0·56	0·36	1·52	1	0·59
Q305	58/III to 72/III	6·09	3·82	1·59	1	0·53
Q309	58/III to 72/III	1·99	1·37	1·45	1	0·40
Q366	55/I to 72/II	1·42	0·81	1·76	1	0·89

[1] A detailed explanation is given in Julius Shiskin, *Electronic Computers and Business Indicators*, New York, NBER, 1957.

Table C.2. *Measures of smoothness for shortlisted monthly indicators*

Series no.	Period beginning[a]	$\bar{I}$	$\bar{C}$	$\bar{I}/\bar{C}$	MCD	$\bar{I}/\bar{C}$ for MCD span
M1	48/7	22·96	10·43	2·20	3	0·83
M7[b]	61/6	2·07	1·05	1·98	3	0·67
M8		1·16	0·28	4·19	5	0·82
M10		16·03	7·98	2·01	3	0·72
M15	62/1	0·20	0·11	1·81	3	0·67
M21		0·20	0·11	1·85	3	0·66
M25	48/1	1·46	2·22	0·65	1	0·65
M37	48/7	2·40	3·95	0·61	1	0·61
M48	59/6	0·11	0·16	0·69	1	0·69
M49		0·08	0·16	0·52	1	0·52
M60[b]	62/1	0·34	0·25	1·35	2	0·75
M70	48/7	1·32	2·01	0·66	1	0·66
M78	63/6	3·53	1·24	2·84	3	0·89
M90	50/1	1·71	2·67	0·64	1	0·64
M91		1·42	2·73	0·52	1	0·52
M99	63/6	2·83	1·28	2·20	3	0·80
M116*	48/1	0·97	0·32	2·98	3	1·00
M120*		1·04	0·38	2·72	3	0·89
M160	49/1	2·60	0·72	3·61	4	0·86
M181		7·36	5·65	1·30	2	0·78
M206	48/1	7·07	2·71	2·60	4	0·74
M267		8·30	3·03	2·74	3	0·86
M287		5·28	1·81	2·91	3	0·83
M313		2·30	1·70	1·35	2	0·91
M378	49/1	0·43	0·26	1·63	3	0·70
M382	63/1	0·32	0·25	1·30	2	0·94
M384	48/1	3·01	2·10	1·44	2	0·92
M409	64/10	6·55	1·82	3·60	4	0·81
M453	56/1	4·65	2·88	1·61	3	0·64
M468	51/12	1·20	0·94	1·27	2	0·87
M474	60/1	5·78	1·37	4·22	5	0·83
M482	48/1	9·00	2·58	3·48	4	0·95
M493	55/1	25·04	4·36	5·74	7	0·97
M557	58/1	0·85	0·82	1·04	2	0·68
M560		0·13	0·19	0·68	1	0·68
M582	55/1	0·65	0·53	1·23	2	0·76
M583		0·99	0·77	1·28	2	0·68

[a] Periods for all series end 72/12 except M48 and M49 which end 71/5.
[b] Measures for M9 are identical with those for M7, and for M66 with those for M60.

APPENDIX D

SERIES INDEX AND SOURCE NOTES[1]

QUARTERLY SERIES

Series	Source
Labour turnover in manufacturing per 100 employed	
Q1 Engagements Q4 Discharges Q7 Net engagements (Q1–Q4)	Department of Employment, from 1948. Not published seasonally adjusted.
Vacancies (1959 = 100)	
Q11 MSL index of advertisements for executives	Management Selection Ltd., London, from 1963. Based on a continuous analysis of advertisements for managerial and technical appointments in 6 major newspapers. Not published seasonally adjusted.
Employment – Great Britain	
Q16 Total employees in employment Q17 Total male employees in employment Q18 Total female employees in employment Q19 Total employees (including unemployed) Q22 Total working population (including unemployed, forces, employers and self-employed) Q25 Total in civil employment (Q22 less forces)	Department of Employment, from 1950.

[1] All series marked with an asterisk are detrended.

	Series	Source
Employment by industry group – United Kingdom (1963 = 100)		
Q34	In metal manufacturing	Department of Employment, from 1960. Employers and self-employed included.
Q35	In engineering and electrical goods	
Q36	In vehicle manufacturing	
Q37	In textile manufacturing	
Q46	Total operatives employed by construction contractors – Great Britain	Department of the Environment, *Housing and Construction Statistics*, from 1956.
Wholly unemployed by duration (inverted)		
Q58	Unemployed 8–26 weeks	Department of Employment, from 1948. Not published seasonally adjusted.
Q59	Unemployed 26–52 weeks	
Q60	Unemployed over 52 weeks	
Q74	Average duration unemployed of those on the register	Specially constructed series, unpublished.
Production and consumption of metals		
Q92	Output index for metal manufactures	Central Statistical Office, from 1952.
Q156	Home deliveries of finished steel	Department of Trade and Industry, from 1950.
Q157	Home consumption of finished steel	
Consumers' expenditure at 1970 prices		
Q158*	On non-durables	Central Statistical Office, from 1949.
Q163*	Total	
Q166*	On durables	
Contractors' new orders at 1970 prices		
Q173	Total new work	Department of the Environment, *Housing and Construction Statistics*, from 1960.
Q176	New private housing	
Q180	New private industrial	
GDP at 1970 prices		
Q193*	Expenditure estimate at factor cost (see also Q230* and Q231*)	Central Statistical Office, from 1955.

	Series	Source
Gross domestic fixed capital formation at 1970 prices		
Q209	Private dwellings	Central Statistical Office, from 1958.
Q212*	Private non-residential	
Q214	In manufacturing	Central Statistical Office, from 1955.
Q214*	In manufacturing, detrended	
Fixed capital expenditure by the manufacturing sector at 1970 prices		
Q223	On new buildings	Department of Trade and Industry, from 1955.
Q224	On vehicles	Department of Trade and Industry, from 1959.
Q225	On plant and machinery	
Q225*	On plant and machinery, detrended	
GDP at 1970 prices		
Q230*	Output estimate	Central Statistical Office, from 1958.
Q231*	Average of output, expenditure and income estimates (see also Q193*)	
Aggregate stock-levels and stock-ratios		
Q247	Manufacturing stocks of materials and fuel at constant prices	Central Statistical Office, from 1956.
Q254	Ratio of manufacturing stocks to output	
Q258	Ratio of manufacturing stocks of finished goods to output	
Q259	Ratio of total stocks to GDP (output estimate)	Central Statistical Office, from 1958.
Steel stocks (merchants' and consumers')		
Q264	Total stocks of finished steel	Derived from Q156 and Q157, from 1950.
Q267	Number of weeks supply in stock	
Changes in aggregate stocks at constant prices		
Q269	Total stocks and work in progress	Central Statistical Office, from 1955.

	Series	Source
Q270	Manufacturing stocks and work in progress	Central Statistical Office, from 1956.
Q275	Manufacturing stocks of materials and fuel	Department of Trade and Industry, from 1956.
Q276	Manufacturing stocks of finished goods	
Q286	Stocks of finished steel	Derived from Q156 and Q157.

CBI industrial trends survey

Q305	Optimism balance	Based on opinions of industrialists included in CBI survey, from 1958.
Q306	Cumulative optimism balance	
Q307	Building investment balance	
Q308	Plant and machinery investment balance	
Q309	Total manufacturing investment balance	

Price–cost ratio – whole economy

Q328	Ratio of final prices to unit wages and salaries cost (see also Q336)	Central Statistical Office and Department of Employment, from 1955.

Consumer prices – annual rates of increase

Q332	All goods and services	Central Statistical Office, from 1958. Derived as implicit price deflators of consumers' expenditure.
Q333	Durable goods	

Price–cost ratio – whole economy

Q336	Ratio of final prices to unit labour cost (see also Q328)	Central Statistical Office and Department of Employment, from 1955.

Company profits

Q345	Companies' gross trading profits	Central Statistical Office, from 1955.
Q345*	Companies' gross trading profits, detrended	
Q366	Ratio of companies' gross profits to GDP	

	Series	Source
	Changes in money supply	
Q375	Domestic credit expansion	Central Statistical Office, from 1963.
Q376	Change in 'M3'	
	Trade balance at current prices (inverted)	
Q455	Visible balance	Central Statistical Office, from 1958.
Q472	Current balance	
	Prices in international trade – annual rates of increase	
Q485	World export unit values	United Nations, from 1950.
Q487	Export prices for world primary commodities	United Nations, from 1955.

MONTHLY SERIES

	Series	Source
	Temporarily stopped (inverted)	
M1	Numbers temporarily stopped	Department of Employment from 1948. Not published seasonally adjusted.
	Overtime and short-time in manufacturing	
M5	Operatives on overtime	Department of Employment, from 1952. M7 only is published seasonally adjusted.
M7	Total hours overtime	
M8	Average hours per operative on overtime (M7/M5)	
M9	Total hours overtime adjusted for changes in normal hours	
M10	Operatives on short-time (inverted)	
	Average hours in manufacturing (1962 = 100)	
M15	In all manufacturing	Department of Employment, from 1956. M15 only is published seasonally adjusted from 1962.
M16	In engineering and electrical goods	
M17	In vehicle manufacturing	
M18	In textiles, leather and clothing	
M20	In other manufacturing (excluding also food, drink and tobacco)	

	Series	Source
M21	In all manufacturing adjusted for changes in normal hours	Department of Employment, from 1956. Not published seasonally adjusted.

Vacancies notified and remaining unfilled

M25	Total adults	Department of Employment, from 1948. Published seasonally adjusted from 1958.
M26	Male adults	
M27	Female adults	
M37	Ratio of total vacancies to total unemployed (M25/M70)	

Employees in employment

M48	In index of production industries	Department of Employment, from 1952. Not published seasonally adjusted.
M49	In manufacturing	
M50	In metal manufacturing	
M51	In engineering and shipbuilding	
M52	In vehicle manufacturing	
M53	In bricks, pottery and glass	
M54	In construction	

Total hours in manufacturing (1962 = 100)

M60	In all manufacturing	Department of Employment, from 1956. M60 only published seasonally adjusted from 1962.
M61	In engineering and electrical goods	
M62	In vehicle manufacturing	
M63	In textiles, leather and clothing	
M65	In other manufacturing (excluding also food, drink and tobacco)	
M66	In all manufacturing adjusted for changes in normal hours	

Wholly unemployed, excluding school-leavers and adult students (inverted)

M70	Total unemployed	Department of Employment, from 1948.
M71	Males unemployed	
M72	Females unemployed	
M73	Total unemployed as a percentage of total employees	

	Series	Source
Wholly unemployed by duration, including school-leavers and adult students (inverted)		
M78	Unemployed under 2 weeks (see also M99 and M100)	Department of Employment, from 1948. Not published seasonally adjusted, and quarterly only up to 1963.
Wholly unemployed by industry group, excluding school-leavers and adult students (inverted)		
M90	In index of production industries	Department of Employment, from 1950.
M91	In manufacturing	
M92	In construction	
M93	In agriculture, forestry and fishing	
M94	In transport and communication	
M95	In the distributive trades	
M96	In catering and hotels	
M97	In other industries	
Wholly unemployed by duration, including school-leavers and adult students (inverted)		
M99	Unemployed under 4 weeks	Department of Employment, from 1948. Not published seasonally adjusted and quarterly only up to 1963.
M100	Unemployed under 8 weeks (see also M78)	
Output and productivity		
M114*	Output per employee in all production industries	Ratio of output indices (M116 and M120) to employment (M48 and M49), from 1952.
M115*	Output per employee in manufacturing	
M116*	Index of production in all production industries	Central Statistical Office, from 1950.
M120*	Index of production in manufacturing	

	Series	Source
Production of commodities		
M147	Of crude steel (weekly average)	Department of Trade and Industry, and British Steel Corporation, from 1948.
M153	Of passenger cars (for home sales)	Department of Trade and Industry, from 1948. Published seasonally adjusted from 1958.
M154	Of passenger cars (including exports)	
M160	Of building bricks	Department of the Environment, from 1949. Published seasonally adjusted from 1962.
Wage rates – annual rates of increase – United Kingdom		
M181	Hourly rates for manual workers in all industries and services	Department of Employment, from 1949.
Retail sales		
M185*	Total volume	Department of Trade and Industry, from 1948.
M189*	Volume in durable goods shops	
M198	Annual increase in total volume	Department of Trade and Industry, from 1958.
M199	Annual increase in total value	
New registrations		
M206	Cars	Department of Trade and Industry, and Department of the Environment, from 1948.
M253	Companies	Department of Trade and Industry, from 1948. Not published seasonally adjusted.
Private housing		
M267	Starts (see also M287)	Department of the Environment, from 1948. Published seasonally adjusted from 1956.

	Series	Source
	Engineering orders (1963 = 100)	
M270	Volume of total orders on hand in the engineering industry	Department of Trade and Industry, from 1958.
	Private housing	
M287	Completions (see also M267)	Department of the Environment, from 1948. Published seasonally adjusted from 1956.
	Share prices (July 1935 = 100)	
M313	Financial Times industrial ordinary share price index	Financial Times, from 1935. Not seasonally adjusted.
	Prices – annual rates of increase	
M363	Wholesale price index of materials and fuel in manufacturing	Department of Trade and Industry, from 1958.
M378	Retail price index (all goods and services) (see also M557 and M560)	Central Statistical Office, from 1948. Seasonal items excluded from 1963.
	Price–cost ratio in manufacturing	
M382	Ratio of wholesale prices for manufactured products to unit wage and salary costs	Department of Trade and Industry, and Department of Employment, from 1963.
	Yields on equities (July 1935 = 100)	
M384	FT dividends yield index	Financial Times, from 1935. Based on same 30 industrial ordinary shares as M313. Not seasonally adjusted.
M385	FT earnings yield index	
	Changes in money supply	
M400	Annual increase in currency in circulation	Bank of England, from 1948.

	Series	Source
Hire purchase and other instalment credit		
M403	Increase in HP debt to finance houses	Department of Trade and Industry, from 1958. 'Other credit retailers' included since 1964. Published seasonally adjusted from 1966.
M407	Total new HP credit	
M409	Increase in total HP debt	
M428	Total HP debt outstanding	
Interest rates (not seasonally adjusted)		
M449	On Treasury bills – average discount	Bank of England, from 1948.
M453	On 3-month Local Authority deposits	Bank of England, from 1956.
M465	On 2½% Consols – gross flat yield	Bank of England, from 1950.
M468	FT–Actuaries redemption yield on debenture and loan stocks with 20 years to maturity	FT–Actuaries Index, from 1952.
Business failures – England and Wales (inverted)		
M474	Total failures, including bankruptcies and voluntary and involuntary liquidations	Department of Trade and Industry, from 1960.
Export orders		
M479	Engineering export orders on hand (1963 prices)	Department of Trade and Industry, from 1958.
M482	Production of passenger cars for export	Department of Trade and Industry, from 1948. Not published seasonally adjusted.
Trade balance at current prices (inverted)		
M493	Visible balance	Department of Trade and Industry, from 1964. Data from 1955 available for 'crude trade gap', i.e. exports f.o.b. less imports c.i.f.

	Series	Source
Volume of exports and imports (1961 = 100)		
M495	Total exports	Department of Trade and Industry, from 1954. Published seasonally adjusted from 1961.
M524	Imports of basic materials	Department of Trade and Industry, from 1961.
Prices – annual rates of increase		
M557	Wholesale price index for basic materials for non-food manufacturing	Department of Trade and Industry, from 1950.
M560	Wholesale price index for manufactured non-food products for the home market	
	(see also M363 and M378)	
Export and import unit values – annual rates of increase		
M580	For exports of manufactures	Department of Trade and Industry, from 1954.
M581	For total exports	
M582	For total imports	
M583	For imports of basic materials	

APPENDIX E

GRAPHS OF SOME SHORTLISTED INDICATORS

(See appendix D for full definitions of the series and all sources)

Chart E.1. *Numbers temporarily stopped and unemployed by duration*

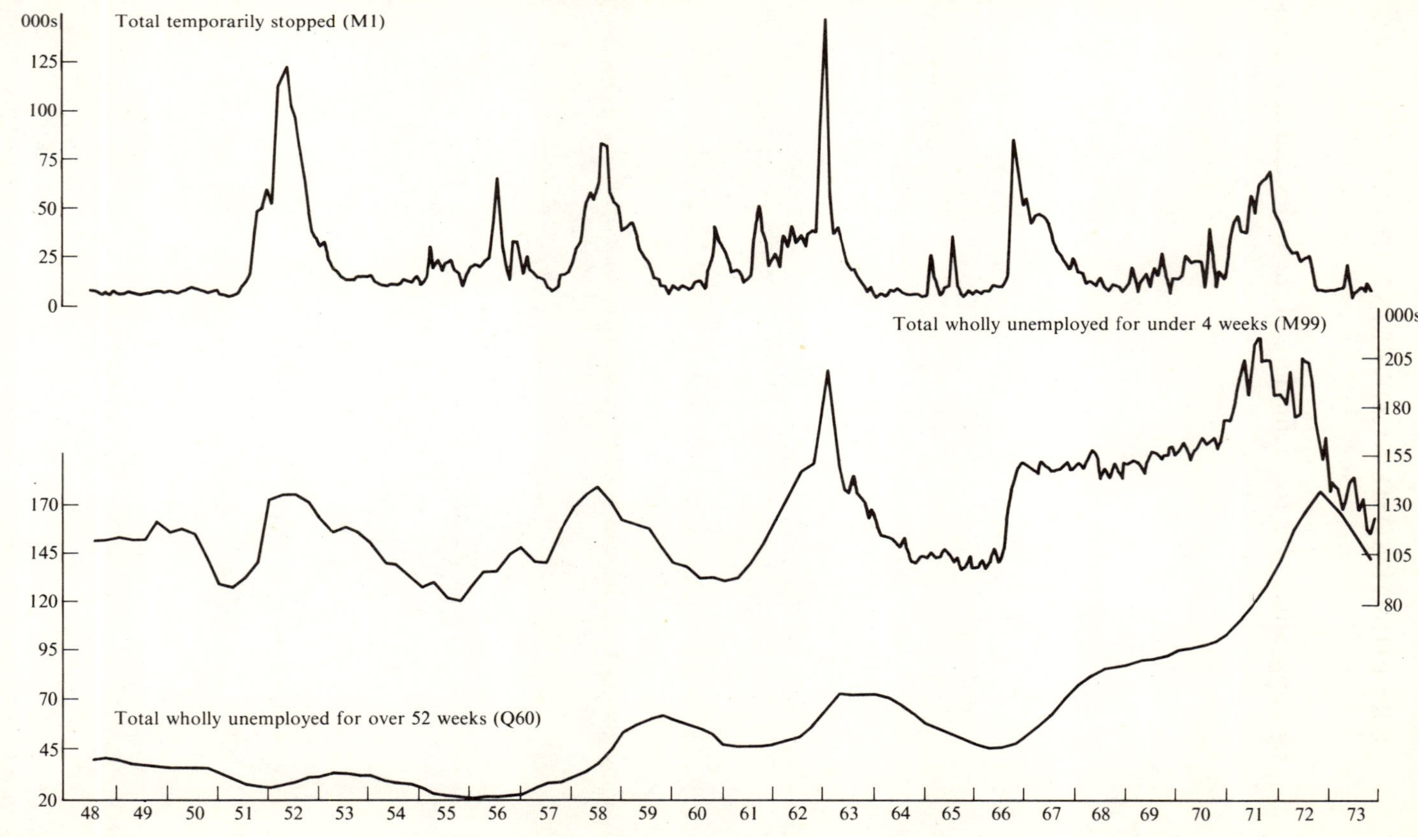

Chart E.2. *Total and net engagements in manufacturing; MSL index of advertisements for executives*

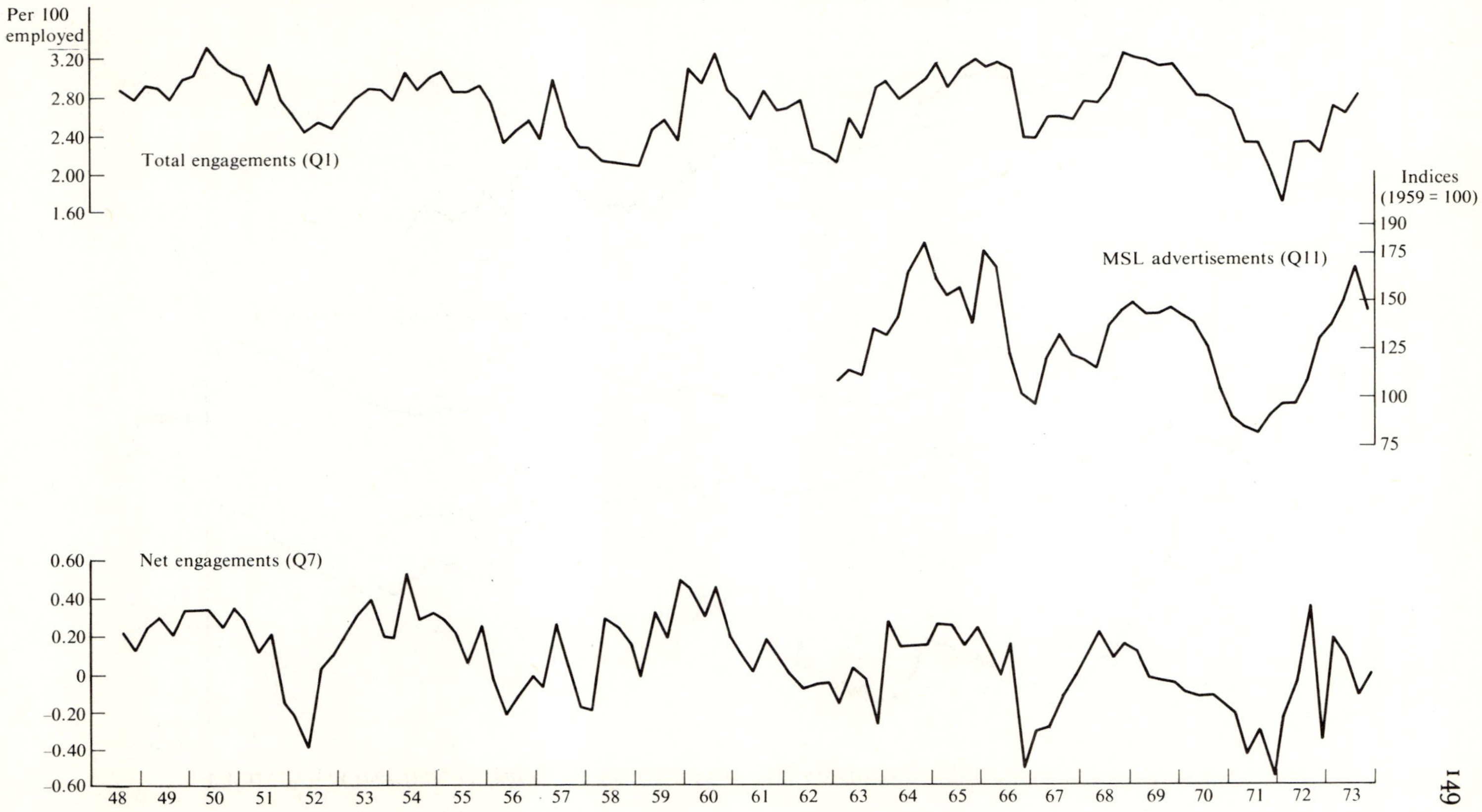

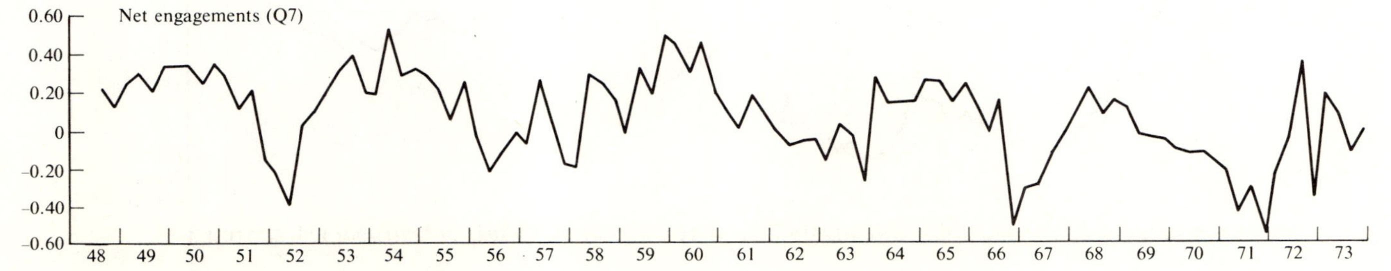

Chart E.3. *Overtime, average and total hours in manufacturing; employees in production industries*

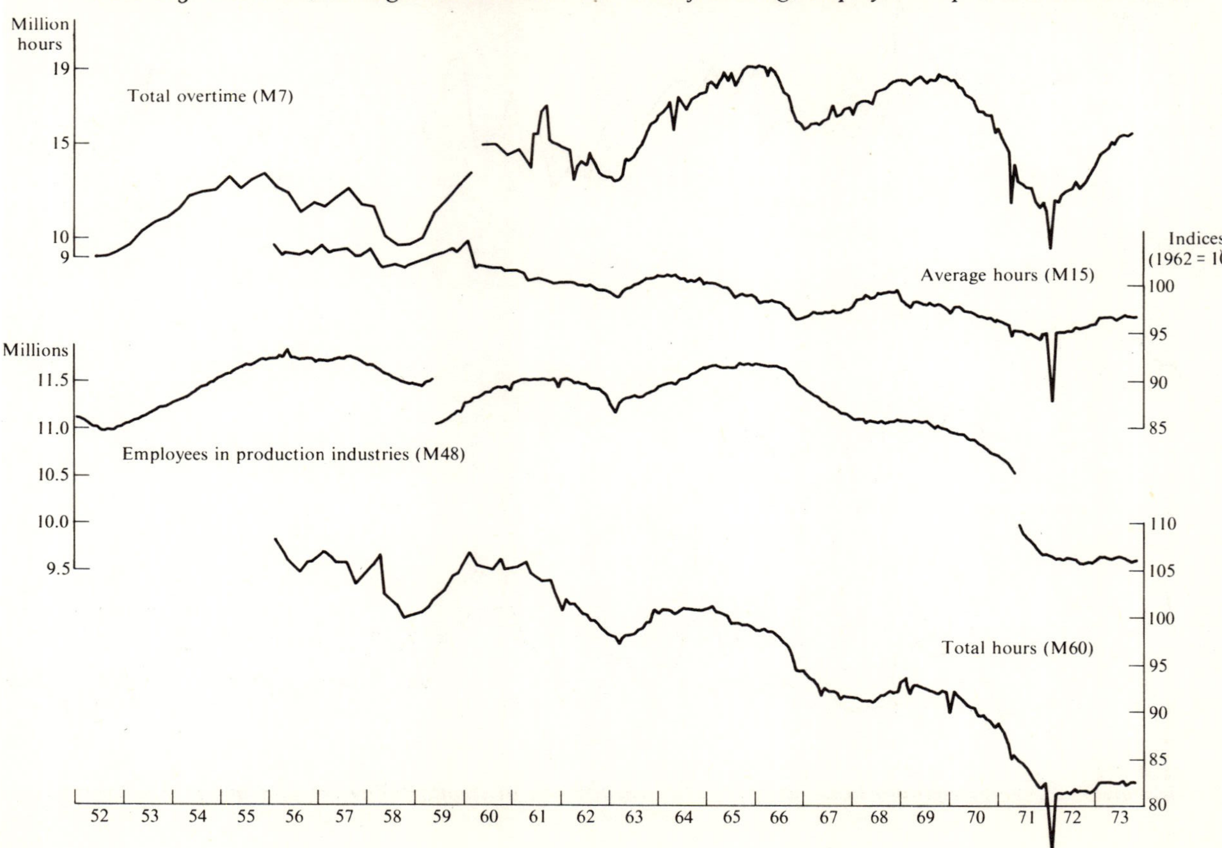

Chart E.4. *New car registrations; gross domestic product (output estimate); change in hire purchase debt; consumers' expenditure*

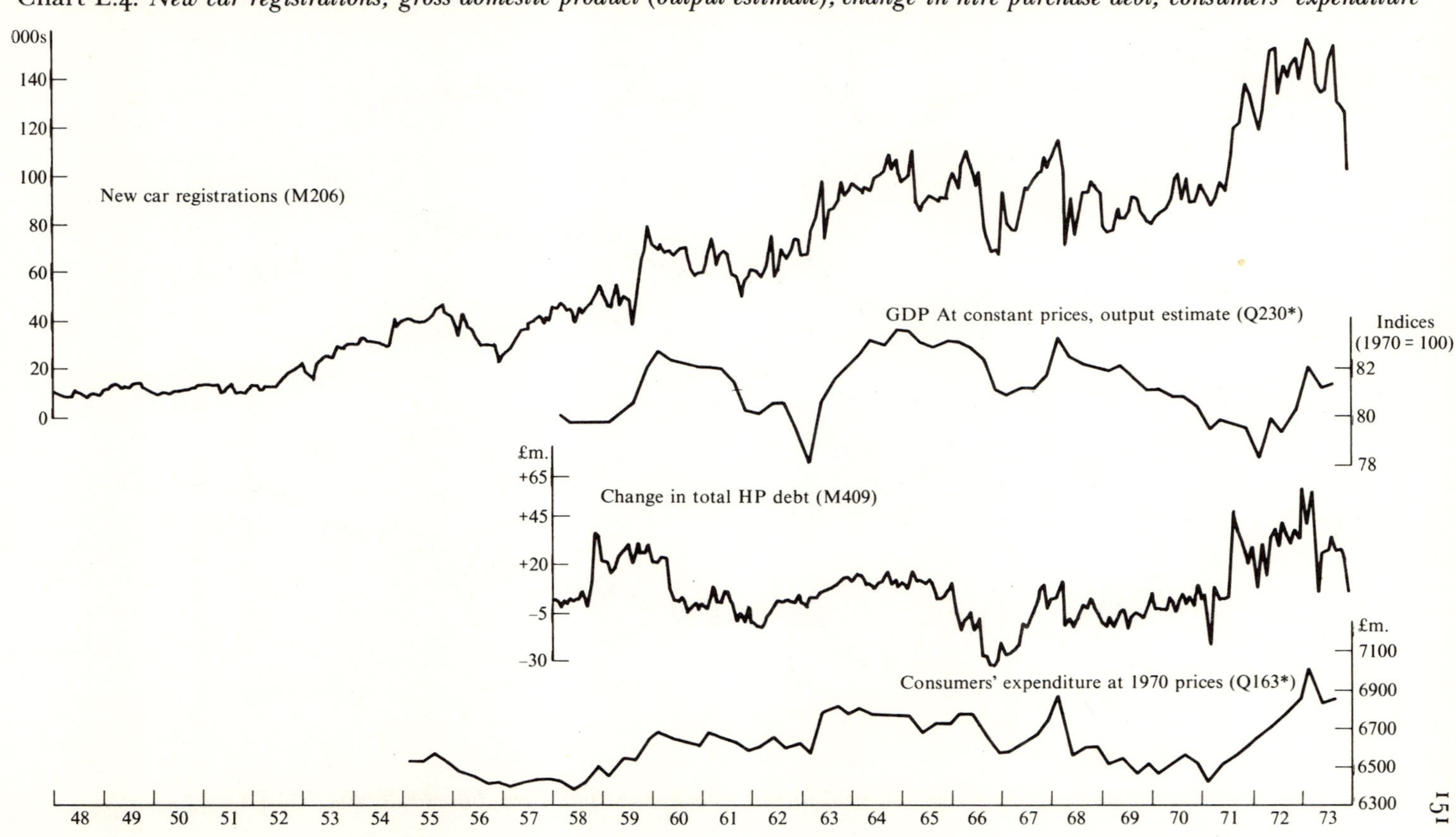

Chart E.5. *Private housing starts and completions; contractors' new orders; production of building bricks*

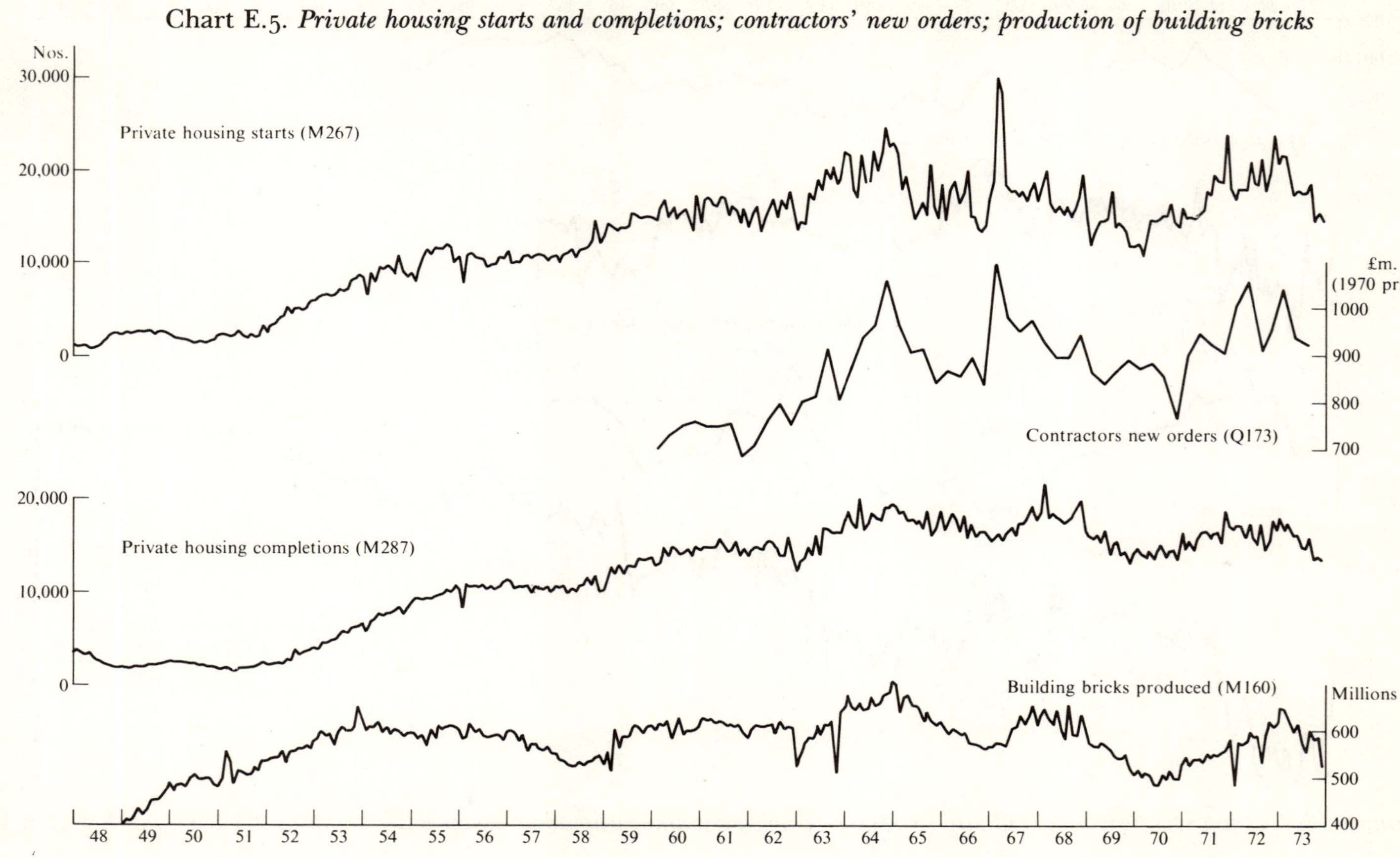

Chart E.6. *CBI balances for optimism and manufacturing investment; ratio of total stocks to gross domestic product (output estimate)*

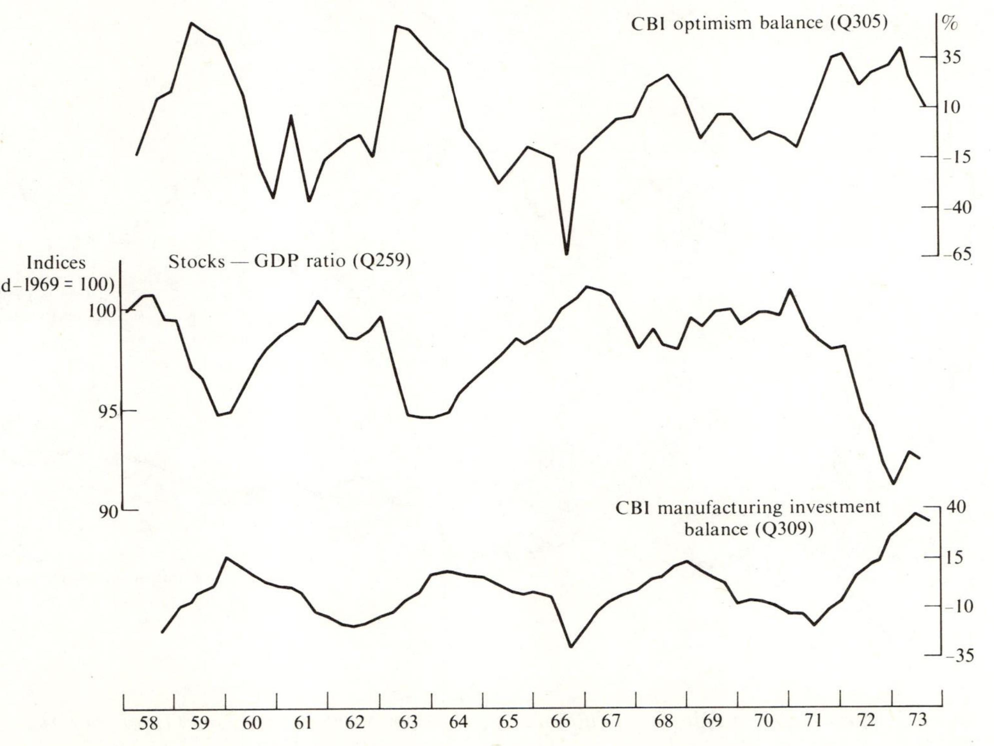

Chart E.7. *Financial Times indices for prices and dividends on industrial ordinary shares; ratio of wholesale prices to unit wage and salary costs in manufacturing; ratio of company profits to gross domestic product*

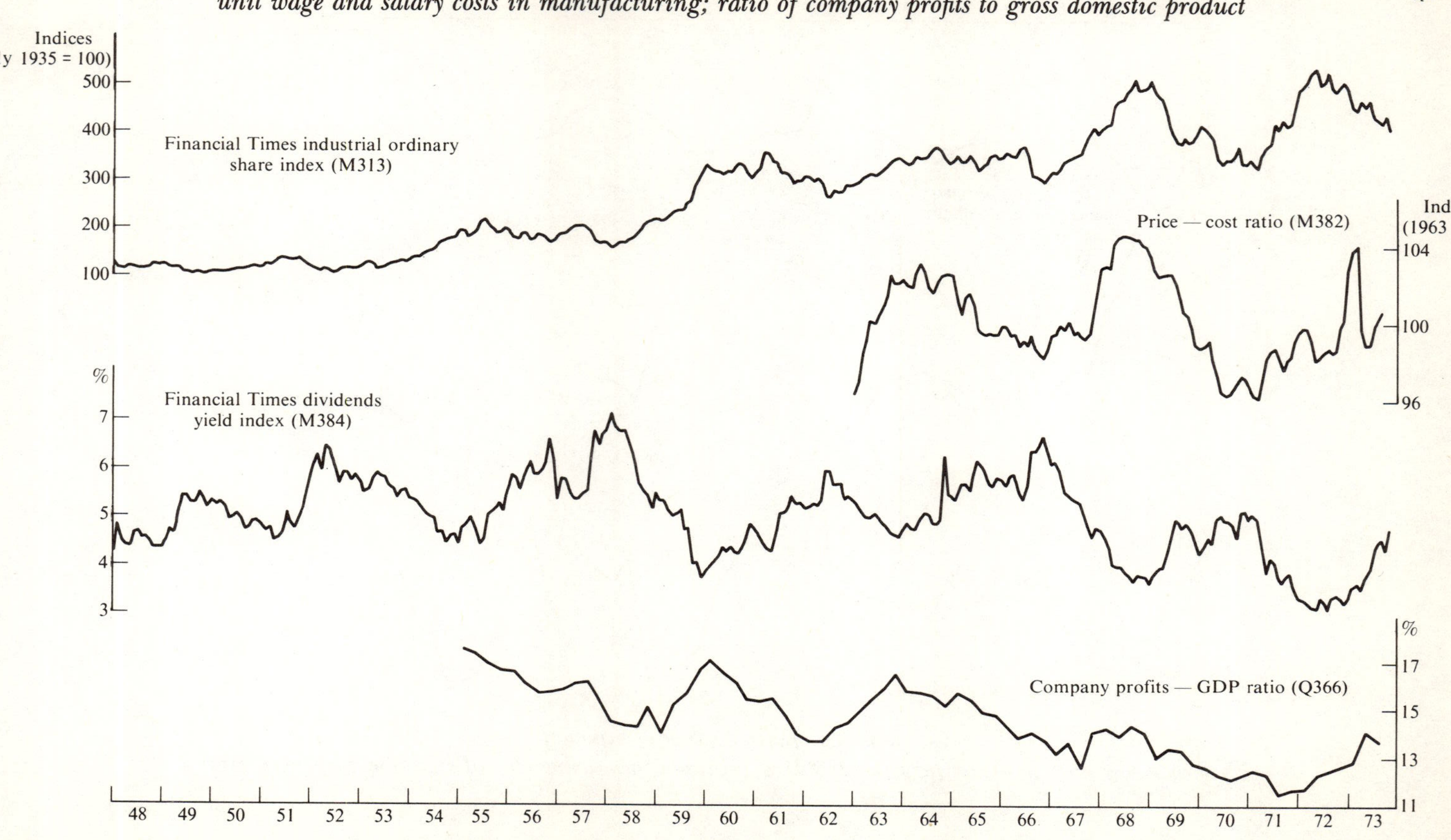

Chart E.8. *Annual increases in import unit values; the retail price index and two wholesale price indices*

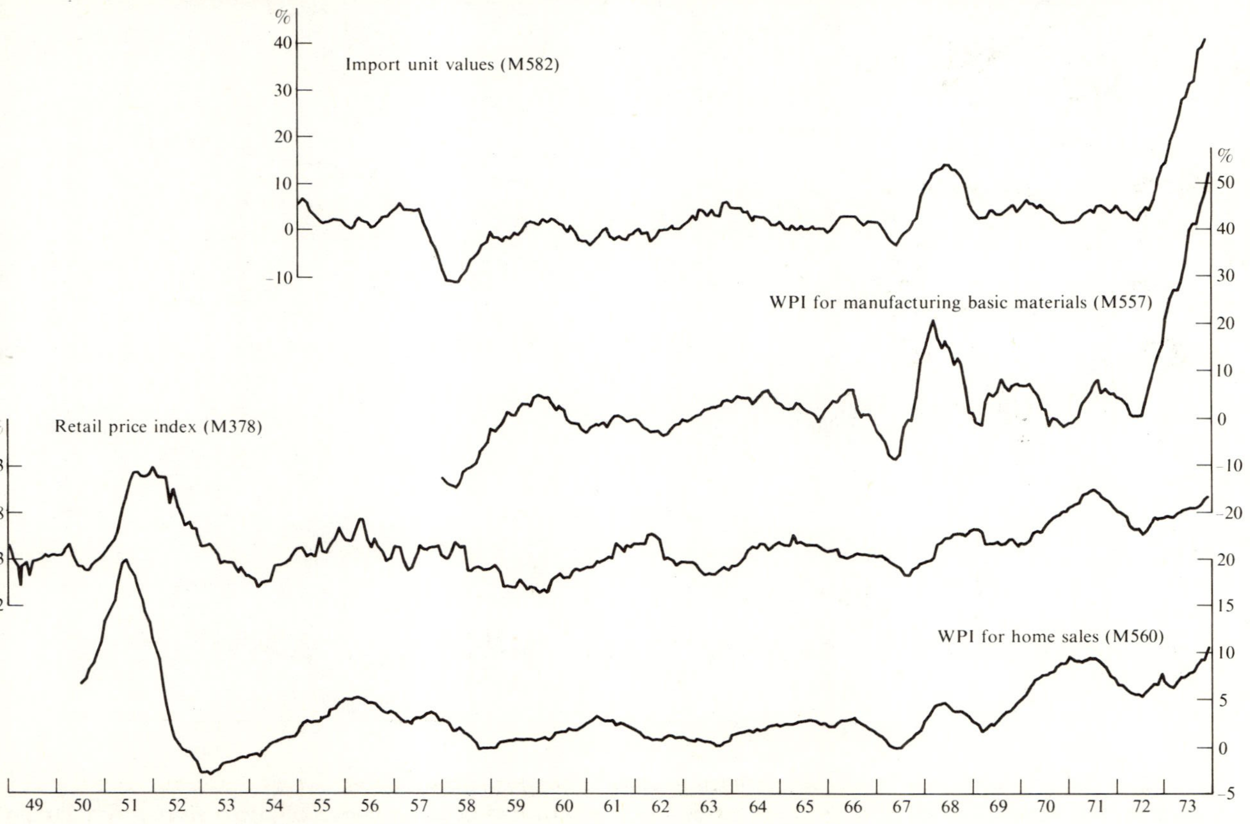

Chart E.9. *Crude trade gap; total business failures; FT–Actuaries index of yield on debentures and loan stock; Local Authority 3-month deposit rate*

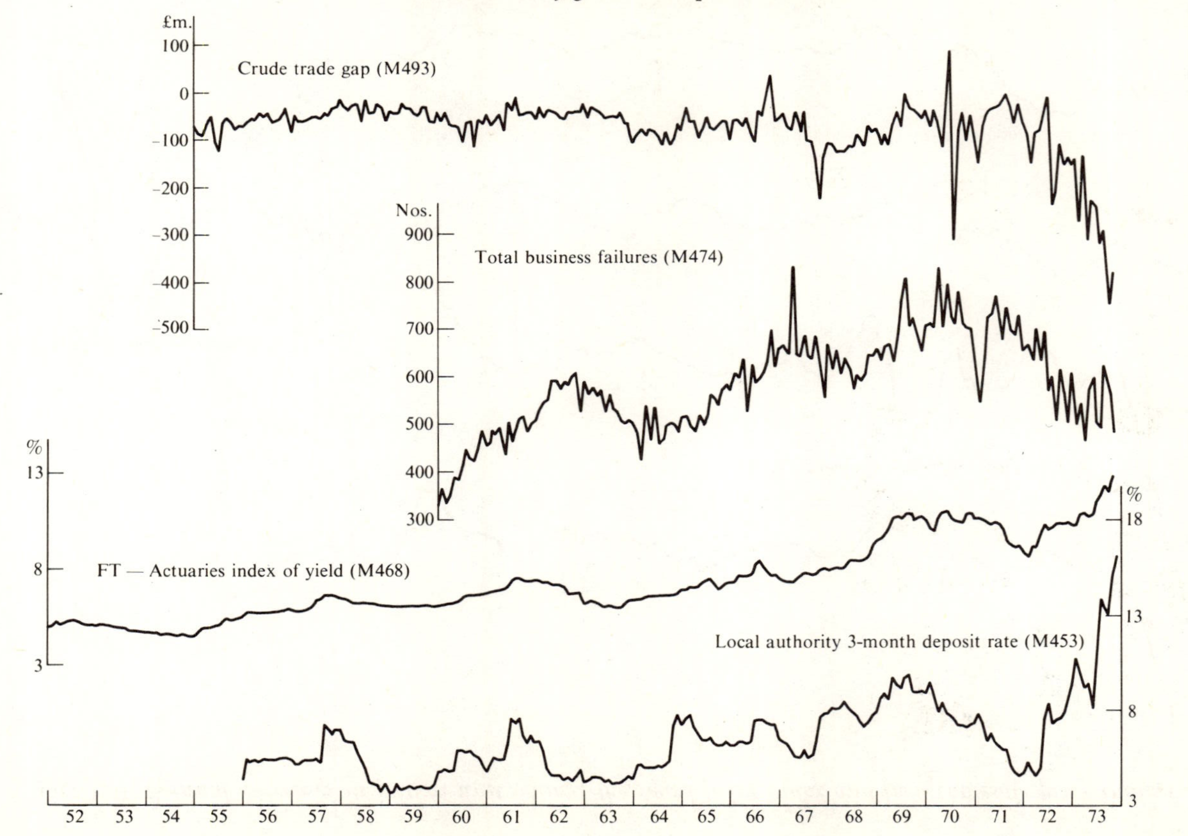

INDEX

PUBLICATIONS OF THE
NATIONAL INSTITUTE OF ECONOMIC
AND SOCIAL RESEARCH

published by
THE CAMBRIDGE UNIVERSITY PRESS

Books published for the Institute by the Cambridge University Press are available through the ordinary booksellers. They appear in the five series below:

ECONOMIC & SOCIAL STUDIES

*I *Studies in the National Income, 1924–1938*
Edited by A. L. BOWLEY. Reprinted with corrections, 1944. pp. 256.

*II *The Burden of British Taxation*
By G. FINDLAY SHIRRAS and L. ROSTAS. 1942. pp. 140.

*III *Trade Regulations and Commercial Policy of the United Kingdom*
By THE RESEARCH STAFF OF THE NATIONAL INSTITUTE OF ECONOMIC AND SOCIAL RESEARCH. 1943. pp. 275.

*IV *National Health Insurance: A Critical Study*
By HERMAN LEVY. 1944. pp. 356.

*V *The Development of the Soviet Economic System: An Essay on the Experience of Planning in the U.S.S.R.*
By ALEXANDER BAYKOV. 1946. pp. 530.
(Out of print in this series, but reprinted 1970 in Cambridge University Press Library Edition, £7.50 net.)

*VI *Studies in Financial Organization*
By T. BALOGH. 1948. pp. 328.

*VII *Investment, Location, and Size of Plant: A Realistic Inquiry into the Structure of British and American Industries*
By P. SARGANT FLORENCE, assisted by W. BALDAMUS. 1948. pp. 230.

*VIII *A Statistical Analysis of Advertising Expenditure and of the Revenue of the Press*
By NICHOLAS KALDOR and RODNEY SILVERMAN. 1948. pp. 200.

*IX *The Distribution of Consumer Goods*
By JAMES B. JEFFERYS, assisted by MARGARET MACCOLL and G. L. LEVETT. 1950. pp. 430.

*X *Lessons of the British War Economy*
Edited by D. N. CHESTER. 1951. pp. 260.

*XI *Colonial Social Accounting*
By PHYLLIS DEANE. 1953. pp. 360.

*XII *Migration and Economic Growth*
By BRINLEY THOMAS. 1954. pp. 384.

*XIII *Retail Trading in Britain, 1850–1950*
By JAMES B. JEFFERYS. 1954. pp. 490.

*XIV *British Economic Statistics*
By CHARLES CARTER and A. D. ROY. 1954. pp. 192.

*XV *The Structure of British Industry: A Symposium*
Edited by DUNCAN BURN. 1958. Vol. I. pp. 403. Vol. II. pp. 499.

*XVI *Concentration in British Industry*
By RICHARD EVELY and I. M. D. LITTLE. 1960. pp. 357.

*XVII *Studies in Company Finance*
Edited by BRIAN TEW and R. F. HENDERSON. 1959. pp. 301.

*XVIII *British Industrialists: Steel and Hosiery, 1850–1950*
By CHARLOTTE ERICKSON. 1959. pp. 276.

* At present out of print.

XIX *The Antitrust Laws of the U.S.A.: A Study of Competition Enforced by Law*
By A. D. NEALE. 2nd edition, 1970. pp. 544. £4.80 net.

*XX *A Study of United Kingdom Imports*
By M. FG. SCOTT. 1963. pp. 270.

XXI *Industrial Growth and World Trade*
By ALFRED MAIZELS. Reprinted with corrections, 1971. pp. 563. £4.20 net.

*XXII *The Management of the British Economy, 1945–60*
By J. C. R. DOW. 1964. pp. 443.

XXIII *The British Economy in 1975*
By W. BECKERMAN AND ASSOCIATES. 1965. pp. 631. £4.00 net.

*XXIV *Occupation and Pay in Great Britain, 1906–60*
By GUY ROUTH. 1965. pp. 182.

XXV *Exports and Economic Growth of Developing Countries*
By A. MAIZELS, assisted by L. F. CAMPBELL-BOROSS and P. B. W. RAYMENT. 1968. pp. 445. £3.00 net.

XXVI *Urban Development in Britain: Standards, Costs and Resources, 1964–2004*
By P. A. STONE. Vol. I: *Population Trends and Housing.* 1970. pp. 436. £3.00 net.

XXVII *The Framework of Regional Economics in the United Kingdom*
By A. J. BROWN. 1972. pp. 372. £4.00 net.

XXVIII *The Structure, Size and Costs of Urban Settlements*
By P. A. STONE. 1973. pp. 304. £4.50 net.

XXIX *The Diffusion of New Industrial Processes: An International Study*
Edited by L. NABSETH and G. F. RAY. 1974. pp. 346. £4.00 net.

OCCASIONAL PAPERS

*I *The New Population Statistics*
By R. R. KUCZYNSKI. 1942. pp. 31.

*II *The Population of Bristol*
By H. A. SHANNON and E. GREBENIK. 1943. pp. 92.

*III *Standards of Local Expenditure*
By J. R. HICKS and U. K. HICKS. 1943. pp. 61.

*IV *War-time Pattern of Saving and Spending*
By CHARLES MADGE. 1943. pp. 139.

*V *Standardized Accounting in Germany*
By H. W. SINGER. Reprinted 1944. pp. 68.

*VI *Ten Years of Controlled Trade in South-Eastern Europe*
By N. MOMTCHILOFF. 1944. pp. 90.

*VII *The Problem of Valuation for Rating*
By J. R. HICKS, U. K. HICKS and C. E. V. LESER. 1944. pp. 90.

*VIII *The Incidence of Local Rates in Great Britain*
By J. R. HICKS and U. K. HICKS. 1945. pp. 64.

*IX *Contributions to the Study of Oscillatory Time-Series*
By M. G. KENDALL. 1946. pp. 76.

*X *A System of National Book-keeping Illustrated by the Experience of the Netherlands Economy*
By J. B. D. DERKSEN. 1946. pp. 34.

*XI *Productivity, Prices and Distribution in Selected British Industries*
By L. ROSTAS. 1948. pp. 199.

*XII *Measurement of Colonial National Incomes: An Experiment*
By PHYLLIS DEANE. 1948. pp. 173.

*XIII *Comparative Productivity in British and American Industry*
By L. ROSTAS. 1948. pp. 263.

*XIV *The Cost of Industrial Movement*
By W. F. LUTTRELL. 1952. pp. 104.

* At present out of print.

XV *Costs in Alternative Locations: The Clothing Industry*
By D. C. HAGUE and P. K. NEWMAN. 1952. pp. 73. £1.05 net.

*XVI *Social Accounts of Local Authorities*
By J. E. G. UTTING. 1953. pp. 81.

*XVII *British Post-war Migration*
By JULIUS ISAAC. 1954. pp. 204.

*XVIII *The Cost of the National Health Service in England and Wales*
By BRIAN ABEL-SMITH and RICHARD M. TITMUSS. 1956. pp. 176.

*XIX *Post-war Investment, Location and Size of Plant*
By P. SARGANT FLORENCE. 1962. pp. 51.

*XX *Investment and Growth Policies in British Industrial Firms*
By TIBOR BARNA. 1962. pp. 71.

*XXI *Pricing and Employment in the Trade Cycle: A Study of British Manufacturing Industry, 1950–61*
By R. R. NEILD. 1963. pp. 73.

*XXII *Health and Welfare Services in Britain in 1975*
By DEBORAH PAIGE and KIT JONES. 1966. pp. 142.

*XXIII *Lancashire Textiles: A Case Study of Industrial Change*
By CAROLINE MILES. 1968. pp. 124.

XXIV *The Economic Impact of Commonwealth Immigration*
By K. JONES and A. D. SMITH. 1970. pp. 186. £1.75 net.

XXV *The Analysis and Forecasting of the British Economy*
By M. J. C. SURREY. 1971. pp. 120. £1.20 net.

XXVI *Mergers and Concentration in British Industry*
By P. E. HART, M. A. UTTON and G. WALSHE. 1973. pp. 190. £2.00 net.

XXVII *Recent Trends in Monopoly in Great Britain*
By G. WALSHE. 1974. pp. 156. £1.80 net.

STUDIES IN THE NATIONAL INCOME AND EXPENDITURE OF THE UNITED KINGDOM

Published under the joint auspices of the National Institute and the Department of Applied Economics, Cambridge.

*1 *The Measurement of Consumers' Expenditure and Behaviour in the United Kingdom, 1920–1938*, vol. I.
By RICHARD STONE, assisted by D. A. ROWE and by W. J. CORLETT, RENEE HURSTFIELD, MURIEL POTTER. 1954. pp. 448.

2 *The Measurement of Consumers' Expenditure and Behaviour in the United Kingdom, 1920–1938*, vol. II.
By RICHARD STONE and D. A. ROWE. 1966. pp. 152. £6.00 net.

3 *Consumers' Expenditure in the United Kingdom, 1900–1919*
By A. R. PREST, assisted by A. A. ADAMS. 1954. pp. 196. £4.20 net.

4 *Domestic Capital Formation in the United Kingdom, 1920–1938*
By C. H. FEINSTEIN. 1965. pp. 284. £6.00 net.

*5 *Wages and Salaries in the United Kingdom, 1920–1938*
By AGATHA CHAPMAN, assisted by ROSE KNIGHT. 1953. pp. 254.

6 *National Income, Expenditure and Output of the United Kingdom, 1855–1965*
By C. H. FEINSTEIN. 1972. pp. 384. £10.40 net.

* At present out of print.

NIESR STUDENTS EDITION

1 *Growth and Trade* (abridged from *Industrial Growth and World Trade*) By A. MAIZELS. 1970. pp. 312. £1.45 net.

2 *The Antitrust Laws of the U.S.A.* (2nd edition, unabridged) By A. D. NEALE. 1970. pp. 544. £2.40 net.

3 *The Management of the British Economy, 1945–60* (unabridged) By J. C. R. DOW. 1970. pp. 464. £1.10 net.

REGIONAL PAPERS

1 *The Anatomy of Regional Activity Rates* by JOHN BOWERS, and *Regional Social Accounts for the United Kingdom* by V. H. WOODWARD. 1970. pp. 192. £1.25 net.

2 *Regional Unemployment Differences in Great Britain* by P. C. CHESHIRE and *Interregional Migration Models and their Application to Great Britain* by R. WEEDEN. 1973. pp. 118. £2.00 net.

3 *Unemployment, Vacancies and the Rate of Change of Earnings: A Regional Analysis* by A. E. WEBB, and *Regional Rates of Employment Growth: An Analysis of Variance Treatment* by R. WEEDEN. 1974. pp. 114. £2.60 net.

THE NATIONAL INSTITUTE OF ECONOMIC AND SOCIAL RESEARCH

publishes regularly

THE NATIONAL INSTITUTE ECONOMIC REVIEW

A quarterly analysis of the general economic situation in the United Kingdom and the world overseas, with forecasts eighteen months ahead. The first issue each year is devoted entirely to the current situation and prospects both in the short and medium term. Other issues contain also special articles on subjects of interest to academic and business economists.

Annual subscriptions, £6.00, and single issues for the current year, £1.75 each, are available directly from NIESR, 2 Dean Trench Street, Smith Square, London, SW1P 3HE.

Subscriptions at the special reduced price of £2.50 p.a. are available to students in the United Kingdom and the Irish Republic on application to the Secretary of the Institute.

Back numbers and reprints of those which have gone out of stock are distributed by Wm. Dawson and Sons Ltd., Cannon House, Park Farm Road, Folkestone. Back numbers cost £2.00 each and reprints £3.00 each, plus postage.

THE IVTH FRENCH PLAN

By FRANÇOIS PERROUX, translated by Bruno Leblanc. 1965. pp. 72. 50p net.

This also is available directly from the Institute.

Published by Heinemann Educational Books

AN INCOMES POLICY FOR BRITAIN

Edited by FRANK BLACKABY. 1972. pp. 260. £4.00 net.

THE MEDIUM TERM: MODELS OF THE BRITISH ECONOMY

Edited by G. D. N. WORSWICK and F. T. BLACKABY. 1974. pp. 268. £4.80 net.

Available from booksellers.